Welsh Literature and the Classical Tradition

Welsh Literature
and the
Classical Tradition

CERI DAVIES

CARDIFF
UNIVERSITY OF WALES PRESS
1995

British Library Cataloguing in Publication Data

A catalogue record for this book is available from the British Library.

ISBN 0-7083-1499-6

Published with the financial support of the Arts Council of Wales.

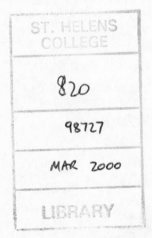
Typeset at the University of Wales Press
Printed in Wales by Dinefwr Press, Llandybïe

For

Michelle, Steffan and Daniel

Contents

Preface   ix

Abbreviations   xi

Glossary of Welsh Literary Terms   xiii

Introduction   1

I   A Roman Twilight: From Gildas and Taliesin to the Sons of Sulien   5

II   Medieval Wales and the Ancient World: Aeneas' Great-grandson and Ovid's Man   25

III   Wales's Humanists and the Classics   53

IV   Clerics and Schoolmasters: The Mid-Seventeenth to the Mid-Nineteenth Centuries   85

V   The University Movement and its Impact: The Classical Heritage since the Mid-Nineteenth Century   115

Notes   157

Bibliography   181

Index   189

Preface

This book has grown out of the union of two interests, one the literature of my own mother tongue, the other the ancient literature of Greece and Rome. Over twenty years and more I have often been asked to talk about aspects of the classical dimension in Welsh literature to a variety of audiences whose main concern was with the Welsh side of things. Conversely, my classical associates, in Wales and outside, have frequently pressed me to tell them more about literature written in the Welsh language and what bearing the classical tradition has upon it. The interest shown by both groups has encouraged me to write this book, and in so doing I have tried to keep members of both types of audience before my mind's eye. I should explain that it is as one whose main professional concern is with the teaching of the Greek and Latin languages and their literature that I have undertaken my self-imposed task. The attention which has been paid in recent decades by classicists to the study of the tradition of their own discipline in specific periods or within particular cultures has borne fruitful results. My hope is that this book may be a small contribution to that collective attempt to understand more fully the place of the classical heritage in the history of European culture. My concern is of necessity with the link between Welsh literature and material which recognizably belongs to the classical world of Greece and Rome. It will also be clear that, with regard to modern literature, 'Welsh' in the book's title means 'Welsh language'.

In writing this book I have been constantly aware of the extent of my debt to others. My interest in these two areas of study owes more than words can express to the encouragement which my parents gave me. Three excellent teachers in Ardwyn Grammar School, Aberystwyth – the late Mr W. Leslie Davies and Mr Gareth Emanuel on the classical side and the late Mr

W. Beynon Davies on the Welsh side – were highly formative influences. Over the years it has been my good fortune to have the opportunity of discussing various aspects of the subject of this book with many friends and associates: I am particularly mindful of the benefits which I have derived from conversations on these matters with the late Professor W. H. Davies, Professor J. Gwyn Griffiths, the late Mr Aneirin Lewis, Dr Peredur Lynch, Professor J. G. F. Powell, Professor B. R. Rees and Dr Brynley F. Roberts. As to my manuscript, Professor David Kirby kindly read a version of the first chapter and Professor D. Simon Evans a draft of the second, and I am most grateful to them for their perceptive and extremely helpful comments. Professor R. Geraint Gruffydd has once again put me immeasurably in his debt. He gave unstintingly of his time to read and discuss each chapter of the book as it was written, always to my immense benefit and to the undoubted enrichment of the work. It goes without saying that the imperfections and inadequacies which remain are to be laid at my door.

It is a pleasurable duty to thank the Leverhulme Trust for the award of a research grant to further the work: the Trust's support not only facilitated my studies but also provided a welcome boost to my morale at a time when I much needed it. I owe a great debt of gratitude for the help which I have received over years from staff at the National Library of Wales in Aberystwyth and the Bodleian Library in Oxford, and especially from the Librarian and his colleagues in the Library of my own University in Swansea. Mr Ned Thomas and Ms Liz Powell of the University of Wales Press, together with the Press's readers, are to be warmly thanked for their advice and for the expertise which they have brought to bear on the production of the book. It is also a pleasure to thank the Committee of the Classical Section of the University of Wales's Guild of Graduates for supporting this project.

My greatest debt of all is to my wife and our two sons for their good-humoured support and encouragement, and for all manner of practical help. The book is dedicated to them.

University of Wales, Swansea   CERI DAVIES

Abbreviations

ALMA	Hugh Owen (ed.), *Additional Letters of the Morrises of Anglesey, 1735–1786* (*Y Cymmrodor* XLIX). 2 vols., 1947–9
BBCS	*Bulletin of the Board of Celtic Studies*
BT	J. Gwenogvryn Evans, *The Book of Taliesin* (Llanbedrog, 1910).
CMCS	*Cambridge* (now *Cambrian*) *Medieval Celtic Studies*
EA	*Efrydiau Athronyddol*
GDG	Thomas Parry (ed.), *Gwaith Dafydd ap Gwilym* (Caerdydd, 1952)
GIG	D. R. Johnston (ed.), *Gwaith Iolo Goch* (Caerdydd, 1988)
GGG	J. Llywelyn Williams (ed.), *Gwaith Guto'r Glyn* (Caerdydd, 1939)
GGH	D. J. Bowen (ed.), *Gwaith Gruffudd Hiraethog* (Caerdydd, 1990)
GST	Enid P. Roberts (ed.), *Gwaith Siôn Tudur* (Caerdydd, 1980)
IGE	Henry Lewis, Thomas Roberts and Ifor Williams (eds.), *Cywyddau Iolo Goch ac Eraill, 1350–1450* (Caerdydd, 1937)
JWBS	*Journal of the Welsh Bibliographical Society*
LB	J. Leclerc (ed.), *Desiderii Erasmi Roterodami Opera Omnia* (Lugdunum Batavorum [Leiden], 1703–6)
LlC	*Llên Cymru*
NLW MS	Manuscript in the National Library of Wales
NLWJ	*The National Library of Wales Journal*
OBWV	Thomas Parry (ed.), *The Oxford Book of Welsh Verse* (Oxford, 1962)

OBWVE	Gwyn Jones (ed.), *The Oxford Book of Welsh Verse in English* (Oxford, 1977)
PBA	*Proceedings of the British Academy*
PBWV	Anthony Conran (transl.), *The Penguin Book of Welsh Verse* (Harmondsworth, 1967)
PRIA	*Proceedings of the Royal Irish Academy*
PWDN	Thomas Roberts and Ifor Williams (eds.), *The Poetical Works of Dafydd Nanmor* (Cardiff, 1923)
Rhagymadroddion	Garfield H. Hughes (ed.), *Rhagymadroddion, 1547–1659* (Caerdydd, 1951)
RhChLl	Ceri Davies (transl.), *Rhagymadroddion a Chyflwyniadau Lladin, 1551–1632* (Caerdydd, 1980)
SC	*Studia Celtica*
STC	A. W. Pollard and G. R. Redgrave, *A Short-Title Catalogue of Books Printed in England, Scotland and Ireland, and of English Books Printed Abroad, 1475–1640.* 2nd edition, 3 volumes (London, 1976, 1986, 1991).
THSC	*Transactions of the Honourable Society of Cymmrodorion*
TYP	R. Bromwich (ed.), *Trioedd Ynys Prydein,* (Cardiff, 1961; second edition, 1978)
WHR	*Welsh History Review*

Glossary of some Welsh Literary Terms

(For greater detail, see *The Oxford Companion to the Literature of Wales*.)

awdl	A long poem in traditional metres, using *cynghanedd*.
cynghanedd	A uniquely Welsh system of sound chiming (lit. 'harmony') and sometimes internal rhyme, essential for strict metres. 'In *cynghanedd* the sound of one word is orchestrated with the sound of another so that the ear quickly divines a pattern which it expects to be completed' (J. E. Caerwyn Williams, *The Poets of the Welsh Princes*, p.43).
cywydd (pl. *cywyddau*)	One of the most popular of Welsh metrical forms. The best known type is the *cywydd deuair hirion*, consisting of rhyming couplets in which each line has seven syllables, in *cynghanedd*.
dyfalu	A device, used especially in medieval *cywyddau*, to effect a description by means of a multiplicity of comparisons.
englyn	The oldest Welsh metrical form. The best known type is the four-line monorhyming stanza, *englyn unodl union*, containing *cynghanedd*.
proest	A form of 'half-rhyme', where consonants correspond, but not vowels.
pryddest	A long poem, not written in any of the traditional metres; *cynghanedd* may or may not be used.
triban	A popular metrical scheme, neither belonging to the traditional metres nor using *cynghanedd*.

Introduction

'I don't know whether you realize it, friends, but we, the Welsh, are really Romano-British in origin!'

Oliver J. Evans[1]

The aim of this book is to provide an account of the part which the tradition associated with the Greek and Latin Classics has played in Wales, especially in literature written in the Welsh language, from the sixth century to the present day. Of primary concern will be to ask what direct links can be traced between Welsh literature and classical literature, and one's first reaction to such a question may be to suppose that the connections have been very slender. Since the era of the Roman occupation of Britain, Wales has been perceived as a marginal area within Europe: so marginal that one might be forgiven for thinking that even during the greatest periods of European awareness of the classical past – the age of Charlemagne, the twelfth century, the age of Renaissance humanism, the eighteenth century – very little of the throb and excitement of rediscovering the literature of antiquity was felt in Wales. Certainly, it cannot be claimed that the world of Greece and Rome has played an immensely formative role in Welsh culture. Its importance bears no comparison with the all-pervasive presence of the Christian tradition, a presence which led one contemporary scholar justifiably to claim that 'before this century, it is difficult to find since the sixth century one Welsh writer who would not own the label "Christian" if required to do so.'[2] Yet there is a definite sense of the classical heritage which runs through Welsh literature. It is usually confined to individuals, or to small groups of writers, rather than manifesting itself in extensive movements. When, however, such individuals or groups have allowed their awareness of the classical past to come into tension with their own native literary tradition, Welsh literature has enjoyed some of its most creative moments.

Wales (or, perhaps more accurately, the geographical territory now known as Wales) was, of course, part of Rome's empire during the Roman occupation of Britain. The legionary fortresses established at Chester (*Deva*) and Caerleon-on-Usk (*Isca Silurum*) were symbols of Wales's position as a frontier area, and the numerous field forts and their connecting roads visibly reminded the native population of the ever-present power of Rome. The response of that native population to the imperial presence was mixed. It appears that the Silures of south-east Wales, after their initial display of great hostility, became more accommodating towards the conquerors, and it is significant that the signs of Roman civilian influences – the town of Caerwent (*Venta Silurum*), the villas at Llantwit Major and Ely – are mainly concentrated in that area. On the other hand, the Ordovices of southern Gwynedd remained more intractable, their behaviour in line with the resistance which the Druids on Anglesey gave to Suetonius Paulinus' attack in AD 61, an event which provided Tacitus with material for one of his most celebrated accounts of a clash between local interests and the Roman military machine.[3]

Roman rule continued until the end of the fourth century, when (in 383) the troops were, at least partially, withdrawn from Wales by the order of Magnus Maximus, commander of the Roman army in Britain. He was proclaimed emperor by his forces, and with their support overthrew in Gaul the increasingly unpopular Gratian. Magnus' position in Britain, Gaul and Spain was initially confirmed, but his attempt to take control of Italy led to his defeat by Theodosius I, emperor in the East, in 388, and his subsequent execution. In later centuries Magnus' withdrawal of troops was seen by many as the act which laid Britain open to enemies from all sides, Irish from the west, Angles and Saxons from the east. However, as 'Macsen Wledig' he was to play a significant part in Welsh mythology. The story of Macsen's dream (*Breuddwyd Macsen*), a medieval composition in the form in which we have it, links him to Wales in a special way, by his marriage to Elen Luyddog ('Elen of the Hosts'), a princess from Segontium, Roman Caernarfon.[4] And in Wales Magnus' withdrawal of Roman troops has been romantically viewed as the act which symbolized the entrusting of the control of Wales to Cunedda, the legendary founder of the Welsh princely dynasties. The real basis both of the tale and of Magnus' symbolic role is flimsy, but the myth of Macsen, 'the creator of Wales', has remained potent to this day. Dafydd Iwan's song about him, 'Yma o Hyd', has been not only a source of entertainment for many audiences but also a powerful expression of Welsh national consciousness.[5]

What is clear is that, when the Romans had finally withdrawn from Britain and the inroads made by Angles and Saxons had driven at least some of the British to the western extremities of the island, Wales remained something of a sub-Roman outpost. Christian inscriptions in Latin testify to the continued use and awareness of the Latin language, an awareness which persisted into the seventh century. Cadfan's tombstone, the 'Catamanus stone' preserved at Llangadwaladr Church near Aberffraw on Anglesey, represents in effect the title deeds of a king of Gwynedd, one who may even have looked back to Roman times for the authority of his kingship: *Catamanus rex sapientisimus opinatisimus omnium regum*, 'Cadfan, the wisest and most renowned of all kings.'[6] The words of the Plaid Cymru campaigner, quoted at the head of this introduction, hardly cut much ice in the Rhondda valleys in the dark days of the 1930s and early 1940s, but they point to an important conviction which continued in Wales into the Middle Ages, namely that the Welsh were in some way the last representatives of *Romanitas* in Britain. The point has been made with characteristic verve by one of the most stimulating of modern Welsh historians, Gwyn A. Williams: 'When Offa of Mercia cut his great dyke in the eighth century as an agreed frontier, he drew a line between two peoples . . . The people to the west of that line knew where they were: they were in Rome.'[7]

The best witness of all to the continued, if unobtrusive, presence of Rome is in the Welsh language itself. Welsh, like Cornish and Breton, belongs to the 'Brythonic', or 'British', group of Celtic languages, and its parent-language was spoken throughout the whole of Britain except for Scotland north of the Firths of Forth and Clyde. There can be little doubt that, during the period of Roman occupation, some British natives, especially upper-class provincials of what Sir Cyril Fox termed the 'Lowland Zone',[8] began to abandon their mother tongue in favour of Latin: one recalls Tacitus' famous remark about Agricola instilling into the sons of British chiefs a desire to be eloquent in Latin.[9] But more lasting was the infusion of Latin words into the vocabulary of the Brythonic tongue, an assimilation made easier by the fact that Brythonic, like Latin, was an inflected language. In the wake of foreign invasions many of the British, of all classes, appear to have moved west to the Highland Zone (which, of course, included Wales), taking their Latin and their mixture of Brythonic and Latin with them. The late Professor Kenneth Jackson, in his monumental *Language and History in Early Britain*, argued that the Latin which flourished in the Highland Zone of Britain during the centuries immediately after the end of Roman rule was not only widespread but also archaic in form, the language of 'educated speakers of rather stilted school Latin'.[10] Many of the details of Jackson's thesis have been questioned, but the basic evidence which Latin loan-words provide for our perception of the Romanization of Wales remains. The evolution of Welsh from Brythonic was probably complete by the end of the sixth century, and in the course of that process the Latin words which had entered the mother tongue went through precisely the same linguistic changes as the native words, becoming part of normal Welsh vocabulary. The extent to which Latin words had entered Brythonic is shown by the presence in Welsh not only of words which belonged to the world of Rome (e.g., Welsh *llyfr* from Latin *liber, ymherawdr* from *imperator, llurig* from *lorica*), but also of words for which there must have been native terms, like the body and its parts (e.g., *braich* from *bracchium, coes* from *coxa*, and *corff* from *corpus*).[11]

That the Greeks and the Romans had, from early times, been intrigued by the Celtic peoples is well documented.[12] How much interaction, however, was there between the literatures of the classical and Welsh worlds in the centuries when the Welsh language began to emerge as a vehicle for literary expression? That will be part of the theme of our first chapter.

I

A Roman Twilight:
From Gildas and Taliesin to the Sons of Sulien

During the fifth and early sixth centuries, the dwindling remnants of what had been the province of Britain still retained certain vestiges of Roman culture. Latin was still spoken, not indeed by everybody, but in sufficient measure to give men like Gildas, Iltud or Paul Aurelian a dim kinship with their contemporaries in Gaul for whom the tongue of Cicero remained a living language. These ultimate representatives of an etiolated Rome . . . may be viewed as bridging a gap between the old order and the new.

R. R. Bolgar[1]

The history of literature composed in the Welsh language begins, not in the part of Britain we now know as Wales, but – perhaps to our surprise – in areas of present-day southern Scotland and northern England. In the later part of the sixth century the poet Taliesin, who is often thought to have hailed from Powys and to have migrated north, established himself as court-poet to Urien, the powerful king of Rheged, the capital of which may have been at or near modern Carlisle. Obscure and confusing as are many of the traditions which later centuries allowed to accumulate around Taliesin, it may be that as many as nine, possibly twelve, poems are to be attributed to the historical Taliesin of the sixth century. Most of these poems are concerned with the praises of Urien, and end with a refrain which sums up Taliesin's devotion to his master:[2]

> Ac yny vallwyf y hen
> ym dygyn agheu aghen.
> ny bydif ymdyrwen
> na molwyf vryen.

And when I'm grown old, with death hard upon me,
I'll not be happy save to praise Urien.

When Taliesin composed his poems the Welsh language was in its infancy, and its evolution from the Brythonic, or British, parent tongue still a recent process.[3] The old Brythonic-speaking areas now became the context within which the new fledgling language opened its wings, and it is not without some significance that the earliest Welsh literary creations rose out of the struggles of the Celtic areas of the 'Old North' to maintain their identity against the assaults upon them by Scottish, Pictish, and – especially – Anglo-Saxon invaders. The lines of communication between the *Cymry* of Wales and of the Old North were soon to be severed by the extension of Anglo-Saxon power into Cheshire and Lancashire, and the 'Cumbric' dialect of the northern territories was destined to become little more than the provider of some local linguistic peculiarities. Strathclyde, *Ystrad Clud*, alone survived as a Brythonic polity until the eleventh century.

Taliesin was to remain a symbolic founder-figure within the literary tradition of Wales itself. His assertion that it is his joy 'to praise Urien' also points to what has been aptly described as 'his seminal contribution to the conceptual content of Welsh poetry'.[4] Taliesin's world was that of a warlike society facing the pressures of enemies bearing down upon a patron's kingdom, and the dominant note of the poetry is Taliesin's praise of Urien as warrior and protector of the community. This tradition of praise and panegyric was to remain vital in Welsh literature for nearly a thousand years, and during the Middle Ages it became fully developed and systematized. Poets formed themselves into a guild, and the function of bestowing praise on one's patron was the special prerogative of the highest class of bards. Such a poet was called upon to give praise, 'whether his praise was of God, of the saints, of the prince, or of his wife or daughter; in later times, of the nobility, the higher clergy, and powerful patrons or their families; to praise his patron in eulogies while he lived, to praise him in an elegy when he died'.[5] The manner of the panegyric was minutely laid down for the poets in manuals (or 'grammars'). As will be seen, the earliest surviving version of these grammars belongs to the fourteenth century and is attributed to one Einion Offeiriad, 'Einion the Priest'.

Before the time of Taliesin, another writer in these islands had something to say about the practice of panegyrical poetry, poetry which in his day may have been composed in an admixture of disappearing Brythonic and newly-emerging Welsh. The writer was Gildas, whose life appears to provide a fine example of the ease of contact between the Romanized parts of Celtic Britain and the European continent. Much uncertainty surrounds the details of Gildas's life and times. The view, long-held, that the period of his maturity was the middle of the sixth century, and that he died c.570, has in recent years been challenged. His *De Excidio Britanniae* ('Ruin of Britain') has been dated by some scholars at c.515–20, by others as early even as 500.[6] Likewise, his ready familiarity with northern Britain is not nearly as certain as it once appeared, whereas his acquaintance with southern areas is much more established.[7] If tradition is to be relied upon, he knew south Wales, and later in his life he is said to have migrated to Brittany.

Gildas's *De Excidio Britanniae* contains an outline (chapters 2–26) of the history of Britain during and after the Roman occupation, but the bulk of the work (chapters 27–110) is a harsh diatribe against the sinful wickedness which had hastened the decline of the Britons before the inroads of Angles and Saxons and others. In the manner of an Old Testament prophet Gildas castigates kings and clergy for neglecting their duties, and he lashes out in particular against five *tyranni* ('tyrants') who were primarily responsible for the ruination of the British people. Maelgwn, in Latin *Maglocunus*, 'the island dragon' (*insularis draco*, 33.1), is the butt of an extended and rhetorically devastating attack, especially because he allowed bards and poets to give him the praise which rightly should be ascribed to God alone:[8]

Arrecto aurium auscultantur captu non Dei laudes canora Christi tironum voce suaviter modulante neumaque ecclesiasticae melodiae, sed propriae, quae nihil sunt, furciferorum referto mendaciis simulque spumanti flegmate proximos quosque roscidaturo, praeconum ore ritu bacchantium concrepante, ita ut vas Dei quondam in ministerio praeparatum vertatur in zabuli organum, quodque honore caelesti putabatur dignum merito proiciatur in tartari barathrum.

Your excited ears hear not the praises of God from the sweet voices of the tuneful recruits of Christ, not the melodious music of the church, but empty praises of yourself from the mouths of criminals who grate on the hearing like raving hucksters – mouths stuffed with lies and liable to bedew bystanders with their foaming phlegm. Hence a vessel that was once being prepared for the service of God is turned into an instrument of the devil, and what was once thought worthy of heavenly honours is rightly cast into the pit of Hell.

Gildas's sympathy with the leaders of Celtic Britain is minimal. It is evident that the attitudes adopted by him and by Taliesin towards the praise of princes are diametrically opposed to each other.

Of equal significance is their difference in language, coupled as it is with the cultural variance which that linguistic difference connotes. Taliesin – or, perhaps more accurately, several poets whose work was subsumed under the name 'Taliesin' – composed in Welsh, the first (as we have seen) of a line of writers who were to play their part in developing a literature which, in many regards, would be 'metrically, thematically and stylistically distinct from the rest of Europe'.[9] Gildas, on the other hand, wrote in Latin, *lingua nostra* ('our language') as he proudly calls it (23.3). The epithet *sapiens*, 'wise', which was applied to him, was the mark of a man who belonged by birth to the world of Celtic culture, 'but conquered the new one of Latin, written learning'.[10] He handles Latin with a linguistic command which is both confidently innovative and also firmly rooted in the tradition of the grammatical and rhetorical training given to the educated administrative classes throughout the centuries of the Roman Empire.[11] Far from being a work of eccentric and cloying Latinity, as it has often been represented, *De Excidio Britanniae* bears many of the hall-marks of a writer well-trained in the sophistication of the schools of the late Empire. In the opening words of the first chapter, which constitutes a preface to the work, Gildas refers to his book as a letter in which he would 'bewail rather than declaim' (*in hac epistola quicquid deflendo potius quam declamando . . . fuero prosecutus*). The work is indeed a Jeremiad, but Gildas's words do not deny its rhetorical properties. Recent scholarship has demonstrated that the style and structure of the work are to be seen in terms of a Roman declamation, the kind of quasi-forensic speech which was produced as the stock-in-trade of Roman oratorical training from the days of Cicero onwards. The *De Excidio* is renowned for its use of biblical texts. It also demonstrates that in the sub-Roman Britain of the century after the departure of the Roman legions there remained those who not only appreciated echoes and resonances of Virgil (the account of the sack of Troy in *Aeneid* II is particularly used to effect in *De Excidio*)[12] and other Latin writers, but also knew how to use Latin as a powerful medium for the persuasive expression of strongly held opinions.[13]

That Gildas received somewhere, from someone, a training which was in line with that given by the *grammatici* and *rhetores* of the Roman world is established beyond question. The bold style, the dramatic force of his use of hyperbaton and antithesis and alliteration, the regular employment of startling imagery and poetic resonances, all point to a writer whose rhetorical armoury is uniquely well-stocked in Britain in the early sixth century. At the same time, the prophetic theme of Gildas's message lends support to the view that he may have come under monastic influence, and his denunciation of Maelgwn and other Welsh princes strongly suggests that he had direct knowledge of the Welsh scene.[14] The *Life* of Gildas, written in the eleventh century by a monk of Ruis in Brittany (where Gildas was reputed to have founded a monastery), records that Gildas was 'entrusted by his parents to the charge of St Hildutus, to be instructed by him' (*ipse a suis parentibus beato Hilduto traditur imbuendus*).[15] It can hardly be doubted that 'Hildutus' is one of many Latin forms of the name of 'Illtud', the eponymous founder of the monastic school associated with Llanilltud Fawr (Llantwit Major) in the Vale of Glamorgan. The *Life of Gildas* contains material which is common to other hagiographical texts relating to Illtud and his foundation, notably Illtud's connections with Ynys Bŷr (Caldey Island) as well as with Llanilltud Fawr. The picture which the *Life* gives of the reception given by Illtud to his new pupil stresses the liberal as well as the theological training which was imparted:[16]

Qui suscipiens sanctum puerulum sacris litteris coepit instruere illum, et videns eum formae specie fulgentem ac liberalibus studiis instantissime intentum benigno amore dilexit et attento studio docere curavit. Beatus igitur Gildas sub disciplina magistrali in schola divinae scripturae et liberalium artium constitutus,

conspiciens utriusque doctrinam elocutionis divinis curavit magis
erudiri doctrinis.

He took the holy child to himself, and began to teach him in sacred
literature; and seeing he excelled in outward beauty, and was most
eagerly bent upon the liberal studies, he loved him with tender
love, and strove to teach him with attentive zeal. The blessed
Gildas was, therefore, established under a master's training in a
school of divine scripture and of the liberal arts. Observing,
however, the knowledge imparted in both kinds of teaching, he
was anxious to be taught rather in the divine doctrines.

It is difficult to gauge the reliability of the information about
Gildas's education which the *Life* presents. The most sceptical
view would regard the account in the *Life* as hagiographical
fable and question the historicity of any link between Gildas and
Illtud. Indeed, if the *De Excidio Britanniae* is to be dated as early
as 500, then the historicity of any link between Gildas and Illtud
must be in doubt. In any case, one wonders whether Llanilltud
Fawr alone could have given Gildas access to all the resources of
classical literature and rhetoric which his work so amply
displays. It should, however, be noted that the words which
have just been quoted from the *Life* appear to go out of their way
to suggest that Illtud did not draw over-harsh distinctions
between the classical and theological aspects of the education
which he imparted, and that the liberal arts enjoyed an
important place in his scheme of things. Rather it is Gildas who
chooses to concentrate on 'the divine doctrines', thereby
fulfilling all that a later age expected of him as a saint.

A possible hint of Gildas's sense of debt to Illtud may lie
behind the way in which he refers (*De Excidio*, 36.1) to Maelgwn
Gwynedd having for his teacher 'the refined master of almost all
Britain' (*paene totius Britanniae magistrum elegantem*). The *magister
elegans* has traditionally been taken to be Illtud. This explanation
has been questioned by Michael Lapidge, who has persuasively
argued that the adjective *elegans*, a word which often connotes
refinement of rhetorical style, 'could scarcely be used to describe
a monastic instructor'.[17] On the other hand, *elegans* is used here
in the specific context of reminding Maelgwn of the scriptural
warnings which he has received thanks to the *magister* who
taught him. *Elegantia* need not be limited to the sphere of refined

speech, and the reference may be as much to graciousness of life and demeanour, qualities (35.2–3) which Maelgwn had apparently long since forgotten.

Whether Gildas and Maelgwn had connections with Illtud or not, the pre-eminence of the school of Llanilltud Fawr as the foremost centre of learning in post-Roman Wales is clear. Among pupils of whom it can be said with some degree of confidence that they were taught at Llanilltud are Samson (the saint of Dol in Brittany) and Paul Aurelian (of St-Pol-de-Leon). The first version of the *Life* of Samson is a more reliable source than most of the Welsh saints' *Lives*, many of which (like the *Life* of Illtud himself) were composed early in the Norman period and throw more light on their own time than on the age of the saints. The *Life* of Samson was probably written much nearer the time of the saint whom it celebrates than is the case with most *Vitae* of this kind, and is – in some measure at least – based on material handed down within Samson's own family. Of particular importance here is the picture which the *Life of Samson* offers of the education and training which the saint received (Chapter 7). It is recorded how his parents took the young Samson *ad scholam egregi magistri Britannorum, Eltuti nomine* ('to the school of the famous master of the Britons, Eltut [= Illtud] by name'), an expression which may be echoed in the *totius Britanniae magistrum elegantem* of the *Life of Gildas*. It is also stated that Illtud himself was a disciple of Germanus of Auxerre; if the claim is correct, then Illtud had been in contact with one who was not only an important Christian leader in Gaul but also a trained Roman advocate. The *Life of Samson* then proceeds:[18]

Ille vero Eltutus de totis Scripturis veteris scilicet ac novi Testamenti et omnis philosophiae generis, metricae scilicet ac rhetoricae, grammaticaeque et arithmeticae, et omnium artium philosophiae omnium Britannorum compertissimus erat.

In truth Illtud was the most accomplished of all the Britons in the Scriptures of both the Old and the New Testaments, and in the writings of philosophy of every kind, namely geometry, rhetoric, grammar and arithmetic, and of all the arts of philosophy.

The detail is doubtless over-coloured, but the delineation of an educator who was concerned with both the sacred and the secular is unmistakable. Illtud is presented as one who combined the monastic life with openness to learning in the widest sense. This is in contrast to the more austere asceticism which became the hall-mark of the Welsh saints. And it is no accident that Llanilltud Fawr and neighbouring Llancarfan, both in the Vale of Glamorgan, developed as places of learning in the very part of Wales where Roman civilian influences had been most pervasive. After the end of the Roman period the Celtic Church was the guardian of the *Romanitas* which embraced classical as well as Christian values, and the Latin language was integral to that guardianship.

What part, however, would any awareness of the specifically classical heritage play in Wales from the seventh to the tenth centuries, especially as Europe emerged from the (so-called) Dark Ages, and the effects of the Carolingian revival of learning spread beyond the area of Charlemagne's empire?[19] That learning was, of course, controlled by the Church, and it is not surprising that the earliest manuscript book associated with Wales is a Latin manuscript of the Gospels of St Matthew and St Mark and part of the Gospel of St Luke, now kept in the Cathedral library at Lichfield, and known as the Lichfield Gospel-Book (or the Book of St Chad, after the saint to whom the Cathedral is dedicated). It was written in the first half of the eighth century, possibly in Wales, more probably in Ireland or Northumbria; by the early ninth century it was in the church of Llandeilo Fawr, where it acquired its Old Welsh and Latin glosses.[20] Other remains, although few in number, bear witness to the continuity of the more directly classical aspects of the Latin tradition. For example, the anonymous *Historia Brittonum* (*c*.829), formerly attributed to 'Nennius', a work whose Latin belongs to a different world from that of Gildas, is nevertheless a scholarly compilation which catches the occasional echo of classical literature.[21] Then, a ninth-century manuscript of Martianus Capella's *De Nuptiis Philologiae et Mercurii* ('On the Marriage of Philology and Mercury'), source in great measure of medieval teaching about the Seven Liberal Arts, was the product of a Welsh scriptorium, possibly St David's, and contains Welsh glosses on the text.[22] Another ninth-century Latin manuscript, containing a copy of the *Evangeliorum libri* (written *c*.330) of the Spanish poet Gaius Vettius Aquilinus Juvencus, has glosses in both Welsh and Irish; a colophon names its scribe as one Nuadu, probably an Irishman who knew Welsh and worked in the context of a Welsh scriptorium.[23] Of even greater interest, and very intriguing in view of the presumption that the copying of manuscripts was under Church control, is the manuscript of Ovid's *Ars Amatoria*, Book I, which was copied in Wales from a continental exemplar during the ninth or early tenth century. It too contains Welsh glosses which establish its use by a Welsh reader of Latin before it was acquired by St Dunstan of Glastonbury in the second half of the tenth century.[24] Furthermore, it is no insignificant tribute to Latin learning in ninth-century Wales that when King Alfred of Wessex wished to engage a contemporary Suetonius or Einhard to write his biography, he entrusted the task to the cleric Asser, one of the finest products of a scholarly *clas* in western Wales, probably St David's.[25]

Clasau, the monastic foundations of the Celtic Church, were to remain the guardians of Latinity and of such slender classical awareness as continued to the end of the eleventh century. This was largely thanks to Wales's close, if often disrupted, link with Ireland and Irish learning. For example, the court of some kings of Gwynedd, notably of the ninth-century Merfyn Frych and his son Rhodri Mawr, was an important meeting-point for Irish scholars on their way to the continent. Evidence points to elementary knowledge of the Greek alphabet in Merfyn's court, and Sedulius Scottus, one of the most attractive of Europe's *Scotti peregrini*, wrote in praise of Rhodri Mawr.[26] The survival of learning associated with the *clas* at Llancarfan is attested by the articulate and highly engaging *Life* of St Cadoc, the fifth-century founder of the settlement.[27] This work is attributed to one Lifris, who can be identified with the 'Lifricus' who is thrice mentioned in the *Liber Landavensis*.[28] He was the son of Herwald, bishop of 'Gwlad Morgan' (later Llandaff) at the end of the eleventh century, and himself held the office of archdeacon and master of the monastery of Llancarfan (*magister sancti Catoci de Lanncarvan*).

As might be expected, the *Life of Cadoc* is full of the wonders and miraculous deeds which are commonplace in hagiography of this kind. It was also probably meant to extol the ancient claims of Llancarfan before the Normans swept into south-east

Wales, bringing their new order. Also throughout the material there is a picture of Cadoc as a man of learning, and his monastery as a repository of that learning. He himself is said to have been born of royal stock, and his cultural attitudes are depicted as those of the sub-Roman ruling classes. He is entrusted (chapter 4) by his father Gwynllyw, prince of Gwynllŵg, to an Irish hermit, Meuthi (who is probably to be identified with St Tatheus of Caerwent), to be instructed – like Gildas – 'in the liberal arts and in sacred learning' (*liberalibus artibus divinisque dogmatibus*). Meuthi's instruction is said (chapter 6) to have involved a twelve-year study of Donatus and Priscian, late-Roman authors of Latin expositions of grammar which were immensely influential throughout the Middle Ages: *illum Donato Priscianoque, necnon aliis artibus, per annos duodecim diligentius instruxit*. A few years after the establishment of his monastery, Cadoc felt the need (chapter 10) for further personal study. He is represented as looking, significantly enough, towards Ireland: 'I am ablaze with a burning desire to cross over to Ireland for the sake of learning' (*iam flagranti desiderio ad Hiberniam discendi gratia transfretare glisco*). His search was for a master to instruct him in the Seven Liberal Arts, a search successfully concluded at Lismore, where he stayed for three years. He then returned (chapter 11) to south Wales, first to the area of Brycheiniog, because he had heard that a famous Italian teacher (*rhetoricus*) named Bachan had arrived there. Cadoc's wish above all else was to receive instruction from him in Latin, 'in the Roman way' (*ab illo Romano more Latinitate doceri non minimum optavit*). On his eventual return to Llancarfan he found it necessary to rebuild the monastery, although his own stay there was interspersed (so the *Life* says) with travels to Greece and Rome and Jerusalem, and a seven-year visit to Scotland.

Many of these details, such as the references to Donatus and Priscian and to the Seven Liberal Arts, reflect the learned interests and concerns of Lifris himself. However, as Hywel D. Emanuel aptly pointed out, it is likely that Lifris embodied in his composition many popular oral traditions which were still current at Llancarfan in his own lifetime.[29] This would seem to be the implication of phrases such as *ut fertur* ('as it is said'), *ut aiunt* ('so they say'), *ut perhibetur* ('as the story goes'), which occur fairly frequently in the *Life*. The references to the world of learning also appear to convey the memory of that commitment to the classical tradition which was represented by Cadoc and his followers.

The most striking of all the indications of this connection with the world of learning of the pre-Norman period comes in the *Passion of St Cadoc* which is appended to the *Life*. This tells of the abrupt end of Cadoc's personal connection with Llancarfan when (chapter 37), like Elijah carried to heaven in a fiery chariot, he was bodily removed in a white cloud *ad Beneventanam civitatem* ('to the Beneventan city'). There can be little doubt that this fantastic story refers to the city of Benevento in southern Italy. Furthermore, the name 'Sophias' which was there given to Cadoc, while aetiologically explained by Lifris on the basis of Cadoc's renowned wisdom, was doubtless ultimately derived from the monastery at Benevento which was dedicated to Sancta Sophia, Holy Wisdom. We are reminded by Hywel Emanuel that the duchy of Benevento had been, from the fifth century onwards, a vital guardian of the flame of learning, as barbarian forces swept down through Italy. In the early sixth century St Benedict of Nursia founded his abbey of Monte Cassino in the northern part of the duchy. A few years later Cassiodorus' settlement of Vivarium, on his estates at Squillace, was to be another haven of scholarship in southern Italy. Although these centres suffered much in the following centuries, the restoration of Monte Cassino in the year 949 led to a period of immense prosperity for that monastery and her daughter-abbeys. Manuscripts – especially those of classical texts – produced in these abbeys of the duchy of Benevento became known and prized throughout Europe, and the vigour of Beneventan script remained distinctive until the thirteenth century.[30] Whatever one makes of the traditions recorded by Lifris (they are further complicated by the revisions of his work which were made in the twelfth century by Caradoc, also of Llancarfan), they certainly bear witness to a tradition of great learning which Lifris saw encapsulated in the link between Llancarfan and Benevento. To quote Hywel Emanuel:[31]

> The implications of the acquaintance shown by Lifris with the city and duchy of Benevento are of the utmost importance to the early history of learning in Wales . . . It may well be that Llancarfan, in

common with many other centres of learning in western Europe, had benefited from the literary activities of the monastic houses of the duchy of Benevento, and that some of the manuscripts studied in the monastic school and preserved in the library at Llancarfan had been executed by Beneventan scribes.

The Beneventan story also attests that, well before Lifris's own time, there was a sense of classical learning associated with Llancarfan.

Lifris's work, in the second half of the eleventh century, stands on the very threshold of the arrival of Norman influence in Welsh life and culture. The same may be said of the work of the family of Sulien (1011–91), bishop of St David's for two periods, 1073/4–8 and 1080–5. Sulien raised the *clas* of his native Llanbadarn Fawr, near Aberystwyth, to be for the eleventh century what Llanilltud Fawr had been in early post-Roman Wales. Under Sulien's inspiration Llanbadarn grew to become an immensely important centre of scholarship and of manuscript production.[32] The notice of his death in 1091, recorded in *Brut y Tywysogion* (the Chronicle of the Welsh Princes), refers to him as 'the most learned and most pious of the bishops of the Britons, and the most praiseworthy for the instruction of his disciples and his parishes.'[33] Sulien was personally responsible for the education at Llanbadarn of his own four sons, of whom Rhigyfarch and Ieuan have left Latin literary remains, both prose and poetry, which bear priceless testimony to the vibrancy of Latin learning in Wales just before the Norman period.[34] Rhigyfarch is best remembered for his prose *Life* of St David,[35] but three Latin poems which survive from his pen attest even more clearly to his command of classical Latin verse form and diction. Two of Rhigyfarch's poems are preserved in a twelfth-century manuscript which contains the text of the part of the sixth book of Cicero's *De Republica* known as the *Somnium Scipionis*, together with Macrobius' influential Neoplatonist commentary on the Cicero text.[36] In particular, Rhigyfarch's *Planctus*, a lament on the effects of the Norman conquest of Wales, reveals a writer whose style and choice of metre are shaped by Boethius' *Consolation of Philosophy* and whose expression is informed with echoes of classical Latin literature.

There also remain, in an autograph manuscript which contains the text of St Augustine's *De Trinitate*, three poems (or parts of poems) by Rhigyfarch's younger brother Ieuan, notably a poem of 159 hexameters on the life and family of Sulien. As is apt for a manuscript produced by Ieuan of the text of a work on the Trinity, the poem begins with an august invocation to the triune God. However, the imagery of the divine nod (*nutus*, translated below as 'command'), of the globe of Phoebus ('the sun'), and of the moon as sister to the sun, belongs – as do later references to Tartarus (line 30) and to God 'the Thunderer' (line 33) – to the world of classical literature. The invocation is couched in phrases and cadences which carry echoes of major classical poets like Virgil and Ovid, as well as of later Latin works, including the British (or Breton) *Hisperica Famina* ('Western Sayings'):[38]

> Arbiter altithrone, nutu qui cuncta gubernas
> ut nunquam ualeant modulum transire repostum,
> qui cursu propero sustentas iure potenter
> stelliferi centri uergentia culmina circum
> non cassura solo, cursum retinentibus astris,
> flammantemque globum Phoebi, lunamque bicornem
> flexibus ambiguis reptantum more draconum
> celatum lustrare polum glebamque patentem,
> solem dans luci clarum noctique sororem,
> sidera concedis necnon splendescere summa;
> quique manens semper iam summa sede coruscus,
> telluris molem circundans equore tanto
> lymbo consimili clari ceu tegminis oram,
> occianum prohibes minitantem murmure multo,
> undisono fremitu rumpat ne proxima terre:
> tu mihi poscenti sophiam concede supernam,
> uotiuas grates ualeam tibi reddere, Christe,
> qui me scriptorem libri uenerabilis asstans
> nomine quem trino uocitant e iure fideles.

Lofty-throned Judge, who govern all things by your command so that they may never exceed their assigned positions, who mightily sustain in its swift course the turning zenith of the starry heaven at all points, (which) will never crash to earth (so long as) the stars retain their course; and (sustain) the flaming globe of the sun, and the two-horned moon in its ambiguous (i.e. two-way: waxing and waning) movements after the manner of crawling dragons to illuminate the embossed heavens and the receptive earth, (thus) giving the clear sun for light (in day-time) and its sister (the moon) at night; you also grant that the highest stars are resplendent; and who, remaining always gleaming (on your) supreme throne, bounding the mass of earth with such (a body of) water, like a fine hem, just as the margin of a coverspread (bounds it), you restrain the ocean threatening with a great murmur so that it does not break in upon the near-by land with a flood-tide roar. Grant heavenly wisdom to me who beseech (so that) I may be able to return my promised thanks to you, O Christ, you who are assisting me the writer of this reverend book, (you) whom the faithful rightly call by threefold name.

(lines 1–19)

Later in the poem Ieuan recalls his father's pursuit of learning in Scotland and Ireland. The Irish connection was almost certainly of immense influence on the early development and flowering of Llanbadarn as a cultural centre. Ieuan tells of his father's return home:

> protinus arguta thesaurum mente recondens,
> post hec ad patriam remeans iam dogmate clarus
> uenit, et inuentum multis iam diuidit aurum,
> proficiens cunctis discentibus undique circum,
> reges, quem populi, cleri, cunctique coloni,
> omnes unanimes uenerantur mente serena.
> quattuor ac proprio nutriuit sanguine natos
> quos simul edocuit dulci libaminis amne
> ingenio claros, iam sunt hec nomina quorum:
> Rycymarch sapiens, Arthgen, Danielque Iohannes.

Then, storing this treasure in his shrewd mind he thereafter came home, returning (a man) distinguished in learning; he came and divided the gold he had discovered among many, being of use to all disciples on every side, he whom kings, the people, the clergy and all land-dwellers venerated unanimously with serene mind. And he nurtured four sons of his own stock, intellectually distinguished, whom he instructed with the sweet stream of (learning's) libation. These are their names: Rhigyfarch the wise, Arthgen, Daniel, and Ieuan.

(lines 120–29)

Michael Lapidge, whose masterly edition and translation of

the text are quoted above, has demonstrated how the poems of Rhigyfarch and Ieuan show ready familiarity with the works of Virgil, Ovid, Lucan and probably Statius among classical poets, as well as Juvencus, Prudentius, Caelius Sedulius, Boethius and other Christian writers. In style they are more one with the work of Carolingian writers of the ninth century, poets like Theodulf of Orléans, Walahfrid Strabo and Hrabanus Maurus, than with that of contemporary Latin poets in Europe. In that regard Sulien's sons are truly the last witnesses to pre-Norman responses to classical Latinity in Wales.

We have mainly reflected hitherto on the classical continuum in Latin works connected with Wales before the Norman period. Latin had remained the language of ecclesiastical record and of officialdom since the departure of the Romans. Learned readers' grasp of the language often appears to have been somewhat uncertain, as the presence of the Welsh glosses in Latin manuscripts shows. Nevertheless, in the face of ever-increasing isolation, it was the religious centres and their quiet devotion to the things of the mind and the spirit which kept Wales in touch with the wider world of Latin learning.

What, however, of classical influence on literature in the Welsh language before c.1100? No manuscript devoted to a literary work in Welsh remains from the pre-Norman period, although (as we have seen) some Latin manuscripts contain Welsh material. In terms of literary significance, the most important of such insertions are the two series of (mainly) three-line *englynion* preserved in the manuscript of Juvencus' *Evangeliorum libri*.[39] Nevertheless the bulk of early Welsh literature, such as the poetry of Taliesin and the other *Cynfeirdd*, is preserved in later manuscripts of the thirteenth century. That poetry, most of it composed in the heroic mode of early Celtic verse, appears to be immune from classical influence. Some small parallels, however, are worthy of note. For example *Y Gododdin*,[40] the late-sixth-century poet Aneirin's great celebration of the defiant but tragic heroism of *Gwŷr a aeth Gatraeth*, 'men who went to Catraeth', has elements in common with the Greek and Roman epic tradition of Homer and Virgil. For the followers of Mynyddog Mwynfawr the demands of a code of honour were as great as for Achilles or

Hector. It has also been pointed out that *Y Gododdin* 'can be read as an expansion'[41] of the consolation offered, by the contemporary Latin writer Venantius Fortunatus, Bishop of Poitiers, to a father whose two sons had fallen in battle:

> nec graviter doleas cecidisse viriliter ambos,
> nam pro laude mori vivere semper erit.

Do not grieve heavily that both have fallen like men, for to die for the sake of praise will be to live for ever.

(Carmina VII.16.51f.)

It is most unlikely that there is any direct connection between the composition of *Y Gododdin* and the poetry of Fortunatus. However, it need not be 'inherently improbable' (to use Professor Sims-Williams's apt expression)[42] that Latin literature should influence native poetry, whether directly or indirectly.

Saunders Lewis, in a typically exhilarating study entitled 'The Tradition of Taliesin',[43] suggested that the historic Taliesin may himself have indirectly derived some of his imagery and style from Virgil. The argument is made to rest both on accepting a very late dating for Gildas and Maelgwn Gwynedd and on supposing that both Gildas and Taliesin together enjoyed the protection of Urien's kingdom of Rheged. It is then surmised that Taliesin acquired echoes of Virgil from Gildas, whereas Taliesin's panegyrics of Urien provided Gildas with the basis of his character study of Maelgwn and of the moral condemnation of him in the *De Excidio Britanniae*. Saunders Lewis's claim that 'the evidence is there that Gildas and Taliesin were in touch' is not proven. But the wider implications of his argument, that Taliesin and other native poets may have known something of the forms of classical rhetoric, and may even have dimly caught echoes of specific Virgilian themes (whether via Gildas's work or not), cannot be categorically discounted. To quote Patrick Sims-Williams again: 'If the leaders of the Goths and Franks softened their Scythian ways by learning Vergil, speaking Latin to perfection, and trying their hands at poetry, it is likely that some British kings had similar leanings.'[44] We know that Maelgwn not only enjoyed the teaching of 'the refined master of almost all Britain' but also revelled in the panegyrics bestowed upon him by native bards. It is surely not inconceivable that those bards themselves may have been open to similar classical influences, however attenuated.

We are on somewhat firmer ground when we turn to three poems, composed between the ninth and eleventh centuries, which have been preserved in the manuscript compilation known as 'The Book of Taliesin'.[45] This is an early fourteenth-century manuscript containing the poems which have been identified as authentically the work of the historical Taliesin, but including also poems connected with the legends that gathered around the persona of Taliesin as well as a range of poems on religious and panegyrical and other themes. The three poems which were mentioned contain material which is about two of the greatest figures of classical antiquity: Alexander the Great (two poems) and Hercules (one poem). These works have been authoritatively studied by Dr Marged Haycock.[46] The Alexander poems differ in their emphasis. The first (*BT* 51.1–52.5, without a title) contains material relating to the historical Alexander and is based on incidents in his life which can be traced back to sources such as Quintus Curtius Rufus' *Life of Alexander* and especially the *History against the Pagans* of the fifth-century Christian historian, Paulus Orosius. The second (*BT* 52.18–53.2, entitled 'Anryuedodeu Allyxand[er]', 'The Marvels of Alexander') owes its matter to the creators of the Alexander myth which became so popular in the Middle Ages, especially to the *Historia de Preliis*, the tenth-century Neapolitan Archpriest Leo's version (which went through several redactions) of Pseudo-Callisthenes' Alexander Romance and the Letter to Aristotle (about India).[47] The Letter to Aristotle may also have contributed, along with other sources, to the short 'lament' for Hercules (*BT* 65.24–66.8), especially to the sense of wonder associated with his 'pillars'.

Details of Alexander's conquests are recounted by the knowledgeable poet, or poets, in the first, and longest, poem:[48]

> bu deu tec ar wlat gwledychyssit
> bu haelhaf berthaf or ryanet.
> bu terwyn gwenwyn gwae ygywlat.
> ef torres ardar teir gweith yg kat.
> ac ef ny vyd corgwyd ywlat
> dar plufawr pebyr pell athechwys coet
> gyrth ygodiwawd alexander.

> He reigned over twelve foreign realms.
> He was the most prodigal and splendid man [ever]
>   born.
> He was a fierce slayer, woe upon his neighbour.
> He defeated Dareius three times in battle
> And there are not [even] shrubs left in his land.
> Darius of the flashing feathers/wings retreated far
> [But] Alexander furiously overtook him.
>
> (lines 2–8)

The shorter poem about Alexander goes beyond the bounds of the known world, and takes him on his celebrated submarine journey and his celestial flight:[49]

> Aeth dan eigyawn.
> Dan eigawn eithyd
> y geissaw keluydyt.
> Ageisso keluydyt
> bit oiewin y vryt.
> Eithyd oduch gwynt.
> rwg deu grifft ar hynt
> ywelet dremynt.
>
> He went beneath the ocean,
> Beneath the ocean he went
> To pursue learning/art.
> Whosoever may seek learning
> Must be intrepid of purpose.
> He went above the wind
> Flying between two griffins
> In order to see a sight.
>
> (lines 8–15)

The three poems, on Alexander and Hercules, do not draw directly on classical sources. They demonstrate, however, that knowledge of the classical world in pre-Norman Wales was not completely confined to those who wrote in Latin or whose education was ecclesiastical in its orientation. This is far from saying that classical learning was widespread among early Welsh poets, but an over-harsh dividing line should not be drawn between the Celtic world of the bards and the more Latinate world of Church and *clas*. At the same time, such meagre evidence as we have suggests that there was very little, if any, direct commerce between the corpus of Latin classical writings as we think of them and the world of literature composed in the Welsh language before the Norman period.

II

Medieval Wales and the Ancient World: Aeneas' Great-grandson and Ovid's Man

Antiquity has a twofold life in the Middle Ages: reception and transformation. This transformation can take very various forms. It can mean impoverishment, degeneration, devitalization, misunderstanding; but it can also mean critical collection, schoolboyish copying, skilful imitation of formal patterns, assimilation of cultural values, enthusiastic empathy.

E. R. Curtius[1]

Sulien and his sons stood, as we have seen, on the bridge between the Celtic world of the *clas* and the changes which were wrought in Wales as elsewhere by the coming of the Normans. In 1081 Sulien, as Bishop of St David's, received King William I during what *Brut y Tywysogion* calls his 'Menevia pilgrimage',[2] a thinly veiled opportunity for the Conqueror to receive homage and fealty from Rhys ap Tewdwr, prince of Deheubarth. Whatever the civilities observed on that occasion, the real reaction of Sulien's family to the Norman Conquest is seen in Rhigyfarch's *Planctus*, 'Lament', which views as an unmitigated disaster the change that was sweeping even into western Wales. The poem is written in the same verse form (called asynarteton) as the second metrum of Boethius' *Consolation of Philosophy*. Its opening words echo the beginning of Boethius' poem, leaving (as Michael Lapidge says) 'no doubt that Boethius was Rhigyfarch's model'.[3] Like Boethius imprisoned in Pavia and awaiting death, Rhigyfarch sees his world coming to an end:[4]

> Cur nos fata mori ceca negarunt?
> cur non terra uorat, non mare mergit?
> nunc inopinus adit rumor ad aures:
> libera colla iugo subdere fatur.
> nil mihi nunc prestat, ni dare possim:

non ius, non studium, fama nec ingens,
non decus altisonum nobilitatis,
non honor ante habitus, diuitieque,
non doctrina sagax, facta nec artes,
nonque dei cultus, nonque senectus.
nulla locum retinent posse nec ullum.
nunc dispecta iacent ardua quondam;
dispicitur populus atque sacerdos
uerbo, corde, opere Francigenarum.

Why have the blind fates not let us die? Why does the earth not consume us, nor the sea swallow us? Now an unheard-of rumour comes to our ears: it says that free necks are subjected to the yoke. Nothing is of any use to me now, but the power of giving: neither the law, nor learning, nor great fame, nor the deep-resounding glory of nobility, not honour formerly held, not riches, not wise teaching, not deeds nor arts, not reverence of God, not old age; none of these things retains its station, nor any power. Now the labours of earlier days lie despised; the people and the priest are despised by the word, heart and work of the Normans.

(lines 4–17)

The changes clearly entailed many challenges for a family like Sulien's, and much of what they valued seemed to be in peril. On the other hand, this was also to be a time of immense cultural opportunity, and the cross-fertilization of ideas between the Welsh and Anglo-Norman worlds had in it the potential for great developments. In fact, the Latin works of Sulien's sons were themselves harbingers of this new opportunity. Ieuan, in his poem on the life and family of Sulien, likens his father's pursuit of learning to the bee sipping honey from the flower:[5]

haut secus assiduo persistens nocte dieque
exsugit puro septeni gurgitis amne
pocula mellifluo flatu flagrantia longe.

Not otherwise Sulien, persisting diligently (in his studies) by night and day, extracted continuously from the pure stream of the sevenfold fountain cupfuls fragrant with mellifluous aroma.

(lines 109–111)

The 'pure stream of the sevenfold fountain' refers to the Seven Liberal Arts, the *trivium* and the *quadrivium*, which were to

continue as the basis of education in Europe into the High
Middle Ages, as they had been since Late Antiquity. In the
twelfth century Wales was increasingly drawn into the world of
Norman culture, becoming more and more open to influences
and ideas from the European continent. Even the conservative
scriptorium at Llanbadarn Fawr soon displayed Norman styles,
and continental influences were at work there. The manuscript
(London, British Library, MS Cotton Faustina C 1, Part Two)
which contains Rhigyfarch's *Planctus* also includes Macrobius'
commentary on Cicero's *Somnium Scipionis*. It has been
established beyond reasonable doubt that it was written in
Llanbadarn,[6] but the script which it displays is a form of
Caroline minuscule markedly different from the 'flat-topped'
Insular minuscule used in the earlier products of Llanbadarn,
such as Ieuan ap Sulien's copy of the *De Trinitate* or the
magnificent Psalter and Martyrology which was copied (at
Rhigyfarch's request) by a certain Ithael.[7] Likewise, a fragment
of Bede's *De natura rerum*, also written in Caroline minuscule but
containing features of Insular script, is almost certainly a
product of Llanbadarn in the first half of the twelfth century.[8]

Not least among the cultural currents which crossed Wales in
the wake of the coming of the Normans was a heightened sense
of the classical past, and a greater awareness – sometimes at first
hand, frequently from *florilegia*, grammars and other sources – of
classical Latin literature. Undoubtedly, the single most important
agent in creating this awareness was the Church: not now the
native Welsh *clas* with its own indigenous roots but an
organization unified under papal authority and one with
developments which were happening over the whole continent
of Europe. The Church had a monopoly of education, and the
ecclesiastical uniformity imposed upon Europe meant that
Britain, including Wales, became increasingly open to fresh
cultural influences. Throughout Europe, as Professor Glanmor
Williams has succinctly put it, 'new social energies were being
generated in many different directions: the economy, politics,
religion, art and education all bear the marks of the
unmistakable prosperity and vitality of the new and seminal
civilization of that period we know as the Middle Ages. Wales
shared in this achievement along with the other European
countries.'[9]

At the heart of that sense of new vitality in Europe in the twelfth century was a massive revival of interest in the ancient world and in the heritage of Latin literature. The growth of schools and universities, coupled as it was to the gradual but perceptible shift of the focus for education and learning from the monasteries to urban churches, meant that an increasing number of able young men could benefit from a clerical education without of necessity embracing the monastic life.[10] Two twelfth-century Englishmen, among the finest Latin writers of the age, represent the alternative avenues which were possible for an aspiring scholar: William of Malmesbury (died *c*.1143) appears to have spent his life at the monastery in Malmesbury, surrounded by an excellent library which enabled him to write his historical works; on the other hand, John of Salisbury (*c*.1110–80), one of the most brilliant Latin stylists of his day, travelled for his education to Chartres and Paris, returned to England and became chief secretary to Archbishop Thomas Becket, and later went back to France and became Bishop of Chartres.

The twelfth-century Renaissance, and its renewed interest in classical Latin, impinged also upon Wales. A good deal of Latin writing was produced in Wales during the century, much of it functional in its purpose: law-books, religious writings (such as saints' Lives, and also works rooted in issues of ecclesiastical politics like the *Book of Llandav*) and chronicles.[11] Most significant of all, for the quality of their Latin style and for their degree of classical awareness, are the works of two distinguished Latin writers who certainly maintained some connection with Wales, even if their writing was mostly done elsewhere. They are Geoffrey of Monmouth and Gerald of Wales.

Geoffrey, although possibly of Breton descent, was clearly connected with southern Wales. On three occasions (I.1; VII.2; XI.1)[12] in his celebrated *Historia Regum Britanniae* ('History of the Kings of Britain') he refers to himself as Geoffrey 'of Monmouth', and it is reasonable to suppose that his family played some part in the Norman occupation of the Monmouth area. In the course of the *Historia* he mentions Carmarthen, and St Peter's Church in that town (VI.17), Llandaff (IX.15) and Llanbadarn Fawr (XI.3). Most significant of all is the prominence which he gives to Caerleon-on-Usk, *Urbs Legionum*, as the location of King Arthur's court. Situated some twenty miles from Monmouth,

Caerleon may have been particularly well known to Geoffrey. There is unusual detail, enhanced by Geoffrey's fertile imagination, in the description of Caerleon as the scene of the plenary court at which Arthur, wearing his crown, welcomes the kings and leaders of Europe (IX.12):[13]

In Glamorgantia etenim super Oscam fluuium non longe a Sabrino mari ameno situ locata pre ceteris ciuitatibus diuiciarum copiis habundans tante sollennitati apta erat. Ex una nanque parte predictum flumen nobile iuxta eam fluebat per quod transmarini reges et principes qui uenturi erant nauigio aduehi poterant. Ex alia uero parte pratis et nemoribus uallata regalibus prepollebat palaciis ita ut aureis tectorum fastigiis Romam imitaretur. Duabus autem eminebat ecclesiis quarum una in honore Iulii martyris erecta uirgineo Deo dictatarum choro perpulchre ornabatur. Alia quidem in beati Aaron eiusdem socii nomine fundata canonicorum conuentu subnixa tertiam metropolitanam sedem Britanniae habebat. Preterea ginnasium ducentorum phylosoforum habebat qui astronomia atque ceteris artibus eruditi cursus stellarum diligenter obseruabant et prodigia eorum temporum uentura regi Arturo ueris argumentis predicebant. Tot igitur deliciarum copiis preclara festiuitati edicte disponitur.

Situated as it is in Glamorgan, on the River Usk, not far from the Severn Sea, in a most pleasant position, and being richer in material wealth than other townships, this city was eminently suitable for such a ceremony. The river which I have named flowed by it on one side, and up this the kings and princes who were to come from across the sea could be carried in a fleet of ships. On the other side, which was flanked by meadows and wooded groves, they had adorned the city with royal palaces, and by the gold-painted gables of its roofs it was a match for Rome. What is more, it was famous for its two churches. One of these, built in honour of the martyr Julius, was graced by a choir of most lovely virgins dedicated to God. The second, founded in the name of the blessed Aaron, the companion of Julius, was served by a monastery of canons, and counted as the third metropolitan see of Britain. The city also contained a college of two hundred learned men, who were skilled in astronomy and the other arts, and who watched with great attention the courses of the stars and so by their careful computations prophesied for King Arthur any prodigies due at that time. It was this city, therefore, famous for such a wealth of pleasant things, which was made ready for the feast.

Geoffrey's imaginative mind has gone to work on the ruins of *Isca Silurum*. He has populated it with magi, and elevated it to the position of a metropolitan see, a claim which played a not insignificant part in twelfth-century church politics.[14] But most striking of all about the passage is its balanced Latinity (*ex una parte . . . ex alia parte; una . . . alia*) and the warmth with which its author develops his description of his *locus amoenus*.

Whatever Geoffrey's precise connection with south Wales, it is known with certainty that most of his adult life was spent in Oxford or its neighbourhood. His name appears in name-lists and charters of religious houses in the area: the priory of Oseney, for example, and the college of canons of the church of St George.[15] These houses may have played a part in the early beginnings of what developed into the University of Oxford, and Geoffrey was in the city when scholars (who are by now somewhat obscure figures) like Theobald of Etampes and Robert Pullen kept schools in the vicinity of St Mary's Church. It was also at Oxford that Geoffrey met the learned Walter, Archdeacon of Oxford, *vir in oratoria arte atque in exoticis historiis eruditus*, 'a man skilled in the art of public speaking and well-informed about the history of foreign countries' (I.1). Walter gave him, he claims, *quendam Britannici sermonis librum vetustissimum*, 'a certain very ancient book written in the British language' – presumably Welsh, possibly Breton (it hardly matters) – which he then translated into Latin. It is now generally agreed that the claim that the work is a translation, itself a *topos*, is the opening shot of an ingenious literary hoax. To quote Dr Brynley Roberts: 'Today, after some detailed studies of the *Historia*, there can be no doubt that Geoffrey of Monmouth was a writer with a lively and creative imagination, able to make imposing bricks with very little straw. He seems to have been able to see the possibilities inherent in a few suggestive sentences, to combine and adapt different sources and to create a story from the mere record of a name.'[16]

Geoffrey's *Historia Regum Britanniae* was completed in the 1130s, and the only other work by him which has come down to us is a Latin poem of over 1500 hexameters, *Vita Merlini*, composed about 1150.[17] The title *magister* which is regularly given to him suggests that he taught, probably as a secular canon, in Oxford. His involvement with the ecclesiastical politics of his day led, in 1152, to his ordination as a priest and immediate consecration as Bishop of St Asaph, although he never visited his diocese. His natural ambience was the world of scholars and of bishops' councils and of the Plantagenet royal household.

The *Historia* merits a place, however, in a study of the classical tradition in Wales not only because of its author's early connections with south-east Wales or on account of the work's fluent and unstrained use of the Latin language. True, the work may have been largely designed to provide Geoffrey's Norman masters with a glorious past which they might emulate and regard as their own, free from the encumbrance of the traditions of Angles and Saxons. King Arthur, as presented by Geoffrey, could be viewed by the Norman conquerors as the ideal pattern for their own imperial aspirations. But the *Historia Regum Britanniae* also had a Welsh objective, namely to secure for the Welsh nation 'cultural respectability within an essentially English state dominated by the French-speaking descendants of the conquerors of 1066'.[18] This objective was largely realized through the forging of a classical link. Geoffrey's work begins by wondrously developing the account in the *Historia Brittonum* of Brutus (alias Britto), the supposed great-grandson of Aeneas.[19] A summary is given of Aeneas' flight from Troy (I.3), followed by an account of the birth of Brutus to Silvius, son of Ascanius, and a niece of Lavinia, daughter of Latinus. Brutus is said to have been the cause of the deaths of both his mother and his father. He was therefore driven into exile from Italy, and arrived in Greece. There he came upon some descendants of Helenus, Priam's son, held in captivity by Pandrasus, a Greek king. By cunning stratagem and decisive fighting Brutus secured the release of the Trojans, and, after a series of adventures, he brought them to the island of Albion, shortly to be renamed 'Britain' after him. Geoffrey proceeds to tell how Brutus and his Trojan followers inhabited the island, and how Locrinus, Camber and Albanactus, three sons of his marriage to Innogen (or Ignoge), daughter of Pandrasus, became rulers of the three parts of the island after their father's death. Fantastic though it all is, Geoffrey's account contrived to place Britain on the same footing as Rome, with the same Trojan, heroic ancestry. As Aeneas was the leader of a band of Trojans and became the founder of the Roman race, so too his descendant Brutus was the founder of the British people. Geoffrey puts it thus, in words spoken by Julius Caesar (IV.1): '*Hercle! Ex eadem prosapia nos Romani et Britones orti sumus quia ex Troiana processimus gente*', 'By Hercules, those Britons come from the same race as we do, for we Romans, too, are descended from Trojan stock'. Even in the days of King Arthur, the British are represented as still observing the ancient customs of Troy, *antiquam . . . consuetudinem Troie servantes* (IX.13). In all this, the *Historia* provided for Britain a foundation-myth whose credentials were on the same level as those provided for Rome by the greatest of classical Latin poems, Virgil's *Aeneid*.

Not surprisingly, the *Historia Regum Britanniae* held an immense appeal throughout the Middle Ages for the Welsh, who viewed themselves as uniquely 'British', the true descendants of Brutus. In the words of Hubert, Archbishop of Canterbury, in 1199, 'the Welsh, being sprung by unbroken succession from the original stock of the Britons, boast of all Britain as theirs by right.'[20] The *Historia* was translated into Welsh at least three times before the end of the thirteenth century, and its place in the Welsh imagination is clear from some sixty manuscript copies of those Welsh translations which have survived. Thus, indirectly, names and material which belonged to the Trojan cycle of legends were introduced into Wales: Aeneas, Ascanius, Priam, Dardanus, Anchises, Antenor. The names are not always used in a manner which is consistent with their place in classical literature. For example, the name of Assaracus, in Virgil an august ancestor of Aeneas, provides Geoffrey (I.3) with a young man, *ex Troiana matre natus* ('born of a Trojan mother'), who helps Brutus in his opposition to Pandrasus. Likewise Corineus, who is to become the eponymous founder of Cornwall, appears to be named after Virgil's Corynaeus, a name used in the *Aeneid* of two separate Trojan companions of Aeneas. Geoffrey's use of classical names is not, of course, confined to epic or mythological characters. In Books IV and V, where the Roman occupation of Britain is discussed, the reader meets Julius Caesar, Claudius, Vespasian and many other Roman historical personages.[21] Of greater significance than the use of classical names are the specific echoes of classical writers and their themes with which Geoffrey presents his readers. No allusion is surprising, but all serve to show that Geoffrey amply shared in the education and Latin culture of the twelfth century. He quotes Lucan (IV.9) and Juvenal (IV.16) by name; he has one king of Britain, Cadwallo, address (XII.6) Salomon, king of Brittany, with words that are a virtual quotation of Horace's address to Maecenas in the first line of the first of his *Odes*; a speech delivered by Arthur is described (IX.17), possibly with some irony, as *deliberatio Tulliano liquore lita* ('a speech dripping with Ciceronian flow'); fugitives from Maxentius begin an address (V.7) to Constantine in Britain with an echo of the famous beginning of Cicero's first speech against Catiline; there is even some awareness of Homer, *clarus rhetor et poeta* (II.6).

Pre-eminent among the classical authors whose work permeates Geoffrey's writing is Virgil.[22] In itself this is not surprising, as the *Aeneid* was the most studied and revered of Latin literary works throughout late antiquity and into the Middle Ages. More significant is the fact that an account of the descent of Brutus from a Trojan line was bound to invite use of and comparison with the *Aeneid*. Not that Geoffrey was the first to provide his people with a Trojan descent, as witness many other 'national' genealogies which emerge from the Dark Ages, and Brutus already existed in the *Historia Brittonum*. But the imaginative and adroit way in which Geoffrey has used that basic tradition preserved by 'Nennius', and has woven into it Virgilian themes, makes the *Historia* a work of unique brilliance. This is especially evident in the earlier part of the work. The Brutus story, as Geoffrey tells it, is a foundation-myth, following in the line of Virgil's account of Aeneas' departure from Troy to establish his new city. The account of Brutus' voyage, for example, and of his adventures on the way, contains regular echoes of situations in *Aeneid* III, the book which tells of Aeneas' adventures between leaving Troy and arriving in Carthage. Brutus and his followers reach the deserted island of Leogetia (I.11), where he visits a temple of Diana and makes his appeal – in elegiac couplets – to the goddess's statue, opening his address to her in language reminiscent of the opening of Horace's *Carmen Saeculare* and a hymn to Diana (*Odes* III.22). The goddess subsequently appears to him, and gives him instructions (also in elegiacs) during his sleep (technically known as an *incubatio*) in the temple:[23]

Brute, sub occasu solis trans Gallica regna
Insula in occeano est undique clausa mari.
Insula in occeano est, habitata gigantibus olim,
Nunc deserta quidem, gentibus apta tuis.
Hanc pete: namque tibi sedes erit illa perennis;
Hic fiet natis altera Troia tuis.
Hic de prole tua reges nascentur, et ipsis
Totius terre subditus orbis erit.

Brutus, beyond the setting of the sun, past the realms of Gaul,
there lies an island in the ocean, completely surrounded by sea. An
island there is in the ocean, once occupied by giants; now it is
deserted and ready for your folk. Seek it: for down the years this
will be your abode; here will be a second Troy for your
descendants. A race of kings will be born there from your stock
and the round circle of the whole earth will be subject to them.

The situation, while not slavishly imitative, is modelled on the
account (*Aeneid* III.73ff.) of the arrival of Aeneas' men at Delos,
the island sacred to Apollo, Diana's brother, and the information
given to them there about their future journey. Likewise, the
reference to Brutus coming upon the descendants of Helenus
(I.3) recalls, with intriguing alterations, the account of Helenus,
son of Priam, in *Aeneid* III.299ff., with the detail of the slight
which Assaracus suffered at the hands of his brother supplied
from the picture of Jugurtha in Sallust's *Bellum Iugurthinum*. Nor
is use of the *Aeneid* confined to the Brutus story. The telling of
the love of Locrinus for Estrildis (II.2–5) has in it ingredients
which recall the Dido episode in Virgil's epic. In short,
Geoffrey's *Historia* is (to quote Jacob Hammer) 'a eulogy of the
past, a prose-epic, a Welsh *Aeneid* in prose'.[24]

The other major writer of Latin to emerge from twelfth-century
Wales was Gerald de Barri (Giraldus Cambrensis/Gerald of
Wales, c.1146–1223).[25] He is one of the most readable Latin
authors of the Middle Ages, although within Wales itself his
work remained untranslated and consequently did not enjoy a
popularity to compare with Geoffrey's *Historia*. Gerald is a
typical representative of the ethnic and cultural mix of the years
which followed the Norman occupation of parts of Wales. His

father, William de Barri, was a knight whose family had participated in the Norman conquest of Glamorgan, before settling further west at Manorbier in south Pembrokeshire. On the other hand, Gerald's mother, Angharad, was a granddaughter of Rhys ap Tewdwr, prince of Deheubarth, a spirited opponent of ever-greater Norman encroachments. His daughter Nest, 'the Helen of Wales', was married – after her father's death – to Gerald of Windsor, castellan of Pembroke, and they were the parents of Angharad. Gerald was born at Manorbier, a place which always retained a special place in his affections: he concludes his famous description of it by saying that, throughout the whole of Wales, it was 'the most pleasant place by far' (*locus amoenissimus*).[26] But he was also painfully conscious of his mixed ancestry and a victim of the complexes which that created. 'Both peoples regard me as a stranger, and one not their own', he sadly complains.[27]

The education which Gerald received was certainly that of one who belonged to the privileged world of the Norman overlords. He entered the monastic school of the Benedictine abbey of St Peter's, Gloucester, an establishment which had been enriched by the grant to it of the estates and endowments of those two notable Welsh *clasau*, Llancarfan and Llanbadarn Fawr. At Gloucester he studied under 'that most learned scholar, Master Haimo',[28] before proceeding to Paris, the greatest centre of learning in the Europe of his day. His many years in Paris, both as a student and later as a teacher, were ones of great academic success. Of the years there he writes, in his autobiography, that he spent them 'in the study of the liberal arts and at last equalling the greatest teachers, taught the *Trivium* there most excellently, winning especially fame in the art of rhetoric'.[29] His experiences in Wales and Ireland, in Gloucester and Hereford, in Rome and Lincoln, were to be the sources of immense cultural enrichment for Gerald. It was the Paris experience, however, which made a great writer of him. In the succinct and totally apposite words of Robert Bartlett: 'It was Gerald's training at Paris, and his acquisition there of the highest learning that the Latin West could offer, that enabled him to articulate and analyse his own society in the way he did.'[30] The great innovative days of the Parisian schools of Peter Lombard, Hugh of St Victor and Peter Abelard were over, but it was into their rich scholastic legacy that Gerald entered. Bartlett describes it thus:[31]

> The education available at Paris in the later twelfth century was
> diverse and sophisticated. The initial stage, the arts course,
> provided a training in self-expression and logical thought. It also
> gave the student a chance to become familiar with a broad range of
> classical literature, and Gerald's ready use of Roman authors has
> been frequently commented upon. In this respect he can be
> characterized as a 'humanist' in the same sense as John of
> Salisbury. John, Gerald, and other twelfth-century authors wrote
> fluent, forceful Latin, deeply influenced by classical as well as
> biblical models. They take their place in the great efflorescence of
> literary culture, both Latin and vernacular, which occurred in this
> period.

Gerald's devotion to the classical tradition is amply shown in his
writings, which are as varied as they are prolific. Many reflect
his years in royal service and his ecclesiastical concerns, some
belong to the protracted battles concerning St David's and
Gerald's arguments about the status of the see and his own
claims to it, others are pieces of hagiography to which he
devoted his quieter years. Of greatest appeal to a modern reader
are four of his early works: two concerned with Ireland,
Expugnatio Hibernica (*The Conquest of Ireland*) and *Topographia
Hibernica* (*The Topography of Ireland*),[32] two with Wales, *Itinerarium
Kambriae* (*The Journey through Wales*) and *Descriptio Kambriae* (*A
Description of Wales*).[33] These last two are important not only
because in them Gerald brought his training in Paris and
elsewhere to bear upon his writing about Wales, but also because
they served to present Wales and the Welsh to a wider world.

The *Itinerarium Kambriae* is based on incidents which occurred
and material gathered during the course of the journey which
Gerald, then Archdeacon of Brecon, made through Wales in 1188.
He travelled as the companion of Archbishop Baldwin of
Canterbury, their mission the preaching of the Third Crusade.
Like the *Descriptio*, a more reflective work on both the
praiseworthy and the unpraiseworthy characteristics of the
Welsh, the *Itinerarium* is remarkable for the author's acute
powers of observation. Both works also testify to Gerald's
devotion to *literata eloquentia*, the love of literature (*amor
literarum*) which he says he had known from childhood.[34]

Contained in them are hundreds of classical quotations, drawn from a much wider range of authors than is the case in Geoffrey's *Historia Regum Britanniae*. The ancient texts are often cited as 'authorities' rather than used thematically in the way Geoffrey makes use of the *Aeneid*. But Gerald's familiarity with the Latin classics – even if some of his knowledge is bound to be based on *florilegia* and grammars – is formidable, as is shown by nearly every page of his works. For example, the 'first preface' of the *Itinerarium* contains quotations from Persius, Terence, Aulus Gellius, Virgil (*Eclogues* and *Georgics*), Sidonius Apollinaris, Ovid (*Amores* and *Ars Amatoria*), Statius and Juvenal, as well as referring to Galen, Justinian, Marius, Jerome and others from the ancient past. When he discusses (*Itinerarium* I.3) a perceived decline in the adherence of the religious orders to their vows of holiness and purity, he draws not only on the Bible to support his strictures but also on Seneca, Horace, Lucan and even Ovid and Petronius! Significant also is Gerald's acute philological sense, which leads him to speculate in a knowing way about the relationship between Welsh, Latin and Greek.[35]

Gerald's philological observations, like his few quotations in Welsh, show that he had some knowledge of the language. He would have heard, in Welsh, the many folk-tales which he enjoys recounting, and it is reasonable to suppose that Welsh would have been his language for communicating with the Welsh side of his family. On the other hand, we are not told that he preached in Welsh during the course of the *Itinerarium*. Indeed it is specifically stated that 'Alexander, Archdeacon of Bangor, acted as interpreter for the Welsh'.[36] However, he did make use of Latin sources about Wales, not least Geoffrey of Monmouth's *Historia*. Gerald's attitude towards Geoffrey is ambivalent, often disparaging, but that he relied on parts of the earlier writer's work is quite clear. Gerald's dependence on Geoffrey, but also their pronounced difference of attitude towards historical fact, can be seen from comparing Gerald's account of Caerleon with that of the *Historia*, quoted above. Gerald draws on Geoffrey, but there is in the *Itinerarium* a truer sense of the reality of the place and its genuine Roman past:[37]

Dicitur autem Kaerleun Legionum urbs. *Kaer* enim Britannice urbs vel castrum dicitur. Solent quippe legiones, a Romanis in insulam missae, ibi hiemare; et inde Urbs Legionum dicta est. Erat autem haec urbs antiqua et authentica, et a Romanis olim coctilibus muris egregie constructa. Videas hic multa pristinae nobilitatis adhuc vestigia; palatia immensa, aureis olim tectorum fastigiis Romanos fastus imitantia, eo quod a Romanis principibus primo constructa, et aedificiis egregiis illustrata fuissent; turrim giganteam, thermas insignes, templorum reliquias, et loca theatralia; egregiis muris partim adhuc exstantibus omnia clausa. Reperies ubique, tam intra murorum ambitum quam extra, aedificia subterranea, aquarum ductus, hypogeosque meatus. Et quod inter alia notabile censui, stuphas undique videas miro artificio consertas; lateralibus quibusdam et praeangustis spiraculi viis occulte calorem exhalantibus . . . Situs urbis egregius, super Oschae flumen; navigio, mari influente, idoneum. Silvis et pratis urbs illustrata. Hic magni illius Arthuri famosam curiam legati adiere Romani.

Caerleon is the modern name of the City of the Legions. In Welsh 'caer' means a city or encampment. The legions sent to this island by the Romans had the habit of wintering in this spot, and so it came to be called the City of the Legions. Caerleon is of unquestioned antiquity. It was constructed with great care by the Romans, the walls being built of bricks. You can still see many vestiges of its one-time splendour. There are immense palaces, which, with the gilded gables of their roofs, once rivalled the magnificence of ancient Rome. They were set up in the first place by some of the most eminent men of the Roman state, and they were therefore embellished with every architectural conceit. There is a lofty tower, and beside it remarkable hot baths, the remains of temples and an amphitheatre. All this is enclosed within impressive walls, parts of which still remain standing. Wherever you look, both within and without the circuit of these walls, you can see constructions dug deep into the earth, conduits for water, underground passages and air-vents. Most remarkable of all to my mind are the stoves, which once transmitted heat through narrow pipes inserted in the side-walls and which are built with extraordinary skill . . . Caerleon is beautifully situated on the bank of the River Usk. When the tide comes in, ships sail right up to the city. It is surrounded by woods and meadows. It was here that the Roman legates came to seek audience at the great Arthur's famous court.

Geoffrey and Gerald represent, as we have seen, the emergence of writers whose classical awareness and fluent Latin were largely the products of years spent in great 'university' centres like Paris and Oxford. Gerald, like his friend Walter Map, was trained in Paris but also had some Oxford connections. In his autobiography Gerald tells of a visit he made to give a reading of his *Topographia Hibernica* 'before a great audience at Oxford, where of all places in England the clergy were most strong and pre-eminent in learning'.[38] During the medieval centuries Oxford (and Cambridge too – but to a much lesser extent because of its geographical position) attracted many Welshmen. It has been estimated that at least 390 Welsh students attended Oxford during the Middle Ages, and some of the most notable among them went also to Paris or other continental universities.[39] The growth of the orders of friars in the thirteenth century gave a big boost to educational concerns. One of the most notable of their number in the later thirteenth century was the Franciscan scholar John of Wales, Johannes Wallensis, who hailed from the border country of southern Wales and rose to be a leader in his order in both Oxford and Paris. This great preacher, teacher and scholar, who was honoured with the title *Arbor Vitae* ('Tree of Life'), has left in Latin important ethical and homiletic works which are imbued with classical learning. He drew especially on the ancient philosophers.[40] Nor should one forget the contribution of Welsh monasteries to the copying and preservation of some classical texts. Manuscripts of Cicero's *De Senectute* and *De Amicitia* are connected with the Dominican convent of Haverfordwest and the Augustinian priory at Llanthony.[41] The Cistercian abbey at Margam, the richest of Welsh monastic houses, possessed many of the works of Seneca.[42]

What, however, of literary concerns within Wales, and in the Welsh language, during the Middle Ages? The Norman period was a time which brought not only the influence of a European, and Latin, revival of learning to Wales, but also saw a remarkable flowering of native literature. The best-known prose works are the so-called *Mabinogion*: of these, *Pedair Cainc y Mabinogi* (The Four Branches of the Mabinogi) are the most celebrated, tales which belong entirely to the Celtic world, largely unaffected by the legacy of classical writing. Likewise the poetry of the *Gogynfeirdd*, the court poets who sang in honour of the Welsh princes of the period between the Norman conquest and the loss of Welsh independence in 1282, stands firmly in the tradition of Taliesin's poetry of praise. As to knowledge of classical literature among such poets, it has been accurately and aptly stated, by Professor Ceri Lewis, that 'no evidence exists to prove that prior to the fourteenth century the Welsh professional bards, in general, had more than a very superficial knowledge of Latin and its literature, acquired mainly from the Church services and from some familiarity with the life of the monasteries.'[43]

Nevertheless it is clear, as Professor Lewis implies, that some small degree of classical awareness did impinge on intrinsically native and indigenous literary forms, and would gain further momentum in the fourteenth century. The bardic schools, which for centuries maintained strict control over the production of Welsh poetry and whose methods of instruction were largely those of a closed guild, used a framework derived from the classical grammarians Donatus and Priscian for formulating parts of their teaching of 'grammar'. This was crystallized in the texts of the bardic grammar attributed to Einion Offeiriad, 'Einion the Priest' (who flourished in the first half of the fourteenth century), and subsequently to a more nebulous figure, Dafydd Ddu of Hiraddug. The complexities of the bardic grammars and their composition are beyond the compass of this study. It is, however, worth noting that Einion and Dafydd Ddu, in their use of the two classical grammarians, were combining learning derived from their clerical, and essentially Latinate, training with their analysis of the traditional Welsh bardic craft. However unsuitable the classical structures of Donatus' *Artes* and Priscian's *Institutiones* were to meet the needs of Welsh poets, their works gave Welsh poetry the distinction of being one with medieval Latin culture. In the fifteenth century the bardic grammar came to be known as *dwned*, derived from Donatus' name.[44]

Another classical dimension which enriched the work of the *Gogynfeirdd*, and continued in subsequent poets' work, was the use of names of heroes who belonged to the ancient world, heroes who were seen to typify the qualities and attributes of a prince or patron whose virtues were being extolled. Thus Hector (*Ecdor*, *Echdor*), Hercules (*Ercwlff*), Achilles (*Echel*), Aeneas

(*Eneas*), alongside biblical characters and figures from Celtic legend, became part of the stock-in-trade of medieval poets. So, for example, in the late twelfth century Llywarch ap Llywelyn, alias Prydydd y Moch, sings in this way in praise of Rhodri ab Owain Gwynedd:[45]

> Ni bu bryd eisiau Absalon
> Nac Alecsander na Iason,
> Bu cedeirn o'r Tri Trinheion:
> Traul Efrai, afrddwl Groëgion
> Ercwlff a Samswn, seirff galon,
> Ac Echdor gadarn, gad wyllon.

Absalon was not lacking in beauty, nor *Alexander* (= *Paris*), nor *Jason*. Of the Three Warriors, strong were *Ercwlff* and *Samson*, serpent-heart, and *Echdor* the Strong, frenzied in battle – destroyer of the Hebrews and terror of the Greeks.

Many of the names found their way into the lists of *Trioedd Ynys Prydain* ('Triads of the Island of Britain'), 'in effect a kind of catalogue of the names of the traditional heroes, classified in groups of three',[46] originally devised by bardic teachers as mnemonics for their pupils. There one reads, for example:[47]

> Tri Dyn a gauas Kedernit Adaf:
> > Ercwlf Gadarn,
> > Ac Ector Gadarn,
> > A Sompson Gadarn.
> Kyn gadarnet oedynt yll tri ac Adaf ei hun.

> Three men who received the Might of Adam:
> > Hercules the Strong,
> > and Hector the Strong,
> > and Samson the Strong.
> They were, all three, as strong as Adam himself.

In a list of 'the nine bravest and most noble warriors of the whole world', three are 'Pagans': Hector of Troy, Alexander the Great and Julius Caesar.[48] Three men 'who received the Beauty of Adam' were 'Absalom son of David, Jason son of Aeson and Paris son of Priam'.[49] Three women 'who received the Beauty of Eve in three third-shares' were:[50]

Diadema, gorderch Eneas Yscvydwyn,
ac Elen Uannavc, y wreic y bu distriwedigaeth Tro
   drvyy phenn,
a Pholixena uerch Priaf hen vrenhin Tro.

Diadema, mistress of Aeneas White-Shield,
and Elen, the Magnificent, the woman on whose account
   was the destruction of Troy,
and Polixena, daughter of Priam the Old, king of Troy.

Diadema seems to refer to Dido, although there is probably confusion also with Deidameia, mother of Neoptolemus by Achilles.

The power of these classical names, like those of biblical and other figures, was not confined to the poets. The chronicler of *Brut y Tywysogion* (The Chronicle of the Princes), in an eulogy which accompanies his recording of the death of the Lord Rhys in 1197, breaks out thus:[51]

Och am ogonyant y ryueloed a tharyan y marchogion, amdiffynnwr y wlat, tegwch arueu, breich kedernyt, llaw haelyoni, llygat adwyndra, blaenwyd mawrvryt, ymdywynnygrwyd dosparth, mawrvrydrwyd Herkwlff! Eil Achel herwyd garwder y dwyvronn, hynawster Nestor, glewder Tydeus, kedernyt Samson, dewred Hector, llymder Eurialius, tegwch a phryt Paris, huolder Vlixes, doethineb Selyf, mawrvryt Aiax!

Alas for the glory of battles and the shield of knights, the defender of his land, the splendour of arms, the arm of prowess, the hand of generosity, the eye and lustre of worthiness, the summit of majesty, the light of reason, the magananimity of Hercules! A second Achilles in the sturdiness of his breast, the gentleness of Nestor, the doughtiness of Tydeus, the strength of Samson, the valour of Hector, the fleetness of Eurialius, the comeliness and face of Paris, the eloquence of Ulysses, the wisdom of Solomon, the majesty of Ajax!

The classical names quoted in the passage from *Brut y Tywysogion* belong, as can be seen, to the legends associated with the fall of Troy. Translations of Geoffrey's *Historia* undoubtedly heightened Welsh awareness of these ancient figures. The popularity of Geoffrey's work also led to the translation into

Welsh of another Latin text which became the provider of even more names from the classical past. The Welsh work was known as *Ystorya Dared*, a translation (which circulated in many different versions) of the Latin text of the *Historia de Excidio Troiae* attributed to Dares Phrygius.[52] According to Homer's *Iliad* (V.9) Dares was a priest of Hephaestus in Troy, but in later ages he was reputed to be the author of a pre-Homeric account of the Trojan War, written from the Trojan side. The supposed Greek work was lost, but a Latin version became known in the late fifth century AD, prefaced by a letter in which the writer Cornelius Nepos (first century BC) is made to address the historian Sallust and claim that he has translated Dares' Greek into Latin. This is mere convention, not unlike Geoffrey's claim about the *liber vetustissimus*: there is little doubt that Dares' *De Excidio Troiae*, while it drew on scraps of earlier material, is a work which essentially belonged to the world of Late Antiquity.

Welsh versions of *Ystorya Dared*, many in number and falling into three groups, gave Welsh readers a glimpse of the ancient world before the fall of Troy, the point at which Geoffrey of Monmouth's *Historia Regum Britanniae* begins. Dares' story provided, in effect, a 'preface' to Geoffrey's work, and it is not surprising that *Ystorya Dared* is usually found together with a copy of *Brut y Brenhinedd*, one of the Welsh translations of Geoffrey.[53] Dares begins his work with the voyage of the Argo and the adventures of Jason, tells of Hercules' expedition against Laomedon of Troy, and expatiates – with a romantic feel for his tale – on the events of the Trojan War. It is evident that *Ystorya Dared*, more than any other source, provided Welsh poets with names of classical heroes and heroines with whom they might compare their own patrons. It is also the most important source of the lists contained in the Welsh Triads, especially those assembled in the later Middle Ages.

Just as *Ystorya Dared* acted as a preface to the Welsh version of Geoffrey's *Historia*, so *Brut y Tywysogion* – the Chronicle of the Welsh princes, up until the disaster of the end of Welsh independence in 1282 – was conceived as a sequel to it. *Brut y Tywysogion* begins, where Geoffrey's *Historia* ends, with Cadwaladr the Blessed's death in Rome: 'and thenceforth the Britons lost the crown of kingship, and the Saxons obtained it.'[54] *Brut y Tywysogion* is itself a work which testifies to the vibrancy of indigenous Welsh scholarship in the thirteenth century.[55] The lost Latin version of the chronicle was almost certainly compiled at the Cistercian abbey of Strata Florida (or Ystrad Fflur), a religious house which appears to have assumed many of the cultural responsibilities of the *clas* of Llanbadarn Fawr. Before 1400, usually in monastic scriptoria but sometimes by lay scribes in the homes of men of standing (*uchelwyr*), were written some of the most important Welsh manuscript compilations, such as the Hendregadredd Manuscript and the Red Book of Hergest.[56] These are, in their very essence, preservers of Welsh literary works – including the poetry of the *Gogynfeirdd* and the text of *Pedair Cainc y Mabinogi* – which were gloriously and uniquely native. It is, however, noteworthy that some of the prose works contained in the Red Book have a Roman, if not strictly classical, aura: *Breuddwyd Macsen* ('The Dream of Macsen') and *Chwedlau Saith Ddoethion Rhufain* ('Tales of the Seven Sages of Rome'), as well as *Ystorya Dared* and Geoffrey's *Brut*.

One cannot, of course, claim that these indications of classical awareness, interesting and significant though they are, meant that ancient classical authors exerted a major influence on native Welsh literature in the Middle Ages. The bardic schools ensured that Wales had its own 'classical' tradition of poetry, extending back to Taliesin. That poetry was inherently free from outside influences, and followed its own strict canons of metre and style, especially the peculiarly Welsh system of alliteration and sound-chiming known as *cynghanedd*. The Welsh language, too, was a language upheld by rulers and princes, safeguarded by school traditions, dignified by its own learned books – all signs that it shared some of the distinctions of Greek and Latin, as writers of the sixteenth century would emphasize.

It was out of such a situation that the greatest of all Welsh poets arose, namely Dafydd ap Gwilym (*fl.* 1320–70). Dafydd was a master of *cynghanedd*, and, as might be expected, much of his work belongs to the mainstream of Welsh praise-poetry: for example, a group of fine poems to Ifor Hael (Ifor the Generous) of Basaleg, a patron whom he sees fulfilling the role of Urien to his Taliesin. But to think of Dafydd is also to think of a poet whose extraordinary exuberance led him to explore his two main themes of love and of nature through a host of situations and experiences. His love poems, for example, are often expressions of frustrated love, with the poet himself a kind of anti-hero, lost in the mist, laughed at by the girls of Llanbadarn, left out in the rain waiting for his girlfriend as the eaves dripped rainwater over him.

In the context of this study, the importance of Dafydd ap Gwilym lies in the fact that his chosen word to describe his poetry, especially the love poetry, is *Ofyddiaeth*, 'the art of Ovid'.[57] Many strands, both native and European, went into the making of this great poet, and integral to his work is his innovative blend of Ovidian elements and Welsh tradition. Dafydd is a supreme example of the way in which Welsh literature has enjoyed some of its most creative moments when the native tradition has come into tension with a part of the classical heritage.

Ovid is the only external literary authority whom Dafydd ap Gwilym cites for his work, naming the Roman poet fourteen times in all in the corpus of his work. He is himself *dyn Ofydd*, 'Ovid's man'; the lore which he keeps safe is a 'psalm from Ovid's book' (*Salm yw 'nghof o lyfr Ofydd*); he is no coward when it comes to 'the work of Ovid's book' (*Nid gwas . . ./Llwfr wyf ar waith llyfr Ofydd*).[58] There is no doubt that Dafydd, like his near-contemporary Chaucer, was profoundly influenced by the Ovidian tradition which pervaded both the Latin and the vernacular literatures of Europe, notably their love poetry, and made an *aetas Ovidiana* of the twelfth and subsequent centuries. The *Ars Amatoria* was supremely popular, and we have already seen that a manuscript of *Ars Amatoria* I had been copied in Wales as early as the ninth or tenth centuries. There were also numerous translations of the *Ars* into the vernacular languages. It was translated into French alone four times during the Middle Ages, and Ovid's legacy also permeated the later Middle Ages and helped to shape its *courtoisie* through the influence of the thirteenth-century *Roman de la Rose* of Guillaume de Lorris and Jean de Meun.[59] Llywelyn Bren (d. 1317), lord of Senghennydd, is known to have possessed a manuscript copy of the *Roman de la Rose*, and the intermingling of native and Norman culture certainly produced Welshmen who were more than capable of speaking and reading French. Dafydd himself had family connections with parts of Wales which were influenced by Norman-French culture, and it is certain that he himself knew

French. It is therefore quite possible that his knowledge of Ovid, and of the Ovidian tradition, came through translations and also through works like the *Roman de la Rose* which were imbued with the Ovidian spirit.

Very perceptive insights into Dafydd ap Gwilym's relationship to Ovid's *oeuvre* have come from a series of distinguished studies by Dr Rachel Bromwich.[60] She has pointed out that some of Dafydd's poems have a striking resemblance not only to themes in the *Ars Amatoria* but also, and more specifically, to some of Ovid's *Amores*. Dafydd's *cywydd* (*GDG* 39) about a dream allegorically interpreted is paralleled in *Amores* III.5; a cywydd (*GDG* 58), already quoted, to which Sir Thomas Parry gave the title 'Merch yn edliw ei lyfrdra' ('A girl mocks his cowardice', R. M. Loomis), the poet's debate with a girl who regards a soldier as a more desirable lover than a poet, is paralleled in *Amores* III.8; and poems on the theme of the *exclusus amator* (*GDG* 80; 89) are paralleled in *Amores* I.6 and II.12. These were all common themes in classical Latin love elegy, and, as Dr Bromwich shows, there are plentiful examples of their use in medieval literature. The most significant parallel to which Dr Bromwich draws attention is one which was first noticed by Mr Gerald Morgan. It is between *Amores* III.6, in which Ovid addresses an Italian river whose swollen waters prevent him from going to visit his girl, and Dafydd's *cywydd* (*GDG* 71), 'Y don ar Afon Dyfi' ('The wave on the River Dovey'), where Dafydd pleads with the Dyfi in flood to allow him to return to Llanbadarn to visit Morfudd. Ovid's elegiac poem begins thus (lines 1–12):[61]

> Amnis harundinibus limosas obsite ripas,
> > ad dominam propero: siste parumper aquas.
> nec tibi sunt pontes nec quae sine remigis ictu
> > concaua traiecto cumba rudente uehat.
> paruus eras, memini, nec te transire refugi,
> > summaque uix talos contigit unda meos;
> nunc ruis adposito niuibus de monte solutis
> > et turpi crassas gurgite uoluis aquas.
> quid properasse iuuat, quid parca dedisse quieti
> > tempora, quid nocti conseruisse diem,
> si tamen hic standum est, si non datur artibus ullis
> > ulterior nostro ripa premenda pede?

Halt, muddy river! Rest awhile among your reeds.
Make way for a lover in a hurry,
for you haven't a bridge, or a chain-ferry,
to take me across without oars.
I remember you as a little stream, easily forded,
hardly deep enough to wet my ankles.
Now you're in spate, swollen by melting snow from the
    mountain,
swirling along brown and turbid.
Why did I hurry, scanting sleep,
journeying night and day,
to mark time here, without a hope
of setting a foot on the far bank?

And so Dafydd ap Gwilym:[62]

Y don bengrychlon grochlais,
Na ludd, goel budd, ym gael bais
I'r tir draw, lle y daw ym dâl,
Nac oeta fi, nac atal.
Gad, er Duw rad, ardwy ri,
Drais y dwfr, fi dros Dyfi.
Tro drachefn, trefn trychanrhwyd,
Dy fardd wyf, uwch dwfr ydd wyd.

Loud-voiced, rippling, crested Wave,
do not prevent me – portent of success –
from fording to the other side, whence comes my
    recompense:
do not delay me, do not hinder me.
For God's sake, the Lord of succour,
[you] watery tyrant, let me cross the Dyfi.
Turn back, home of three hundred nets,
I am your poet: the foremost of all rivers you.

Dr Bromwich writes of the parallel treatment:[63]

Each poet, in apostrophizing the river, claims that it ought to sympathize with him as a lover: Ovid points out that rivers too have been in love, and gives a long list of the loves of various rivers for nymphs, while Dafydd claims that no one has praised the wave of the Dyfi so much, or compared it to so many different things – its strength to the shoulder of a horse or a man, its voice to a harp or an organ, and so on.

She then makes the following important point:

> I am not aware that any close parallel, other than Ovid, can be found for Dafydd's *cywydd*, and I think that this by itself offers at any rate a presumption that Dafydd knew of the *Amores* in some form.

One must not, of course, discount the obvious fact that Dafydd ap Gwilym's fertile genius was more than capable of creating the imaginative treatment which he gives to his theme entirely from his own resources. Professor D. J. Bowen has aptly noted that crossing rivers, and the effects of stormy weather, are themes in other poems by Dafydd.[64] Nevertheless, the collection of parallels with the *Amores* is remarkably striking. It is also worth noting, with Dr Bromwich, that the *Amores* were not nearly as much translated into the vernacular languages as the *Ars Amatoria*. The possibility is surely there that Dafydd ap Gwilym knew something of Ovid's love poetry, including the *Amores*, in the original Latin, although too much should not be built on such a hypothesis. Of real importance is the fact that Dafydd, whether he was totally familiar with Ovid's Latin or not, recognizes that he is one with so many other devotees of 'Venus' Clerk Ovyde' and that it is the Ovidian spirit which he is infusing into his love poetry and poems of situation. It is the Ovidian spirit too which he uses to revolutionize the old tradition of Welsh poetry, with its strict rules about the proper way of praising *rhianedd*, the young ladies of the court. This is what Dafydd himself acknowledged in calling himself 'Ovid's man'.

Dafydd ap Gwilym's awareness of Ovid, not only as a classical authority for idealized *amour courtois* but also as a witty and unashamedly erotic writer whose subject is love's realities, gives its special colour and shape to the Welshman's poetry. The novelty of the Ovidian strain is also underlined by the way in which Dafydd conventionally refers to those classical heroes and heroines whose names were handed down in Geoffrey's *Brut*, in *Ystorya Dared*, and in the Triads: Hector (*Ector/Echdor*) and

Hercules (*Ercwlff*),[65] and especially the triad of women at the beginning of the *cywydd* to which Sir Thomas Parry gave the title 'Rhagoriaeth ei gariad' ('His love's pre-eminence').[66] Dafydd bases his theme on the material contained in the Triad quoted above:[67]

> Tair gwragedd â'u gwedd fal gwawn
> A gafas yn gwbl gyfiawn
> Pryd cain, pan fu'r damwain da,
> A roes Duw Nef ar Efa.
> Cyntaf o'r tair disgleirloyw
> A'i cafas, ehudras hoyw,
> Policsena ferch Bria,
> Gwaisg o grair yn gwisgo gra.
> A'r ail fu Ddiodemaf,
> Gwiwbryd goleudraul haul haf.
> Trydedd fun ail Rhun yrhawg
> Fu Elen feinwen fannawg,
> Yr hon a beris cyffro
> A thrin rhwng Gröeg a Thro.

> Three women with their face like gossamer
> Got in full proportion
> The fine beauty, when the good state was,
> That God of Heaven gave Eve.
> The first of the brilliant three
> Who won it (lively, fleeting gift)
> Was Polixena, daughter of Priam,
> A bright treasure wearing fur.
> And the second was Deidameia,
> Her lovely face like the light-expending summer sun.
> That third girl, for long a second Rhun,
> Was white and slender Elen Fannog,
> The one who caused commotion
> And war between Greece and Troy.

Needless to say, the girl who has caught Dafydd's eye outstrips all three.

Dafydd ap Gwilym's work also contains two references to 'Fferyll', i.e. Virgil: not Virgil as a literary authority and major classical poet of Augustan Rome, but rather in the role of magician and wonder-worker with which he was invested in the

Middle Ages.[68] Dafydd describes the colours and shapes on a garland of peacock feathers which his beloved gave him as *drychau o ffeiriau Fferyll*, 'mirrors from Virgil's fairs'.[69] And in a *cywydd* in which the girl is herself seen, very significantly, as a wonder-working enchantress, Dafydd says of a silver harp that will be given to her:[70]

> Ei chwr y sydd, nid gwŷdd gwŷll,
> O ffurf celfyddyd Fferyll.
>
> Its frame (?) not made of forest wood
> but conjured by Virgilian art.

These are not isolated references in medieval Welsh literature to the tradition about Virgil as a magician. The folk-tale and the (later) poetry which grew around the persona of Taliesin present him as the son of Ceridwen, a witch well-versed in *celfyddyd llyfrau Pheryllt*, 'the art of Virgil's books', while Taliesin himself is made to find grounds for personal jubilation *o erymes Fferyll*, 'because of Virgil's prophecy'.[71] The tradition of Virgil the wonder-worker – as, for that matter, the use of the heroic names encapsulated in the Triads – was to continue also in the work of masters of the *cywydd* after Dafydd ap Gwilym. Thus Guto'r Glyn, in the fifteenth century, in a poem which also contains references to Diogenes and Alexander the Great, likens the workmanship on the house of one of his patrons to *gwaith Fferyll*, 'Virgil's work'; and Tudur Aled, at the beginning of the following century, refers to a craftsman as *câr i Fferyll*, 'a friend of Virgil'.[72] Meanwhile, in other *cywyddau*, Guto'r Glyn likens the travels of Sieffrai Cyffin to those of *Iason ab Eson*, 'Jason son of Aeson', and compares Dafydd Mathau of Llandaff and his burgeoning family with Priam and his children.[73] Likewise the legends about Alexander find their place in the poets' work: for example, in a *cywydd* by Dafydd Nanmor to the infant Henry Tudor.[74] Interest in Alexander was particularly maintained in Europe by the translation from Arabic into Latin, under the intriguing name *Secretum Secretorum* ('Secret of Secrets'), of the letter supposedly sent by Aristotle to the young Alexander. This was translated into Welsh during the fourteenth century.[75] Legends concerning Alexander were also made popular in the

Middle Ages by Walter of Châtillon's poem, *Alexandreis*. The work was known in Wales, and – as will be seen later – the part of Book I which was based on the *Secretum Secretorum* was translated into Welsh in the sixteenth century.

It is difficult to tell to what extent some of the medieval *cywyddwyr* had direct knowledge of classical Latin texts. We have seen that there are reasons for supposing that Dafydd ap Gwilym may have known the elegies of Ovid's *Amores* in their original form. Iolo Goch (*c.*1320–98), Dafydd's younger contemporary, appears to have received some form of clerical education – possibly in the *schola cantorum* at St Asaph[76] – and his training is reflected in the smattering of Greek and Latin words in his poems and his knowledge of the popular *Elucidarium* of the twelfth-century scholastic writer Honorius Augustodunensis.[77] But Iolo's classical learning is limited: conventional allusions to Hercules, Julius Caesar and Ovid; a reference to the Three Fates (although his forms for their names – *Tropos, Cletis, Letisis* – do not inspire confidence); and perhaps some awareness of Virgil's *Georgics* – or, at least, of the tradition associated with that poem – in the *dyfalu* of the plough in the celebrated *cywydd* to the Labourer and in the detailed equine descriptions in his poems requesting, or thanking for, the gift of a horse.[78] In the early fifteenth century another of the *cywyddwyr*, Siôn Cent, a powerful and often acerbic discerner of the human predicament, made use of some Latin phrases in his poetry. In a famous prophetic *cywydd, Gobeithiaw a ddaw ydd wyf* ('I place my hope in that which is to come'), he makes splendid use of the myth of Trojan origins, displaying knowledge of detail that goes far beyond what is contained in the Triads.[79]

An attractive case was made by Saunders Lewis for thinking that Siôn Cent was educated at Oxford and that his rejection of the quasi-Platonic idealism of the Welsh tradition of praise-poetry reflected the influence of the Nominalist approach to metaphysical theory, an approach which he learnt from his study at Oxford of the *via moderna* of William of Ockham and his followers.[80] 'The theory is a highly ingenious one,' writes Professor Glanmor Williams, 'though the evidence adduced in its support seems hardly strong enough to bear the weight of interpretation placed upon it.'[81] What is, however, clear is that during the later fifteenth and early sixteenth centuries more and more Welshmen, including poets, were drawn to the universities. Ieuan ap Hywel Swrdwal (*fl.*1430–80) went to Oxford and there wrote the 'Hymn to the Virgin', an English poem whose orthography is Welsh and which is composed in full *cynghanedd*. It appears that the poem was meant as an answer to the jibes of English students who taunted the Welsh for lack of literary talent.[82] An older contemporary, Ieuan ap Rhydderch, in 'Y Fost', a *cywydd* which emulates the boastful *Gorhoffedd* of Hywel ab Owain Gwynedd, lists his own intellectual and academic achievements, probably attained at Oxford: mastery of the subjects of the *Trivium* and *Quadrivium*, study of Ptolemy and Aristotle, skill in the accomplishments of a gentleman.[83]

The century between 1435 and 1535 was memorably termed, by Saunders Lewis, 'y ganrif fawr' ('the great century') for the remarkable poetic creativity of a succession of outstanding *cywyddwyr*.[84] Their sensitivity to the legacy of their craft, their command of the technical requirements of *cynghanedd*, their loyalty to their patrons, all meant that they essentially worked within a native Welsh tradition. The little classical influence which impinged upon them was subordinated to the requirements of that tradition. Nevertheless, during that same century, some faint echoes of continental humanism began to reach a few Welsh ears. Tudur Aled, acknowledged master of the *cywyddwyr* who flourished in the early 1500s, praised Rhobert ap Rhys of Dôl Gynwal for his learning by saying that he was one 'whose nest was in the language of humanism' ('A'i nyth mewn iaith uwmana').[85] One Welshman, Richard Whitford of Flintshire, came into close contact with Erasmus in Paris in 1498. Together with William Blount, Lord Mountjoy, he was instrumental in bringing Erasmus to England in 1499, and remained a close friend of the great Dutch humanist.[86] It was in the middle of the sixteenth century, however, that Renaissance influences became a force in the literature of Wales, and with them developed a heightened sense of classical antiquity. The interplay between native Welsh tradition and the classicism of the humanists will be the subject of the next chapter.

III

Wales's Humanists and the Classics

Since the time of Henry VII and Henry VIII that we were emancipated, as it were, and made free to trade and traffic through England, the gentlemen and people in Wales have greatly increased in learning and civility, for now great numbers of youths are continually brought up and maintained at the Universities of Oxford and Cambridge and in other good schools in England, where some prove to be learned men and good members of the Commonwealth of England and Wales . . . Many good Grammar Schools in divers parts of the country are now to be found throughout Wales, whereby the country is grown and shortly like to be as civil as any other place of this land.

George Owen (of Henllys)[1]

On the evening of 7 April 1485 the young Henry Tudor landed with his troops from France at a bay near Milford Haven in Pembrokeshire. Henry had been born at Pembroke Castle, and doubtless it was of symbolic as well as strategic significance that the march to Bosworth should begin in his native county. Just over a fortnight later King Richard was defeated and Henry immediately laid claim to the throne. The Tudor Age, which was to continue until the early seventeenth century, had begun.

The arrival of the new dynasty marked the beginning of a period of remarkable optimism for many Welshmen. Henry's descent from Owain Tudur led poets and politicians alike to see in him the tangible fulfilment of the prophecy made to Cadwaladr, at the end of Geoffrey of Monmouth's *Historia Regum Britanniae*, that the day would come when the Britons – by which the Welsh understood themselves – would again rule over the whole island. Thus the ageing Lewys Glyn Cothi hailed Henry as the restorer of the Trojan line to its former glory:[2]

Efô yw'r ateg hir o Frutus,
ef wedy Selyf o waed Silius,

> o ddynion Troea, lwyddiannus – fonedd,
> ac o ais Gwynedd ac Asganius.

He is the long bulwark from Brutus, he following Solomon is of the
blood of Silvius, of Trojan stock, a successful pedigree, and from
the ribs of Gwynedd and Ascanius.

Nor was such enthusiasm confined to writers in Welsh. The
unknown author of a pageant held in Worcester, early during
Henry's reign, wrote thus of him:[3]

> Cadwaladers Blodde lynyally descending,
> Longe hathe bee towlde of such a Prince comyng.
> Wherfor Friendes, if that I shal not lye,
> This same is the Fulfiller of the Profecye.

The support which many Welshmen gave to the Tudor cause
was amply rewarded, often with advancement at court; and
although the Tudors' own sense of their Welsh roots should not
be overstressed, it would be too cynical to say that Henry made
use of his Welsh connections only when it was politically
expedient for him to do so.[4]

Certainly in the sixteenth and early seventeenth centuries,
especially in the wake of the (so-called) Acts of Union of 1536
and 1543, the educational and cultural horizons of a substantial
number of young Welshmen were greatly widened. In more
recent times there has been an understandable tendency on the
part of some Welshmen, notable scholars among them, to view
the Acts of Union as the beginning of the end for any distinct
Welsh identity. Very few articulate Welshmen felt like that at the
time. The words of the Elizabethan antiquarian George Owen,
quoted at the head of this chapter, bear witness to the greater
educational opportunities for Welshmen in the universities and
in schools like Westminster, Winchester and Shrewsbury (three
schools which were particularly attended by Welsh boys). It
should also be noted that grammar schools were established in
some of the towns and boroughs of Wales itself: Brecon,
Abergavenny, Bangor, Presteigne, Rhuthun, Carmarthen,
Cowbridge. The 'grammar' which was studied at such schools
was, by definition, Latin grammar, together with a modicum of

Greek. The result was that far more Welshmen than ever before came into contact with the classical languages and their literature. It also meant that Wales became more and more open to the new spirit which was abroad in Europe: that is, the spirit of Renaissance humanism resulting from the rediscovery of the Greek and Latin classics and from the attempt to study and understand those classical works on their own terms and within their own context. Such a study meant paying detailed attention to the language and style of the ancient writers and aiming to imitate their work in one's own writing. In northern Europe, and especially in England, no figure was seen to personify the glories of such humanistic learning more fully than Erasmus. In his enthusiasm for classical literature, his concern for change in education and his commitment to the printing press, Erasmus stands 'at the fountain-head of that spate of ideas which flooded Europe in the early sixteenth century'.[5]

Many of the Welshmen who made good in England stayed there, often as teachers. The phenomenon of the Welsh teacher, so familiar in London and the Midlands in the middle of the twentieth century, is not a new one! Shakespeare's best-known schoolmaster is Sir Hugh Evans, the amiable pedagogue in *The Merry Wives of Windsor* (Act IV, Scene 1), trying hard – Welsh accent and all – to instil Latin accidence into his reluctant pupil. Richard Watkins at Eton, Hugh Lloyd and Hugh Robinson at Winchester, John Owen at Warwick, were all notable headmasters who were themselves beneficiaries of the widened horizons. Others came to prominence in the universities and were known for their classical studies. Griffith Powell, of Llansawel in Carmarthenshire, a Fellow (and later Principal) of Jesus College, Oxford – a college established in 1571 by the Welshman Hugh Price and attended especially by Welshmen – was renowned for his works on Aristotle. His studies of the *Posterior Analytics* (1594) and the *Sophistici Elenchi* (1598) played a vital part in the neo-scholastic revival of interest in Aristotle in the sixteenth century. Meanwhile Powell's Oxford contemporary Matthew Gwinne, son of a 'London Welsh' grocer, wrote a Latin play entitled *Nero: Tragaedia Nova* (published 1603) which was based on the Roman historians' account of Nero.[6]

It is estimated that, between 1540 and 1642, as many as 2,200 Welsh students were registered in the Universities of Oxford and

Cambridge, about 85 per cent of them in Oxford.[7] For the majority the benefits of the New Learning led to a not unconscious distancing of themselves from the cultural traditions associated with the Welsh language and its literature. English and Latin would henceforth be their languages, at least for literary self-expression, and the availability in England of printing presses (so markedly absent in Wales until the beginning of the eighteenth century) meant that publishing in the two more widely known languages, for a readership which shared the same cultural tastes, had an attractive appeal. To cite a few examples: the remarkable Leonard Cox (of Monmouth), during an astonishingly varied career, published among other works *The art or crafte of rhetoryke* (1532), based on Melanchthon's *Institutiones rhetoricae;*[8] Ludovic Lloyd (a descendant of the Blayney family of Gregynog), in his 400-page *Pilgrimage of Princes*, drew widely on classical authors to illustrate a study of the growth, authority and decline of the kings and princes of this world;[9] and William Vaughan (of Golden Grove near Carmarthen) published attractive, if conventional, collections of English and Latin poetry, as did Sir John Stradling (of St Donat's in the Vale of Glamorgan).[10] Nor should one forget that Englishmen who settled in Wales in the wake of the Tudor settlement brought English (and continental) interests with them. One of the most notable, in the context of classical pursuits, was Thomas Phaer, a native of Norwich. Phaer was a distinguished physician (his *The Boke of Chyldren,* 1544, became the cornerstone of paediatric studies in Britain) and also a lawyer, by virtue of which he was appointed Solicitor to the Council in the Marches of Wales. He settled in Cilgerran Castle, on the banks of the River Teifi, and there composed in ballad metre an ambitious – if sometimes heavy-going – English verse translation of the first nine books of the *Aeneid*. Books I–VII were published in 1558, books I–IX after Phaer's death in 1560. It appears, however, that Phaer had nothing to do with Wales's own literary and cultural traditions.[11]

The most outstanding example of a Welsh man of letters who gained immense popularity not only in England but also on the continent of Europe was the Latin epigrammatist John Owen, *Audoenus* as he styled himself.[12] He came of a gentle family in north Wales, whence he went to Winchester and New College,

Oxford. He became a fellow of his college, and later (as has already been indicated) headmaster of King Henry VIII's School, Warwick. It seems, however, that early in the first decade of the sevententh century Owen gave up teaching, moved to London, and lived on the not inconsiderable patronage which he could enjoy as a Latin poet. Between 1606 and 1612 he published nearly fifteen hundred Latin epigrams, in four instalments of ten 'books' in all. His witty and often sardonic poems became immensely popular throughout Europe, first in Latin and then in vernacular translations. It has been graphically said of them that 'most Europeans of literary tastes were acquainted with them. On the Continent he was much better known than Shakespeare his contemporary; he was probably the best known British man of letters.'[13] Some Welsh references, and occasionally a Welsh word or expression, occur in his poems. But he is essentially a poet of the one British kingdom. In an epigram addressed to an imaginary Welshman he distances himself from any allegiance to the claim, based on Geoffrey of Monmouth's *Historia Regum Britanniae*, that the Welsh are 'the genuine Britons', and at the same time celebrates the recent Union of the Crowns of England and Scotland:[14]

> Tecum participant in nomine Scotus et Anglus;
> Iam tu non solus, Walle, Britannus eris.

> English and Scots by name are one with thee:
> Now Welch man, sole thou shalt not British be.

To what extent, then, did the Renaissance exert any direct impact on Wales or upon Welsh literary and cultural concerns? Compared with the situation in most of the countries of Europe, including England, the impact was very limited. The great efflorescence in the vernaculars of genres which were rooted in classical literature – drama, epic, lyric – was virtually unknown in sixteenth-century and early seventeenth-century Welsh literature. Several negative factors may be adduced to account for such a situation. The increasing loss of the Welsh gentry into the main currents of English life meant that Wales was deprived of potential patrons for such new developments: *sint Maecenates, non derunt, Flacce, Marones*. Furthermore, the absence of urban centres, poor internal communications, lack of printing facilities, all denied Wales many of the conditions necessary for a full flowering of Renaissance ideals.

It is, however, important to emphasize that many of the young Welshmen who entered the universities and whose perceptions were shaped by the New Learning did not lose their interest in and their concern for their Welsh heritage. That is most graphically seen in the scholarship and humanistic learning which went into the work of translating the Bible into Welsh, rightly described by Professor Geraint Gruffydd as 'a major triumph of humanism as well as Protestantism in Wales'.[15] Richard Davies, William Salesbury, William Morgan, Edmwnd Prys, Richard Parry, John Davies: these were university men who had spent years at either Oxford or Cambridge and were *viri trium linguarum gnari*, noted for their mastery not only of Latin but also of Greek and Hebrew.[16] Clearly, their long study of the classical languages and their literature, while not an end in itself, played a vital role in providing these scholars with the tools necessary for their task. William Salesbury translated Thomas Linacre's Latin version of Proclus's *De Sphaera* into English; William Morgan could turn his hand to producing an elegant Latin epigram, Edmwnd Prys an attractive poem in hexameters; Richard Parry and John Davies were skilled writers of Latin prose.[17] Yet their main concern was to apply their learning to the task of translating the Scriptures into Welsh. In order to fulfil that task they drew not only on their university training but also on their profound knowledge of the language of the Welsh bardic tradition. Their efforts gave their compatriots the most precious jewel in the crown not only of the Protestant Reformation but also of the Renaissance in Wales.

The humanists who concerned themselves with the Welsh tradition also assiduously applied themselves to the study of the language, its grammar and its lexicography. William Salesbury and John Davies, two of the biblical translators already named, were outstanding Welsh philological scholars. John Davies made it his life's work to study the language of Welsh poets down to his own day, and his Grammar (*Antiquae Linguae Britannicae . . . Rudimenta*, 1621) and Dictionary (*Antiquae Linguae Britannicae . . . et Linguae Latinae, Dictionarium Duplex*, 1632) are – next to the Welsh translation of the Bible – possibly the finest achievements of Welsh Renaissance humanism. It is important to note that Latin is the language used by John Davies to discuss Welsh grammar, and that it is Latin which is placed alongside Welsh in the Dictionary. Like William Salesbury and Henry Salesbury and others before him, John Davies's purpose was to extend the humanist's interest in classical literature to include the Welsh tradition. In marked contrast to the way in which the rediscovery of the classics led in other countries to something of a rejection of much of the medieval heritage, in Wales many of the humanists were inspired by the New Learning to rediscover their own traditions more fully and more gloriously. The renewal of interest in the Greek and Latin classics led them to search for the manuscripts of their own country, just as Petrarch and the early Italian humanists had avidly looked in monastery and cathedral libraries for classical manuscripts. Many of the Welsh humanists also went on to assert that Wales had a literature of her own which would stand comparison with the noblest of Greek and Latin achievements. This aspect of Welsh Renaissance learning was especially emphasized in seminal studies by Saunders Lewis and G. J. Williams.[18] Professor Williams put the matter with characteristic clarity in a lecture on the history of Welsh scholarship:[19]

> Our humanists . . . were all classical scholars who had mastered the new learning, but that did not prevent them from realizing the excellence of their own literature and of the Welsh traditional learning. They did not ask the poets to forsake the old native literary forms, they encouraged them to retain their traditional methods, and to enrich their work by assimilating the new learning of the period. Although they were classical scholars, and although they had studied under some of the foremost teachers of the period, they regarded the old bardic learning and the Welsh poetic tradition as equal to the learning and literature of the Ancient World. They had their own classical works.

Such an attitude on the part of the Welsh humanists is very different from that of many of their counterparts in France or England. Most important of all it resulted in a productive tension between the Greek and Latin heritage, on the one hand, and the Welsh tradition on the other.

One of the main areas where this tension made itself felt was in relation to Geoffrey of Monmouth's *Historia Regum Britanniae*. The Welsh, as we have seen, found much in the *Historia* which fed their sense of nationhood, and the work's credibility was confirmed by the ample fulfilment of the prophecy to Cadwaladr in the accession of the Tudors. But Geoffrey's book did not escape criticism. Even in the twelfth century itself a historian of the stature of William of Newburgh had been harsh in his condemnation of it. Certainly in the sixteenth century the work was questioned by many scholars whose aim, in keeping with the *ad fontes* principle, was to see the writing of history firmly based on the proper assessment of documentary evidence. Chief among the sceptics was the Italian diplomat and historian, Polydore Vergil. Polydore first came to England early in the sixteenth century and was commissioned by Henry VII to write a history of England, *Anglica Historia*, 'an up-to-date history justifying the Tudors in Latin to the Latin-reading humanists of the courts of the West.'[20] A key element in Polydore's scepticism about Geoffrey's work was the absence of corroborative evidence from classical historians for Brutus and much else. Polydore's work was published several times, the first time in Basel in 1534, and his – usually justifiable – criticisms of Geoffrey engendered a strong reaction among devotees of the *Brut*, English as well as Welsh. The foremost English champion of Geoffrey's work was the eminent antiquarian and classical scholar, John Leland, who angrily defended the British History in a pamphlet entitled *Codrus, sive Laus et Defensio Gallofridi Arturii Monumetensis contra Polydorum Vergilium* (1536), later expanded into a 40-page tract, *Assertio inclytissimi Arturii Regis Britanniae* (1544).[21] Welsh antiquaries were especially stung by the attack on Geoffrey. They were acutely aware that the British past which Geoffrey had been extolling was the epic past which they claimed as their own.

A number of Welsh Renaissance scholars came to Geoffrey's defence, and most of them chose to write in Latin. Geoffrey's *Historia* was itself a Latin work, Polydore Vergil had written in Latin, and Latin was certainly the language in which to engage in a debate that had now been given international circulation. The first significantly to enter the fray was one of the earliest of Welsh humanists, Sir John Price, or Prys (*c*.1502–*c*.1555) of Brecon. A lawyer educated at Oxford and the Inns of Court, John

Price held positions of great authority in Wales, including that of Secretary of the Council in the Marches and of visitor to the monasteries before their dissolution. He is also remembered as the man who was responsible for the printing of *Yny Lhyvyr Hwnn* (1546), the first printed book in Welsh, testimony to his standing as a Renaissance figure who blended public duty and university training with a commitment to Welsh study. And it was John Price who set about writing, in Latin, the fullest of all defences of Geoffrey's work against the calumnies (as he saw them) of Polydore Vergil. That his trust in the truth of Geoffrey's writing was misplaced in no way detracts from the significance of what he says, and his *Historiae Brytannicae Defensio*, 'A Defence of the British History', remains one of the most important of the early writings of the Renaissance in Wales. John Price is known to have worked on the *Defensio* for a number of years before his death, although it remained unpublished until his son Richard saw to having it printed in London in 1573.[22]

One of the most interesting elements of the *Defensio* is the stance which Price adopts with regard to Greek and Latin historical writing. The fact that he was writing in Latin itself encouraged reflection on the relationship between Geoffrey and the classical historians, and at the very outset Price feels obliged to come to grips with Polydore's charge that historians of Rome's expanding empire provide no evidence for many of the events and personalities featured in the *Historia Regum Britanniae*. The following passage comes at the beginning of the work (pp.1–2), and in it Price seeks to establish that Britain had its own annals of the past; there was no need to rely on classical sources, and, in any case, it was not to be expected that classical writers would give much prominence to the affairs of a distant people:

> Quare eorum iniqua iudicia satis admirari non possum, qui tametsi id constanti et diuturna rerum fama, et probatis authoribus abunde testatum sit, tam praeclaros et excellentes viros in hac Insula floruisse non credant, quales vetusti gentis nostrae Annales nobis depingunt, partim hoc innixi argumento, quod a Romanis authoribus silentio praetereantur, partim eo quod nulla credant apud Brytannos extare monumenta, quibus huiusmodi Annalium fides innitatur et fulciatur. Caeterum quam leve sit utrumque illud quod in hoc affertur, facile est perspectu. Quis enim ignorat

Romanos scriptores in hoc potissimum incubuisse, ut suorum res gestas potissimum illustrarent: aliorum vero non nisi carptim atque subsultim nulla perpetuae historiae deductione tantummodo perstrinxisse. Ut igitur in rebus quas potissimum tractare profitentur, scriptoribus Romanis quantamcunque poposcerint fides sit adhibenda, de aliorum tamen rebus verba facientibus non aeque, cum et eas longinqua atque incerta ut plurimum relatione acceperint, et acceptas levi pede pertransierint, ad suorum res gestas commemorandas properantes.

I cannot but be astonished by the hostile opinions of those who, in the face of the abundant evidence of a long and firm tradition and the testimony of excellent written authorities, still refuse to believe that such distinguished and remarkable heroes, of the kind that the old Annals of our nation describe, did once flourish in this island. They produce such objections, partly on the basis of the argument that these heroes are passed over in silence by Roman authors, and partly because they do not believe that there are in Britain any records remaining which support and uphold the credibility of such Annals. But it is easy to perceive how slight are both these arguments. For surely everyone knows that Roman writers primarily exerted themselves in the task of rendering as renowned as possible the deeds of their own people; as for the deeds of other peoples, they only touched upon them occasionally, now and then, without ever producing a continuous history of them. Accordingly, when Roman writers have it as their professed aim to discuss particular matters, we should place in them all the trust which they demand; but similar confidence should not be placed in them when they are dealing with the history of other peoples, as their sources on such matters will be remote – and, for the most part, unreliable – reports; and, furthermore, after hearing about these matters, their treatment of them will be very slight, as their real concern is to press on to recount the deeds of their own heroes.

That is a carefully written paragraph. John Price knew very well the claims made for the unique authority of Greek and Roman historians, and he carefully combines respect for the classical tradition with his insistence on defending Geoffrey's work and all that was bound up with it.[23]

John Price was not the only Welshman to write in Latin in defence of Geoffrey, although his is certainly the longest and most sustained reply to the attacks of critics like Polydore Vergil.

Others devoted their energies to the same cause and were, like Price, greatly exercised by the whole question of the authority of Greek and Latin classical writers and how to reconcile that authority with the matter of the British History. One thinks in particular of two scholars, both from Clwyd, both educated at Oxford: Humphrey Llwyd of Denbigh and David Powel of Rhiwabon. Between them they made major contributions to historical and chorographical studies, and among Powel's writings is a short essay which bears the significant title, *De Britannica Historia Recte Intelligenda, et cum Romanis Scriptoribus Reconcilianda*, 'On correctly understanding the British History, and establishing its compatibility with the work of Roman authors'. Among David Powel's many other contributions to the study of Welsh history was his production of the first printed edition of Gerald of Wales's *Itinerarium Kambriae* and *Descriptio Kambriae* (Book I).[24]

As we have seen, John Price is one of the earliest of the Welsh humanists. He chooses to write in Latin, and is conscious of all the claims of the classical tradition. He is also aware of the humanist aspiration, crystallized in Lorenzo Valla's *Elegantiae Linguae Latinae* (1471), to restore Latin prose to the kind of stylistic and rhetorical glory which it had enjoyed under Cicero. In a prefatory letter to the *Defensio*, addressed to William Herbert, Earl of Pembroke, he alludes to contemporary concern for elegant Latin, and to his own inability to scale such stylistic heights:[25]

Fateor equidem me prorsus infantem, et usque adeo ingenio et eloquentia vacuum, ut haec de quibus disserturus sum nullo prorsus verborum lenocinio cuiquam persuadere me sperem, nisi nuda veritas ipsa, cuius vis tanta est, ut vel invitos ad se trahat, patrocinari videatur. At non hic agitur de verborum sed de rerum controversia, qua in re veritas non eloquentia requiritur. Porro non sum nescius, quam delicatae hac tempestate sint hominum aures, ut nihil arrideat, nisi quod eloquio usquequaque politum et nitidum sit, plusque fere laborent in sermonis ornatu, quam in rerum ipsarum consideratione, quorum ut iudicium ceu praeposterum non probo, sic et eos qui sermonis nitorem cum rerum gravitate coniungunt, maximopere suspicio atque admiror. Verum non cuivis homini (ut est in proverbio) contingit adire Corinthum, neque vitae nostrae ratio, quae negotiorum undis semper a puero agitata est, id concessit, ut utrumque praestare possemus.

I for my part admit that I am only a child, so devoid of ability and eloquence that I could never hope to succeed in using enticing words to persuade anyone concerning the matters I am about to discuss, unless it is clear that I have the support of unadorned truth, whose power is so great as to attract to herself even those who are unwilling. However, we are not here dealing with an argument over words but rather over facts, and in such a matter it is truth, not eloquence, which is needed. Furthermore, I am fully aware how fastidious men's ears are at this time, so that nothing pleases them except what is in all respects polished and refined in its eloquence, and they take nearly more trouble over the adornment of their speech than they do over considering the facts themselves. Just as I do not approve of the well-nigh preposterous opinion of such people, so too I greatly look up to and admire those who join together elegance of speech and gravity of subject-matter. But (as the proverb puts it) it is not granted to all and sundry to enter Corinth, nor has the course of my life, which from childhood has always been tossed about by the waves of responsibilities, allowed me this, namely to be able to fulfil both tasks.

Eloquentia, eloquium, verborum lenocinium, sermonis ornatus, sermonis nitor: these are the qualities which Price recognizes as the desiderata of contemporary Latinity. His periodic style in these sentences shows that there is an element of mock-modesty about Price's claim that his prose is not polished. The reference to *delicatae aures* echoes the first chapter of the third book of Quintilian's *Institutio Oratoria* (III.1.3). Likewise the hexameter quoted from Horace (*Epistles* I.17.36), 'non cuivis homini contingit adire Corinthum', although it was probably mediated by Erasmus' *Adagia* (I.iv.1) yet reveals a sensitive awareness of classical Latin literature.

That an informed interest in the classical world impinged upon the Welsh humanists, whether they wrote in Latin or in Welsh, is revealed by a glance at their range of reference and their quotations from the classics. No single authority contributed more to their openness to the classical past and its literature than Desiderius Erasmus.[26] In 1547, about the same time as John Price was writing the *Historiae Brytannicae Defensio*, William Salesbury, the most prolific and wide-ranging of the earlier figures of the Welsh Renaissance, paid his tribute to Erasmus and the *Adagia*:[27]

Erasmus Roterodamus yr athro dyscedickaf, huotlaf, ac awdurusaf yn Cred oll or a vu in oes ni ac ys llawer oes or blayn, efe a clascadd nyd cant, nyd mil, nyd lleng, nyd myrdd, nyd Riallu, ac nid buna anyd caterua vawr o ddiarebion Groec a Llatin, ac ae kyfansoddes yn vnllyfr.

Erasmus of Rotterdam, the most learned, most eloquent and most acknowledged teacher in all Christendom, both in our own age and in many ages before, collected not a hundred, not a thousand, not a legion, not a myriad, not a hundred thousand, not a million but a vast multitude of Greek and Latin proverbs, and brought them together in one book.

Salesbury's zeal may have got the better of his arithmetic, but there is no mistaking his sense of the greatness of the Dutch humanist's contribution: the detailed knowledge of both Greek and Latin literature, the presentation of his studies in an attractive and palatable form, and the moral and contemporary application of truths derived from the ancient works. In an English letter to Richard Colyngbourne, Salesbury likewise describes Erasmus as 'the head learned man of all our tyme'.[28] Like the later humanists, Salesbury makes full use of the *Adagia*: so, for example, in his short prefatory letter to *Kynniver Llith a Ban* (1551), he quotes two of Erasmus' adages, as well as making use of half a line of Virgil's *Aeneid*.[29]

The use of classical allusions, frequently mediated by Erasmus, gained greater momentum during the second half of the sixteenth century and the early seventeenth century. David Powel, in his address to Sir Henry Sidney (1585), quotes Virgil's *Aeneid* (I.607–9) as part of his praise to the great man.[30] Similarly Henry Salesbury quotes the *Eclogues* (V.32–4) in his prefatory address to Henry Herbert, Earl of Pembroke, at the beginning of *Grammatica Britannica* (1593),[31] and Rowland Vaughan quotes Horace (*Ars Poetica* 58–61) in the course of his Welsh introduction to *Yr Ymarfer o Dduwioldeb* (1630).[32] In itself, this may not appear so different from the use made of classical literature by, say, Gerald of Wales. Certainly the range of ancient authors whose work is quoted is widened to include Greek writers, classical and patristic; John Davies in particular appears to be very familiar with Greek texts.[33] The really significant change, however, is that, for the humanists, classical antiquity becomes a touchstone against which cultural, moral and intellectual concerns (*sapientia*) as well as literary and stylistic principles (*eloquentia*) are to be measured. The Welsh humanists were no exception to this tendency, even when they wished to stress the uniqueness of their own traditions.

No one person from the ancient world more forcibly personified such humanist concerns, from the days of Petrarch onwards, than the great Roman orator and statesman, Marcus Tullius Cicero (106–43 BC): 'y pwyllog a'r ymadroddus Rufeiniwr M. T. Cicero' ('the wise and eloquent Roman, M. T. Cicero') as Huw Lewys aptly describes him.[34] As a philosopher and literary stylist who was not above putting his formidable oratorical skills at the disposal of the world of government and politics, Cicero represented the Renaissance ideal of civilized and civilizing statesman, a prototype of Castiglione's courtier or Thomas Elyot's governor. Cicero provided a pattern to which educated scholar-gentlemen might aspire to conform, and it is not surprising that many of the Welsh humanists were attached to the households of the rising aristocracy of the day: David Powel was chaplain to the family of Sir Henry Sidney, Humphrey Llwyd was closely connected to the Earl of Arundel, Maurice Kyffin (as we shall see) served as tutor to the sons of Lord Buckhurst. Within Wales also there were a few select households – Richard Davies's episcopal palace at Abergwili, the homes of the Salusbury family at Lleweni and of the Wynn family at Gwydir, St Donat's Castle in Glamorgan in the days of Sir Edward and Sir John Stradling – which, in their own way, were small 'Renaissance courts'. The language used by their protégés to describe – and to flatter – the aristocratic patrons is language imbued with the Ciceronian ideal.[35]

The Ciceronian image of the engaged man, devoted both to the things of the mind and to the business of the state, was of such significance to humanists throughout Europe that, during the fifteenth and sixteenth centuries, they set about translating some of Cicero's most influential philosophical and rhetorical works into their native tongues. Such a development is in itself a sign of growing confidence that the vernacular languages could aspire to a position similar to that of Greek and Latin, and the fact that Cicero's works should be so translated marks the cultural importance attached to him. It appears that more translations of his work were made into each of the major continental languages than was the case into English. Nevertheless, by the third quarter of the sixteenth century, printed English translations were available of *De Amicitia*, *De Senectute*, *De Officiis*, *Pro Marcello*, *Paradoxa*, *Tusculanae Disputationes*, *Somnium Scipionis*, *Pro Archia* and a selection of letters.[36] Verse authors too, especially Virgil and Ovid, together with the hexameter poetry of Horace, are also prominent in the lists of translations. The immense influence on English literature of works like Golding's version of Ovid's *Metamorphoses* or Thomas North's Plutarch requires no comment.

What of translations of classical literature into Welsh? Renaissance scholars working in Wales devoted much of their energy, as we have seen, to the task of providing the Welsh people with the Bible in their own language. It appears, however, that they showed little enthusiasm for translating classical literature into Welsh. The earliest version of a classical work put into Welsh is Simwnt Fychan's *cywydd* based on Martial's epigram *Vitam quae faciant* (X.47). The version has been preserved in some manuscripts, and also on a broadside (dated 1571) containing the Latin text and an anonymous English translation. It is unlikely that Simwnt knew much Latin, and it seems that the content of Martial's poem was explained to him by his patron Simon Thelwall.[37] There also exists, in manuscript, a translation of a short section of the first book of the *Rhetorica ad Herennium*, an influential work wrongly attributed to Cicero. The translation is the work of Siôn ap Hywel ab Owain, one of the minor gentry of Eifionydd in the late sixteenth and early seventeenth centuries.[38] Also in manuscript is an unknown translator's version of part of one of Seneca's lesser-known works, *De Remediis Fortuitorum*.[39]

The longest translation of a classical text produced by a humanist who also contributed to Welsh literature is not a translation into Welsh at all, but – not surprisingly – into English. That is Terence's *Andria*, translated by Maurice Kyffin and published in 1588.[40] Kyffin came from Oswestry, and is known to have been given some Welsh bardic training, but must also have somewhere received a classical education. He became a man of affairs who served with the army in Holland and in Normandy, and died with the army in Ireland in 1598. He was also a man of letters. In English he published *The Blessednes of Brytaine*, a poem in praise of Queen Elizabeth.[41] His greatest work is his translation from Latin into Welsh of Bishop John Jewel's *Apologia Ecclesiae Anglicanae* under the title *Deffynniad Ffydd Eglwys Loegr* (1595), a masterpiece of Welsh prose writing of the early modern period.[42] In the early 1580s Kyffin was also tutor to the sons of Lord Buckhurst, and it was during those years that he began to translate the *Andria*. The book which he eventually published contains a dedication to William Sackville, one of Lord Buckhurst's sons, and an address to two other sons, Henry and Thomas.

Terence's plays had, from the days of the Roman Empire, been a staple element in Roman education, especially on account of their fluent use of Latin. That high view of Terence is reflected in the title-page of Kyffin's translation:

ANDRIA. The first Comoedie of Terence, in English. A furtherance for the attainment unto the right knowledge & true proprietie of the Latin Tong. And also a commodious meane of help, to such as have forgotten Latin, for their speedy recovering of habilitie, to understand, write and speake the same.

Likewise in the 'Preface to the curteous Reader' Kyffin declares:

Among all the Roman writers, there is none (by the iudgement of the learned) so much available to bee read and studied, for the true knowledge and puritie of the Latin tong, as Pub.Terentius.

He is well aware of Terence's stylistic merits:

The Latin is pure and eloquent, much commended by Tullie himselfe, and right requisite to be studied, and understood of all such, as would attaine to the knowledge of right speaking, and readiness of wel writing, in the Latin tong.

Kyffin was also unusually sensitive to the challenge which translation posed for one who would undertake it. He reminds Henry and Thomas Sackville how, seven years earlier, he had 'first attempted the translation of *Andria* into English verse'. However, he came to realize 'what difficultie it was, to enforce the pithie and proverbiall sayings of *Terence* into Rime; . . . such manner of forced translation, must needs be both harsh and unpleasant to the Reader, and also not halfe seemly befitting the sweete style and eloquence of the Author.' He therefore chose to publish a prose translation, one in which, as he explains in a prudent section of the 'Preface to the curteous Reader',

> My cheefest care hath bin, to lay open the meaning of the Author especially, in all hard and difficult places of this Comoedie, and to utter the same in such apt, plaine and familiar words, as are most meete, for this low stile and Argument: for to handle a meane matter, with high and lofty phrase, were as great oversight, and lack of iudgement as could be.

Kyffin's sensitivity to registers of language and style is reflected in the colour and verve of his translation. The following brief extract (from Act I, Scene 2), presents two of the play's main characters: Simo, an elderly gentleman, and Davus, a cunning slave, both of whom begin to speak in asides. The passage represents well the method and tone of Kyffin's work:

Da. His purpose was to have us brought underhande into fooles paradise, to the end that now hoping the best, and having cast of all feare, we should suddeinly bee taken napping, in such sorte, as wee might not have time to bethinke us how to preuent the marryage. A suttle fore I warrant him.

Si. What prates this Gallowclapper.

Da. Good Lord my maister is here, and I saw him not till now.

Si. Dauus?

Da. Now, what is the matter?

Si. Come your way hether, to mee.

Da. What a Devill will hee have?

The manner of translation is, of necessity, very different from that of *Deffynniad Ffydd Eglwys Loegr*. In both works Kyffin displays his sensitivity to variations of style and subject-matter, a sensitivity largely born of a classical awareness of what was rhetorically appropriate in a given situation.

In the dedication to William Sackville not only does Kyffin show his knowledge of Terence's standing in the Roman world but he also makes a link between ancient patronage and the support which he received from the Buckhurst family:

Whyle he [i.e Terence] lived at *Rome*, his most company, and conversation, was among the Nobilitie, and most of al other, with those twoo noble and learned gentlemen, *Laelius* and *Scipio Africane*: In like sort, after his death, his woorks were right currantly accounted of, and highly commended, by the two Princes of eloquence, even *Caesar*, and *Cicero*: as their own writings do witness the same unto us. Therefore, sith *Terence*, neither alive nor dead, did ever want a noble Maecenas to protect him: I hope that now, being partly put into english, and having cheefly chosen you for his Patrone in England: you likewise, in regard of your noble birth and vertues, wil graunt him like curteous and frendly fauour, as by these noble men in *Rome*, was heretofore affoorded unto him.

A passage of that kind, couched though it is in the language of flattery, reveals how a humanist like Maurice Kyffin could see his own social relationships with the grandees of his day in the light of the bond betwen patron and poet in Republican Rome.

As we have seen, Wales's humanists were mainly indebted to the two English universities for their learning and awareness of Renaissance ideas. For many, too, it was the support and patronage of an English-based social and cultural élite which enabled them to further their interests in Welsh matters. Humanism was, however, European in its essence, and some of the most notable of its Welsh promoters spent years, whether by choice or because of religious necessity, on the continent of Europe. Richard Davies was, for three years of Mary Tudor's reign, a Protestant exile in Frankfurt, an experience which greatly widened his European perceptions.[43] The young Edward Stradling of St Donat's spent years in Italy and also travelled in other European countries, all of which gave him a dimension which his protégé Siôn Dafydd Rhys saw as the source of his learning and many other virtues.[44] Humphrey Llwyd in 1566 journeyed with the Earl of Arundel to Padua, where the earl hoped to be cured of gout in the medicinal baths. Their outward and homeward journeys were leisurely affairs, and in Antwerp on the way back Llwyd was introduced to the famous Dutch cartographer Abraham Ortelius.[45]

Among the more permanent Welsh residents on the continent was the Oxford-educated Dr Gruffydd Robert, of Milan. He was a Catholic exile, formerly archdeacon of Anglesey and one of the not inconsiderable group of Welsh priests who refused to acknowledge Queen Elizabeth's religious settlement. Gruffydd Robert, like his friend Morys Clynnog, made his way to Rome, where he attracted the notice of the Archbishop of Milan, Cardinal Carlo Borromeo, nephew of Pope Pius IV and a leader of the Counter-Reformation. Borromeo invited the Welshman to Milan as his confessor and to be Canon Theologian at the Duomo. As far as is known, Gruffydd Robert stayed in Milan until his death (post-1598).

The importance of Gruffydd Robert for this study is not so much that, in his exile, he longed for Wales, but that he turned his longing into a reflection upon the Welsh language and its literature. His thoughts were inspired by the literary and linguistic aspects of the Renaissance as he met them in Italy, and the importance of Milan as a centre for printing made the publication of his ideas a realistic possibility. The result was that, in 1567, there appeared from a press in Milan the first part of Gruffydd Robert's Welsh Grammar, *Dosparth Byrr ar y Rhan Gyntaf i Ramadeg Cymraeg*, to be followed (although not with the same degree of circulation) by other parts between then and the 1590s.[46] His work is written in Welsh, but it is very different from both the bardic grammar of Einion Offeiriad and from the grammars, written in Latin, by later humanists like Henry Salesbury and John Davies. Gruffydd Robert's concern is not so much to describe the traditional language and metres of the Welsh bards, but rather to enable his native tongue to take its rightful place among those languages capable of dealing with any literary demands made upon them in the new world of Renaissance culture. Such had been Bembo's concern, with regard to the Italian dialects, in his *Prose della volgar lingua* (1525), and it is no surprise that Gruffydd Robert follows Bembo by couching his discussion of grammar in the form of a dialogue.[47]

The dialogue form also had a long classical pedigree, used especially for philosophical discussion by both Plato and Cicero. The stylistic advantages of Plato's kind of dialogue, in terms both of clarity and comprehensiveness, are appreciated at the start of the second part of the Grammar:[48]

Gweled fod hynn yn wir a wnaeth i Blato a llawer o'r hen philosophyddion gynt i arfer yn gimaint: mal y mae oi weled yn llyfrau Plato sydd wedi sgrifennu o'mddiddan deuddyn, ne fwy rhai yn holi, eraill yn atteb.

It was seeing this to be true which led Plato and many of the other ancient philosophers to practise it [i.e. the dialogue form] so much; this can be seen in the books of Plato which are written in the form of a conversation betwen two men or more – some asking questions, others answering.

Likewise, when (early in Part One) the author presents Morys (Clynnog) and himself withdrawing to a shaded grove to assuage their longings for Wales by 'talking about Welsh things, and seeing what would be of some good to them' (*siarad am bethau Cymreig, ag edrych beth a wnai les iddynt*), their undertaking is compared to the way in which Cicero withdrew perforce from the political world to that of philosophical reflection:[49]

. . . moesswch weled a fyddai bosibl ini wneuthur mal y gwnaeth llawer o'r Groegwyr, a'r Lladinwyr gynt, pan yrrid nhwy ar darfysg i ryw gilfach neilltuawl i dario: yno'r scrifonnent hwy ryw beth i hyphorddi gwyr i gwlad mewn rhinwedd, dysc, ne bethau eraill, a fyddai les, urddas, a gogoniant iddyn, fal y gwnaeth Tullius i lyfrau o philosophyddiaeth gan mwyaf igyd.

Let us see whether it is possible for us to do as did many of the Greeks and Latins of old, when they were driven at a time of tumult to tarry in some secluded nook: there they would write something to instruct the men of their country in virtue, learning, or other things which would confer benefit, dignity and glory upon them. That is how Tullius [Cicero] came to write nearly all his books of philosophy.

The elevation of a language to the level envisaged by Gruffydd Robert meant patterning its style and rhythms upon the classical masters, but doing so in a manner consistent with that language's own character and native genius. Of all the Welsh humanist grammarians, he is the one who is most concerned with prose writing, and within his treatment of the *Questione della lingua* he sees the practice of translation as vital for the process of extending the capabilities of a language to meet all needs:[50]

. . . da oedd, ymarfer o transladu groeg, cynnymchwelyd lladin, cyfieuthu eidaliaeth, ne droi i'r gymraeg yr iaith a fynnai ddyn, a chraphu ar briodoldeb pob iaith, a'r rhagor a fo rhwng y naill a'r llall, yn yspressu yr un pwnc, ne ystyr.

It is an excellent practice to translate Greek, turn Latin, make a version of Italian, or put into Welsh any language that one wishes, and to look carefully at the properties of each language and the difference between one and another when it comes to giving expression to the same subject or meaning.

Gruffydd Robert has left us eight printed pages, the sixth part of his Grammar, in which he puts his ideas on translation into practice. The pages, which have survived in two copies only, contain a translation of the beginning of Cicero's dialogue *Cato Maior de Senectute* ('Cato the Elder, on Old Age'): *Lyfr Marcws Tulliws Sisero, a elwir Caton hynaf, ne, o henaint, at Titws Pomponius Atticws*. The *De Senectute* (as it is usually called), with its blend of philosophy and rhetoric presented in dialogue form, was an immensely popular work both during the Middle Ages and in the Renaissance. Several printed editions of the text appeared before 1500, and by the middle of the sixteenth century there had been published several translations into the main European vernaculars.[51] As Gruffydd Robert's version ends in mid-sentence, it is impossible to tell whether the whole dialogue was at one time translated into Welsh or not. Enough, however, survives to make clear the way in which Gruffydd Robert sought in his translation to capture the periodic style of Cicero's Latin with its finely balanced correspondence of phrases and subordinate clauses. Here is part of one of Cato's contributions (IV.9), set out to show the rhetorically balanced pattern of phrases and correspondences, followed by Gruffydd Robert's very successful attempt at maintaining a similar periodic style:

> Aptissima omnino sunt (Scipio et Laeli) arma senectutis
>   artes exercitationesque virtutum,
>   quae in omni aetate cultae,
>   cum diu multumque vixeris,
>   mirificos ecferunt fructus,
>   non solum quia numquam deserunt,
>   ne extremo quidem tempore aetatis,

quamquam id quidem maximum est,
verum etiam quia conscientia bene actae vitae
multorumque bene factorum recordatio
iucundissima est.

Arfau cyfaddas i henaint (Scipion f'annwyl a Laelius)
yw celfyddydau ag ymarferion o rinweddau;
y rhain wrth i gwrteithio, ai 'mgleddu ymhob oedran,
a ddygant phrwyth diarhebawl,
wedi i un fyw yn hir, a llawer o amser,
nid yn unig am i bod heb ymadel byth a'i perchen
nag yn yr amser diwaethaf o'i hoedl,
(er bod hyn yn beth mawr)
eithr hefyd, am fod y gydwybod o'r fuchedd a wariessid
yn dda,
a meddwl am lawer o weithredoedd
da a wneithid,
yn hyfrydlonaf peth.

Gruffydd Robert's translation is a skilful transposition of
Ciceronian style into a Welsh medium. Even more important is
the way in which he makes use of the same style in his own
original prose. His grammar, couched as it is in the form of a
dialogue between two friends, is a masterpiece of prose
literature that goes far beyond the idea of a technical 'grammar'.
Saunders Lewis, in a notable essay, refers to the first part of
Gruffydd Robert's Grammar as the beginning of modern Welsh
literature, the work through which – more than any other – the
Ciceronianism of Italy came to exert a direct and creative
influence on Welsh prose. He continues:[52]

Yn hanes rhyddiaith Gymraeg y mae rhan gyntaf Gramadeg
Gruffydd Robert, y Dosbarth Byr fel y mae'n hwylus ei alw, megis
mynydd-dir yn gwahanu dyfroedd oddi wrth ei gilydd. Cyn ei
ddyfod yr oedd yn bod ryddiaith yr oesoedd canol; ei ddyfod
oedd dechrau rhyddiaith fodern.

In the history of Welsh prose, the first part of Gruffydd Robert's
grammar is like a watershed. Before it came, we had the prose of
the Middle Ages; its coming was the beginning of modern prose.

The significance of Gruffydd Robert's writing in the first part of his Grammar was soon recognized by the Welsh humanists. Other grammarians refer to his work, and tributes were paid to his style by men who were on the opposite side of the religious divide. Thus even Maurice Kyffin, in 1595, referring to the *Dosbarth Byrr*, says of it:[53]

... yr hwn sydd ddarn o waith dyscedic ynghelfyddyd gramadec, mor buraidd, mor lathraidd, ag mor odidawg ei ymadroddiad, na ellir damuno dim perffeithiach yn hynny o beth.

... a work so learned in the art of grammar, so pure, so polished, and so splendid in its eloquence that one cannot wish for anything more perfect.

One sentence from among many must suffice to illustrate Gruffydd Robert's Ciceronian sense of style and periodic cadence in his own Welsh writing. It is the start of Morys's famous expression of his longing for Wales (followed by Professor T. Gwynfor Griffith's translation):[54]

Er bod yn deg y fangre lle'r ydym, ag yn hyfryd gweled y dail gwyrddleision yn gyscod rhag y tes, ag yn ddigrif clowed yr awel hon o'r gogleuwynt yn chwythu tan frig y gwinwydd i'n llawenychu yn y gwres anrhysymol hwn, sydd drwm wrth bawb a gafodd i geni a'i meithrin mewn gwlad cyn oered ag yw tir Cymru: etto mae arnaf hiraeth am lawer o bethau a gaid yng Nghymru, i fwrw'r amser heibio yn ddifyr, ag yn llawen, wrth ochel y tes hirddydd haf.

Although this spot in which we sit is fair, and delightful though it is to see the green leaves shading us from the sunlight, and pleasant though it is to hear this northerly breeze blowing under the tops of the vines to gladden our hearts in this unreasonable heat, which is hard to bear to anyone born and bred in a land as cool as Wales: yet I long for many things that were to be had in Wales to help one pass the time pleasantly and happily while avoiding the heat of the long summer day.

Gruffydd Robert was not the only humanist scholar who spent a length of time in Italy. One who was there before him was William Thomas (d.1554) of Breconshire, described by Professor

T. Gwynfor Griffith as 'the father of the study of Italian in these islands'.[55] After his return from Italy Thomas was apppointed Clerk to Edward VI's Privy Council, but soon after Mary Tudor's accession he was put to death for opposing the marriage to Philip of Spain. However, it is for his Italian studies that William Thomas is remembered. His *Historie of Italie*, the first English work on the subject, was published in 1549, to be followed by a grammar and dictionary of the Italian language, *Principal Rules of the Italian Grammer, with a Dictionarie for the better under-standynge of Boccace, Petrarcha and Dante* (published 1550). William Thomas's distinctive contribution was his detailed appreciation of the way in which Italian grew to be a literary language capable of meeting all demands made of it. That the Welsh language should likewise be elevated was Gruffydd Robert's prime wish, and close attention to Cicero's matter and style was an integral part of his recommended programme.[56]

The most versatile and colourful of the Welsh humanists who went to Italy was Dr John Davies (1534?–1621?) of Brecon, usually known as Siôn Dafydd Rhys (an alternative form which conveniently serves to distinguish him from Dr John Davies of Mallwyd).[57] Rhys was born in Llanfaethlu on Anglesey, and it appears that he had some family connection with Bishop Richard Davies. He went to Oxford as an undergraduate, but before completing his course left (in early 1557) for Italy where he eventually registered as a medical student at the University of Siena. It would be very interesting to know if he had any contact with Gruffydd Robert during these years. He later refers to Robert with great respect as *ille vir doctissimus, insignisque nostrae aetatis Philosophiae professor*, 'that most learned man and outstanding teacher of our age'.[58] It is known (on the basis of a protocol in the Siena State Archives) that Siôn Dafydd Rhys graduated as Doctor of Medicine from Siena in July 1567, but there is no certainty about his practising as a doctor in Italy.[59] He also made a distinctive contribution to classical teaching. Three books came from his pen during his stay in Italy: a Latin work – now sadly lost – on Greek grammar and syntax; a treatise, written in Italian, on Latin grammar and syntax, *Della costruttione latina*; and a guide, in Latin, to the pronunciation of Italian, *Perutilis Exteris Nationibus De Italica Pronunciatione et Orthographia Libellus* (1569).[60] Such works show beyond doubt that Rhys takes his place among the most dedicated of humanist teachers.

Not long after the publication of *De Italica Pronunciatione* Siôn Dafydd Rhys returned to Wales, and about 1574 was appointed headmaster of Friars School, Bangor, in succession to John Price who had been there, certainly since 1566, possibly since the school was established about 1557.[61] The main purpose of the school, whose statutes were based on those of Bury St Edmund's School, was to train its pupils in Greek and Latin, and the new headmaster doubtless brought much of his Italian experience to bear on his new responsibilities. He did not, however, stay in Bangor for long. About 1576 Rhys moved to south Wales, probably in response to an invitation to join his older kinsman, Bishop Richard Davies, at his episcopal palace in Abergwili. It was here that William Salesbury had co-operated so fruitfully with the bishop to produce the Book of Common Prayer (including the Psalter) and the New Testament in Welsh, both published in 1567. One of the mysteries in the history of the translation of the Bible into Welsh is the reason why, as the work of preparing the translation of the Old Testament went ahead, friendship between Richard Davies and Salesbury grew cool. According to Sir John Wynn of Gwydir, the interpretation of one word caused the rift: '[Davies] was very far onward with the Old Testament and had gone through with it if variance had not happened between him and William Salesbury (who had lived almost two years with him in that business) for the general sense and etymology of one word which the Bishop would have to be one way and William Salesbury another.'[62] Rhys's move to south Wales may have been, in part at least, to fill the gap created by Salesbury's departure. That is a sign of Rhys's stature as a scholar. In Abergwili he would also be able to participate in the life of one of the few households in sixteenth-century Wales where the old hospitality of medieval abbots and *uchelwyr* combined with the Christian humanism of the Renaissance. If Richard Davies had brought home with him some of Frankfurt's Protestant proprieties and introduced them into his episcopal palace outside Carmarthen, Siôn Dafydd Rhys surely took there a share of Italy's Renaissance culture.

A few years later, possibly at Richard Davies's death in 1581, Rhys moved to the Cardiff area, perhaps to practise as a doctor.

There he came in contact with the Herbert family (of Cardiff Castle and Wilton), and especially with Sir Edward Stradling and his family at St Donat's. It has already been pointed out that Stradling had himself been to Italy, and it was perhaps their common experience in that country which brought aristocrat and scholar together. What is certain is that Siôn Dafydd Rhys found in Sir Edward Stradling a matchless patron for his humanistic aspirations. He recalls how Stradling encouraged him to translate from Latin and Italian into Welsh, and promises him *Metaphysices compendium*, a compendium of Aristotelian metaphysics, translated into Welsh.[63] The most important of the scholarly works which Rhys produced thanks to Edward Stradling's support was a grammar of the Welsh language, written in Latin, *Cambrobrytannicae Cymraecaeve Linguae Institutiones*, published at Sir Edward's expense in 1592.[64] By then Siôn Dafydd Rhys had again moved, this time to live in the Brecon area, but in a Latin dedicatory letter he recalls the urbane generosity of his patron's court at St Donat's. He places Edward Stradling in the frame of a Renaissance *cortegiano* as he tells why he felt bound to attempt to carry out his wish and write the grammar:

> Primo quod ipse sis perquam foeliciter in literis versatus, et adhuc illarum ita suavitate deliniaris, ut cunctis eruditis tuae semper pateant aedes. Cum his enim suaviter sermones misces, horum dulci colloquio ingenium exerces, animique lassati vigorem reuocas.

> First of all because you are yourself a man most happily versed in letters, and are so fashioned by the charm which attaches to them that your home is always open to all men of learning. For you find your pleasure in joining in discussion with such men, you exercise your own genius as you delight in talking to them, and thus you summon back the vigour of your tired mind.

Rhys also recalls why it was Sir Edward's wish that he should write his grammar in Latin, 'so that knowledge about the Welsh language might the more easily spread to other nations too' (*quo facilius ad exteras quoque gentes illius linguae cognitio dimanaret*). Learning was a seamless garment for the humanists, and here from among their number was a much-travelled Welshman presenting to Europe some of the threads of his own tradition. Siôn Dafydd Rhys's life, like his writing, serves to highlight many of the positive influences of Renaissance classicism upon the Welsh humanists. He was fully aware of the classical heritage in both its Greek and Roman aspects and taught the languages to the young; his own Latin prose-writing displays his sensitivity to matters of style, a sensitivity which is carried over into his Welsh writing (for example, his long address to his Welsh readers at the start of the Grammar); and he shared with humanists, at home and abroad, a vision of a cultured way of life which was ultimately derived from Cicero and other classical authors.

This chapter has concentrated on the work of some of those Welshmen who, though few in number and limited in the scope of their undertakings, were motivated by the values and ideas of the Renaissance and its rediscovery of the Greek and Roman past. One must, however, return briefly to the Welsh bards, the guardians of that long poetic tradition which traced its ancestry back to Taliesin, and ask to what extent they admitted the classical strains of humanism into their work in the sixteenth and early seventeenth centuries. We have already observed their predecessors' awareness of the names of ancient personages, both mythological and historical. The fascination of stories about heroes like Hercules and Alexander the Great continued in sixteenth-century Wales. Elis Gruffydd, 'the Soldier of Calais', included in his chronicle of the history of the world an account of the exploits of Hercules, *Ystorya Erkwlf*, translated from a French work, *Les proesses et vaillances du preux et vaillant Hercules* (printed 1500, 1508, 1511).[65] Likewise, continued interest in Alexander is illustrated by Welsh translations of part of Walter of Châtillon's *Alexandreis*.[66] Such works clearly held great attraction. Did, however, the more scholarly and strictly classical awareness of the Renaissance have a significant influence on the attitudes of Welsh poets of the age?

That Welsh poetry belonging to the old tradition continued to thrive throughout the Tudor age is beyond doubt. The period after the Acts of Union may not have produced as many outstanding practitioners of the poets' craft as in the 'great century', 1435–1535, but – in Professor Glanmor Williams's graphic words – 'in spite of [the] bubbling springs of enthusiasm for publishing in English and other languages and the diverse threats testing the Welsh language, native literature remained virile and responsive for much of the century between 1540 and 1640'.[67] Committed humanists like William Salesbury, Gruffydd Robert, Siôn Dafydd Rhys and John Davies of Mallwyd held the tradition of Welsh poetry in the highest esteem, and made it part of their mission as men of the New Learning to study that tradition and to make it as open and available as the Greek and Latin classics. What mortified them was the entrenched conservatism of most poets, their blind adherence to the conventions of praise-poetry and their stark refusal to open windows to allow in fresh breezes. That way lay annihilation. Thus Siôn Dafydd Rhys berates the Welsh poets for their indifference with regard to the destruction and death of the language (*o barth distriwiad ac angeu yr iaith*),[68] and appeals to them to seek material for their poetry in the realms of humanistic erudition:[69]

> Ceisiwch eich defnydd gan y sawl a'i gwyppont yn dda ag yn hyfedr ag yn gwbl berffaith o ran gwybodaeth eu celfyddyd, pwy rai bynnag font y rhai hynny, ai theologyddion ai philosophyddion, ai historyddion ai eraill, a chynnyscaeddwch a gwaddolwch chwithau y defnydd hwnnw o fesuron cerddaidd a chynghaneddion, ag odlau a chymmeriadau a chymmwys eiriau.

> Seek your matter from those who are expert in it and know it well, from those who are thoroughly perfect in the knowledge of their art, whether they be theologians or philosophers, historians or others, and then do you enrich and endow that matter with poetic metres and the *cynganeddion*, with rhymes and line-linkings and suitable words.

Such words crystallize the desire of the humanist that his language should claim its rightful place among Europe's learned tongues, and make its own distinct contribution to the European inheritance.

The most memorable expression of the tension between old and new is the poetic debate (*ymryson*) between the *pencerdd* Wiliam Cynwal, representative of the old bardic order, and the

Cambridge-educated Edmwnd Prys, close friend of William Morgan and advocate of blending humanistic values with traditional verse forms.[70] For Edmwnd Prys poetry should have a moral and religious goal (he is best remembered now for his consummate metrical versions of the Psalms), should display learning, and should be made readily available in print. The debate, the most thorough discussion of the art of poetry ever written in Welsh, extended over fifty-four *cywyddau*, some 5,500 lines in all, and the reader finds himself, like Petrarch two centuries earlier, 'as if standing on the border between two peoples and looking in both directions at the same time' (*velut in confinio duorum populorum constitutus ac simul ante retroque prospiciens*).[71] Prys's poems, which form the majority, display his knowledge of authorities both ancient and modern. Detailed references to the works of Plato, Cicero and Horace come as easily as do allusions to and echoes from Petrarch, Erasmus and Sebastian Münster. Prys's appeal to the traditionalists is that they should not only pursue their own craft but also avail themselves of the legacy of the Bible and of the classical poets. Wiliam Cynwal's rather feeble response is that Prys should stick to his own calling as a priest and leave poetry to its accredited practitioners.

It should not be thought that all Welsh poets working within the old tradition were opposed to the influences of the New Learning. Earlier in the sixteenth century Gruffudd Hiraethog, friend of William Salesbury and outstanding bardic teacher of many poets (including, as it happens, Wiliam Cynwal), was noted for his openness to Renaissance influences. He is the author of *cywyddau* in praise of William Salesbury, John Price and Humphrey Llwyd.[72] Gruffudd's work also contains commonplace references to the heroes and heroines of the ancient world, known from *Trioedd Ynys Prydain* and from the *Brut* and *Ystorya Dared*. Thus an *awdl* in praise of Tomas Mostyn of Gloddaith likens him to Hector; the exploits of Siôn Llwyd of Bodidris are compared to those of Jason; and Marged, wife of Robert ap Morys of Alltygadair, is likened in death to Hecuba.[73] But Gruffudd's knowledge of classical myth goes deeper than conventional reference. In a *cywydd* in praise of his formidable patron, Dr Elis Prys of Plas Iolyn, Gruffudd compares at length the defeat of his patron's enemies to the end of Icarus.[74] A *cywydd gofyn* (request-*cywydd*), asking Cadwaladr ap Robert of Rhiwlas for a gift of a ram for Siôn Mostyn of Gloddaith, nicely summarizes the mission of the Argonauts.[75] Gruffudd also makes effective use of historical references to the classical past. Notably, in a *cywydd marwnad* (elegy) for Judge Lewys ab Owain, killed by the Red Bandits of Mawddwy in 1555, Gruffudd views the rise of Siôn, the Judge's son, in the light of Augustus taking the place of his adoptive father Julius Caesar.[76] All these references confirm the view that Gruffudd's learning, so praised by his contemporaries, included more than a passing awareness of the world of Renaissance classicism. Such openness on Gruffudd's part to humanist interests must have been instrumental in bringing him and William Salesbury together. It is no accident that Salesbury, in the preface to Gruffudd's collection of Welsh proverbs, *Oll Synnwyr Pen Kembero Ygyd* (1547), likens him to Erasmus, Polydore Vergil and John Heywood.[77]

The work of Siôn Tudur (*c*.1522–1602), one of the many poets associated with Gruffudd Hiraethog (although probably not a pupil of his) and among the last of the great poets of the gentry, also contains a great range of classical reference: Actaeon; Philomena, Procne and Tereus; the Three Fates; Aeneas and Dido.[78] In one *cywydd*, on a duel fought between John Salusbury of Lleweni and his relation Owain Salesbury of Holt, three classical pairs of enemies (who were related to each other or had close family connections) are named in two couplets.[79] He knows of Ovid's punishment at the hands of Augustus, and compares John Salusbury's command of languages to that of Horace and Cicero.[80] In an *awdl* in praise of Rhisiart Siôn of Buellt, one of Queen Elizabeth's Yeomen of the Guard, Siôn Tudur likens his subject's prowess to that of Hercules and Odysseus, and displays considerable knowledge of the myths associated with the two mythological heroes: Atlas, Hydra, Nessus, Diomedes, Cacus (all connected with Hercules' Labours), the Harpies, the Cyclops, Scylla and Charybdis (Odysseus), as well as references to Daedalus' labyrinth and the Minotaur, and to the Gorgon.[81] Siôn Tudur was himself for a time in royal service as a Yeoman of the Crown, and it has been established (by Dr Enid P. Roberts) that he attended Queen Elizabeth at the performance of masques and other dramatic productions, in London and in Oxford and

Cambridge. It is likely that he derived much of his classical knowledge from the subject-matter of some of these performances. Siôn Tudur's comments on the social life of the court are often acerbic.

Equally scathing are his comments on the degenerate standards of most of his fellow Welsh poets, men prepared to praise all and sundry for money:[82]

> Gwae ni'r beirdd gan air y byd!
> Gwae ail fodd y gelfyddyd!
> Swydd y bardd sydd heb urddas,
> Oedd enwog gynt heb ddwyn cas.

> Alas for our art, scandal
> Is rampant about us all!
> Credit of our calling's gone,
> Prized once without aspersion.

A family of poets who did try to maintain the old standards in the changing world of the late sixteenth and early seventeenth centuries was the Phylip family of Ardudwy. One of their number, Siôn Phylip, has *cywyddau* which have a distinct classical aura to them: one to Bacchus and the drunkard (*I Bacchus duw'r gwin ac i'r meddwyn*), another to Cupid (*Cywydd Cuwpyd*), and a much-copied poem on the mythical phoenix (*Cywydd y Phenix*).[83] Likewise, the much-travelled Tomos Prys, son of the Cambridge-educated Dr Elis Prys of Plas Iolyn, wrote a *cywydd* on the story of Damon and Pythias (*Damon a Phyddias*), the most sustained poetic treatment of a classical 'myth' to emerge from Renaissance Wales.[84]

Such sustained references are, however, rare in the work of poets who belonged to the traditional order, men whose instinct and training led them to retreat to a position which was in essence conservative and inward-looking. Even in the work of Gruffudd Hiraethog and Siôn Tudur the vein of classical interest does not go very deep. It is thanks to writers of prose, especially the translators of the Bible and individuals like Gruffydd Robert and Siôn Dafydd Rhys and Maurice Kyffin, that a real awareness of humanistic scholarship and of classical style, based on a study of the ancient authors, entered Welsh literature. Their efforts also ensured that the Welsh tongue could claim its place, albeit modestly, as one of Europe's languages of learning.

IV

Clerics and Schoolmasters: The Mid-Seventeenth to the Mid-Nineteenth Centuries

In a country which possessed neither a university nor a cultural centre of any kind, and lacked the wealth to dispense to its children that education which might enable them to comprehend the heritage of other peoples and assimilate it to their own, the period from 1650 till the middle of the nineteenth century is merely one unbroken effort to give the Welsh sufficient education for understanding the things which belonged to the salvation of their souls. Literature of every kind had to struggle for existence as it could; sometimes it was disparaged, sometimes ignored, sometimes used for the purpose of religion, but very rarely was it nurtured for the sake of its own special glory.

Thomas Parry, translated by H. I. Bell[1]

The middle years of the seventeenth century saw, in Professor R. Geraint Gruffydd's apt words, 'the effective end of humanism, as well as of professional poetry, in Wales'.[2] The death of Dr John Davies of Mallwyd in 1644 marked the end of that tradition of integrated and judicious scholarship which had been given its initial direction by men like Richard Davies, William Salesbury and John Price. Not only had their scholarship been fostered at the universities or the Inns of Court and was based on careful classical and biblical learning, but they were also deeply committed to the application of the same humanistic principles to the study of the Welsh language and the history of Wales. The fragmentation of the rounded approach of that small succession of Welsh humanists – a fragmentation whose beginnings were already appearing a century earlier – was complete. The beginning of the Civil Wars, two years before John Davies's death, created in Wales, as in other parts of Britain, a sense of religious and political and cultural polarization. True, the Commonwealth period saw Parliament order the establishing in Wales of many new schools, but they were devoted neither to instruction in Welsh nor to teaching classical literature. After the Restoration, the combined effect of the Act of Uniformity (1662) and the Toleration Act (1689) was that a number of Dissenting academies, providing an education which was often both more demanding and more stimulating than that of the two English universities, were established in Wales and the border counties. Greek and Latin had pride of place in the best of these academies: at Brynllywarch in Glamorgan, for example, and in Oswestry and Carmarthen. But their primary concern was not with bringing classical learning to bear upon the study or advancement of Welsh literature.[3]

Meanwhile the Anglicization of the gentry, and their looking towards the schools and universities of England, meant that few of the natural heirs of Renaissance classicism thought in Welsh terms. Thus, for example, the twin brothers Henry and Thomas Vaughan, like George Herbert before them, can hardly be said to view their work as writers and poets in a Welsh light. It is true that Henry Vaughan, the 'Silurist', acknowledged his Welsh ancestry. In one of his many Latin poems he writes:[4]

> CAMBRIA me genuit, patulis ubi vallibus errans
> Subjacet aeriis montibus ISCA pater.

> Wales gave me birth, in the place where Father Usk launches down
> from the windswept mountains to wander in broad valleys.

Nevertheless, Henry Vaughan's work belongs, in essence, not to Wales but to the world of the seventeenth-century English metaphysical poets. Like his brother Thomas (who wrote under the pseudonym 'Eugenius Philalethes') he was drawn into contemporary Hermetic theorizing. Many of his English works are influenced by the form and content of Horace's *Odes*, and he translated much from classical Latin poetry, especially his celebrated version of Juvenal's Tenth Satire and renderings of some of Ovid's poems from exile.[5] Most noteworthy of all his translations are his eighteen poems from Boethius' *Consolation of Philosophy*, verses of a metaphysical nature to match Vaughan's own temperament and interests. Thus he concludes his rendering of Boethius' telling of the story of Orpheus:[6]

This tale of Orpheus and his love
Was meant for you, who ever move
Upwards, and tend into that light,
Which is not seen by mortal sight.
For if, while you strive to ascend,
You droop, and towards earth once bend
Your seduced eyes, down you will fall
Ev'n while you look, and forfeit all.

To translate Boethius belonged to an English tradition which stretched from King Alfred, via Chaucer, to Queen Elizabeth I.

Alongside the demise of an organic commitment to the legacy of humanism within a Welsh context there occurred also the effective end of that tradition of praise poetry which extended back to Taliesin. Gruffydd Philip (d.1666) and his brother Phylip John Phylip (d.1677), sons of Siôn Phylip of Ardudwy, were the last of the itinerant poets who lived by their time-honoured craft. The art of writing in *cynghanedd*, using the traditional strict metres, continued, but some poets began to combine *cynghanedd* with new metres; others followed the pattern associated with the popular carol and ballad in English; yet others worked within a purely folk tradition, *canu gwerin*. Edward Morris, a seventeenth-century master of these popular forms, composed a delightful poem entitled 'Carol Ciwpit, sef Duw'r Cariad' ('Carol of Cupid, God of Love') in which he displays knowledge of the pictorial representations of the winged boy-god with his bow and arrows:[7]

Gŵr gwamal, adeiniog, aur walltiad, modrwyog,
    A bwa cwmpasog, anelog yn nes;
A'i euraid saeth ganddo, mi lefais drwy gyffro,
    Rhag iddo fo ei minio, yn fy mynwes.

Fickle fellow, winged, golden-haired and curly,
his bow opened out, and aimed ever closer;
he had his golden arrow, and I cried out in agitation,
lest he should plant its sharp point in my bosom.

Such composing in free metres, with touches of *cynghanedd*, was set to continue into the eighteenth century. However, as has already been suggested, Welsh poetry of the later seventeenth century showed very few signs of that classically inspired poetic flowering which happened at the same time in England. The lyric poetry of Jonson and Cowley, the satire of Dryden and the epic of Milton did not have their counterparts in seventeenth-century Wales. A lone voice is that of Rhys Cadwaladr (*fl.*1666–90), vicar of Llanfairfechan and friend of the pioneer printer and devoted Anglican, Thomas Jones 'the Almanacker'. In spite of all the decline in traditional poetry, and in the midst of the political and religious turmoils which were happening about him, Rhys Cadwaladr found both time and inclination to produce some outstanding translations, written in *cynghanedd* and in the *cywydd* metre, of classical Latin poetry. Four of his translations have been preserved in the Mostyn collection of manuscripts in the National Library of Wales, and they are a notable achievement.[8] The four translations are of well-known Latin works which were very popular in this period: Horace, *Epode* 2; Horace, *Odes* I.22; part of a choral ode from Seneca, *Thyestes* (lines 392–403); and Petronius, fragment 30 (Buecheler). Horace's *Integer vitae* (*Odes* I.22) was paraphrased by Henry More, the Cambridge Platonist, in his poem 'Resolution'[9] and was familiar to students of Latin as the example of a poem in the Sapphic metre quoted in William Lily's Latin Grammar. The first two lines are quoted by Demetrius in Shakespeare's *Titus Andronicus* (Act IV, Scene 2), whereupon Chiron responds:

> O! 'tis a verse in Horace; I know it well:
> I read it in the grammar long ago.

Petronius' *Satyricon* gained great popularity through being extensively quoted in Burton's *Anatomy of Melancholy* (1621), and part of the poem on dreams, translated by Rhys Cadwaladr, appears in the *Anatomy*.[10] Horace's second Epode and the choral ode from Seneca's *Thyestes* reflect the interest of seventeenth-century poets and scholars in the withdrawn and contemplative side of classical literature, the enjoyment of *otium* rather than a Ciceronian pursuit of *negotium*. Martial's *Vitam quae faciant* (X.47), translated by Simwnt Fychan in the last third of the sixteenth century, was part of the same trend.[11] The poems and essays of Abraham Cowley embody this interest in seventeenth-century England, and both *Epode* 2 and the passage from *Thyestes* are translated by him.[12]

The longest of Rhys Cadwaladr's translations from Latin is his masterly version of *Epode* 2, *Beatus ille*, a poem which created its own tradition in the seventeenth century. The poem's impact has been vividly summarized by Maren-Sofie Roestvig:[13]

> When Horace first conceived the idea of this poem, he could have little visualized the great popularity it would enjoy some 1600 years later, nor could he have guessed the importance which then would be attached by Europeans generally at that distant date to his philosophy of the happiness of a rural existence.

The epode takes the form of a nostalgic eulogy of the countryman's way of life, spoken by one Alfius, a usurer. Alfius' monologue extends to sixty-six lines, but any thought that he is truly converted to a rustic existence is dashed in a *coda* of four lines, as he returns to the getting and spending of the usurer's life. Significantly, the last quatrain is usually omitted by the seventeenth-century translators, and it is not included in Rhys Cadwaladr's translation. This is not his only departure from Horace's original Latin, and both the title given to the *cywydd* in Mostyn MS 96, 'Cywydd i gyfflybu epod Horace, 2' ('A cywydd *to resemble* Horace, Epode 2') and the poet's practice show that Rhys Cadwaladr subscribed to the method of translation recommended by Dryden, 'where the author is kept in view of the translator, so as never to be lost, but his words are not so strictly followed as his sense, and that too is admitted to be amplified, but not altered'.[14] Thus Rhys Cadwaladr omits specifically Roman references, expands the original and changes the order of the epode as he sees fit, and creates a *cywydd* which has the form and pattern of a newly conceived poem. It is also worth noting that his *cywydd* is not restricted by the couplet form, and he uses enjambement with a confidence worthy of Dafydd ap Gwilym. His manner is seen in comparing his opening lines with those of Horace himself, and also with Cowley's version:

> Beatus ille, qui procul negotiis
> ut prisca gens mortalium,

paterna rura bubis exercet suis,
   solutus omni faenore,
neque excitatur classico miles truci,
   neque horret iratum mare,
forumque vitat et superba civium
   potentiorum limina.

Happy the Man whom bounteous Gods allow
With his own Hands Paternal Grounds to plough!
Like the first golden Mortals Happy he
From Business and the cares of Money free!
No humane storms break off at Land his sleep.
No loud Alarms of Nature on the Deep,
From all the cheats of Law he lives secure,
Nor does th'affronts of Palaces endure.

Dedwydd yw'r sawl nid ydyw
Â'i ben mewn dinas yn byw;
Llon yw fo allan o fysg
Y dyrfa a'r mawr derfysg,
Fel yr oedd lluoedd llawen
A bywyd da'n y byd hen;
Heb dreth nac ardreth hirdrom,
Nac ofni trwst, na ffrwst ffrom
Utgorn, na rhyfel atgas
Mindene rhyw gledde glas;
Heb roi'i draserch, brau drysor,
I dan a mellt ar don môr,
Na charu llys, na char llaw,
O'i dyddyn, ddowad iddaw,
Na phlas unrhyw ddinasydd
Ansyber gan falchder fydd.

Rhys Cadwaladr's interest in Latin poetry, combined with his adherence to the craft of the *cywyddwyr*, did not find much emulation among poets of later seventeenth-century and early eighteenth-century Wales. Were it not for the devotion of anti-quarians like Robert Vaughan of Hengwrt, who sought out manuscripts of the medieval period and saw to their preserva-tion, and the researches of a scholar like the Montgomeryshire-born William Baxter and of Edward Lhuyd and his protégés Moses Williams and Iaco ap Dewi, much of the Welsh literary heritage might well have been lost for ever.[15]

In the second half of the seventeenth century the main thrust of creative writing in Wales went into prose literature, largely inspired by the political turmoils of the Civil Wars and the Restoration and by the religious stirrings of Puritanism and reactions to it. Morgan Llwyd (1615–59), descendant of an old family of *uchelwyr* and the most exciting of Wales's Puritan writers, was schooled in Greek and Latin. He was also indirectly influenced by contemporary Neoplatonism, but his rich style owes little to classical rhetorical theory.[16] On the other hand, Charles Edwards (1628–91?), a later Puritan and author of *Y Ffydd Ddi-ffuant* ('A History of the True Faith'), studied at All Souls College and Jesus College in Oxford, and his work displays a fine awareness of the classical and patristic heritage. He is not afraid of drawing imagery from the world of Greece and Rome to illumine his material, and his style has an epigrammatic ring which reflects the influence of Seneca and the rhetorical teaching of Peter Ramus.[17] *Y Ffydd Ddi-ffuant* is one of the greatest works of Welsh prose, and the classical tradition played its part in the way in which Charles Edwards conceived his work. His primary purpose, however, is to trace the work of Divine Providence in history, and his classicism is incidental to his wish to communicate his vision to his fellow Welshmen.

It is for works written in prose that the early eighteenth century too, like the late seventeenth, is mainly noted in the history of Welsh literature. Most of these writings were of a theological and devotional nature, often translated from English and easily made available thanks both to the work of the Society for the Promotion of Christian Knowledge (SPCK) and to the burgeoning of printing-houses in Shrewsbury and in the small towns of Wales at the beginning of the century. Not surprisingly, most of the authors were Anglican priests, a few were Dissenting ministers in the tradition of Morgan Llwyd and Charles Edwards, all had enjoyed the good fortune of an education far beyond the reach of most of their contemporaries in Wales. Two prose works, not primarily religious in their import, stand out among books of the early eighteenth century for their literary artistry. Both also reflect something of the classicism of their authors. Ellis Wynne (1671–1734), the well-educated rector of parishes in the vicinity of his home, Y Lasynys near Harlech, derived the idea for his *Gweledigaetheu y Bardd Cwsc* ('Visions of the Sleeping Bard', 1703) from English versions of the Spanish writer Quevedo's *Dreams*. In three 'visions' – of 'the Course of the World', 'Death in his Lower Court' and 'Hell' – Wynne brilliantly brings all the powers of his satire to bear upon the presentation of aspects of contemporary morality. Many elements make up the rich tapestry of his style, not least the classical legacy of his schooling, probably in Shrewsbury, and his university training at Oxford. It is firmly established that echoes of Virgil's *Aeneid*, especially the sixth book, abound in the second 'vision'.[18] Theophilus Evans (1693–1767), like Wynne a staunch Anglican, works more consciously within a classical, and Virgilian, frame in his most famous work, *Drych y Prif Oesoedd* ('The Mirror of the First Ages', 1st edition 1716, 2nd edition 1740). Evans stoutly adopts Geoffrey of Monmouth's view of early British history as the basis for his own account of the history of Wales, and interprets that history as the providential unfolding of divine purposes. In writing about the Romans in Britain he displays first-hand knowledge of the classical sources. In the 1740 edition of the *Drych*, Theophilus Evans's colourful use of language and the power of his imagery undoubtedly echo the style and content of many of Virgil's most memorable extended similes.[19] Nor were Ellis Wynne and Theophilus Evans alone at that time in their awareness of the potential of classical style. A far less well-known writer, the Dissenter Jeremy Owen (*fl*.1704–44), in *Golwg ar y Beiau* ('A Look at the Faults', 1732–3), a work of religious polemic, artfully turns lines of Virgil and Horace, Ovid and Juvenal, into the Welsh *triban* form. More significant, a fine classical education shines through Owen's Welsh style. His mastery of the Ciceronian period led Saunders Lewis to see him, in the history of Welsh literature, as 'the last and greatest of the creators of a Ciceronian paragraph, the chief of Welsh rhetoricians'.[20]

However enriching in the experience of Ellis Wynne, Theophilus Evans and Jeremy Owen was their awareness of Latin literature, it hardly betokens a major classical impetus behind their writing. Their main concern was neither with the ancient world of Greece and Rome for its own sake, nor with its impact on their own. And as the eighteenth century progressed, the greatest verve in its literature was to be found as much as anywhere in the hymns and other writings of men possessed of a commitment very different from that to the classical world. Ellis Wynne and Theophilus Evans may well have despised their enthusiasm, but the impetus with which Methodist leaders like Morgan Rhys and Dafydd William, and especially William Williams of Pantycelyn, expressed their spiritual insights, has an energy about it which is a far remove from the supposed proprieties of classical literature.

Although Welsh poetry took new directions in the eighteenth century, and became – in the hands of hymn-writers – a vehicle for conveying some of the profoundest experiences and insights, it should not be thought that it had no contact at all either with its own past or with the great flurry of interest in classical literature which took place in contemporary England. According to tradition, Dafydd Nicolas (1705?–74), a poet connected with the Williams family of Aberpergwm in the Neath Valley, translated some of Homer's *Iliad* into Welsh.[21] Much more tangible, a group of Welsh scholars and poets, memorably termed 'A School of Welsh Augustans' by the young Saunders Lewis (in the title of his first scholarly book),[22] brought a keen awareness of classical literature to bear upon their interest in Welsh literature. Most of them were eager to discover all they could about early Welsh poetry. They also knew of the arguments which informed Swift's 'Battle of the Books' and were familiar with the tensions between 'Ancients and Moderns'. All these concerns they related to their wish to see Welsh poetry regaining some of the high ground which it was in danger of losing. The Oxford-educated Edward Samuel, in a *cywydd* which is an elegy for Huw Morys, displays detailed knowledge of ancient poets, Greek and Latin, and of the mythology attached to the nine Muses.[23] Likewise John Morgan, for the last twenty years of his life Rector of Matchin in Essex, composed epigrammatic couplets in Welsh which were based on lines of Latin poetry; he also translated Tertullian's *Ad Martyras* and *Ad Scapulam*, and wrote a religious work, *Myfyrdodau Bucheddol ar y Pedwar Peth Diweddaf* (1714), a fine example of classically inspired Welsh prose.[24]

It is, however, in the work of those 'Augustan' writers who were closely associated with the Morris brothers of Anglesey that we find the finest flowering of classical awareness, with regard to both content and style, among Welsh poets of the eighteenth century. Lewis Morris (1701–65), the eldest brother, by profession a land-surveyor of repute, was by nature a scholar in the tradition of Edward Lhuyd and Moses Williams and is immensely important for the direction which he gave to eighteenth-century antiquarian interest in Welsh history and literature. Witness to his scholarship is the large library which he amassed at his home in north Cardiganshire, during his time as controller of the Cardiganshire lead-mines.[25] Together with his brother Richard, who spent his adult life as a clerk in the Navy Office in London, Lewis Morris was instrumental in establishing in 1751 the London-based Honourable Society of Cymmrodorion. The prolific correspondence, not only between Lewis and Richard and a younger brother William but also with others of their circle, attests to a deep concern for the preservation and study of Welsh literature. Above all else, their lasting contribution was the support which they gave to poets and writers whose eyes were opened to the glories of the Welsh past. In Dr Prys Morgan's succinct and apposite words: 'Encouragement was the mark of the Morris circle. They encouraged young poets and scholars to borrow and copy from their fine collections of manuscripts . . . They put Welsh poets and scholars in contact with one another and, when necessary, with English writers.'[26]

The three most prominent Welsh poets and writers to be so encouraged by the Morris brothers were Goronwy Owen (1723–69), also from Anglesey, a priest who was educated at Friars School, Bangor, and – very briefly, it seems – at Jesus College, Oxford; Edward Richard (1714–77), a fine scholar who kept a school at Ystradmeurig in deepest Cardiganshire and produced a succession of good classicists; and Evan Evans (1731–88), nicknamed by his contemporaries 'Ieuan Fardd' or 'Ieuan Brydydd Hir', one of Edward Richard's pupils at Ystradmeurig, whence he went to Merton College, Oxford. Goronwy Owen and Evan Evans lived troubled lives, and neither found security or contentment in his calling as a priest. That they contributed, however, in a remarkable way to Welsh literature and scholarship is beyond doubt. Particularly important in the context of this work is that for them, as for the more tranquil Edward Richard, their study of Greek and Latin literature contributed in a vital way to their perception of their roles as Welsh poets and scholars. We are also fortunate that much of their correspondence, written mainly in English, has survived and affords us some marvellous glimpses of their interests and motives as men of letters.

Goronwy Owen's extant work includes six poems written in Latin, mainly early exercises.[27] Three are in elegiacs; an ode, in Sapphics, is addressed to Richard Rathbone of Llanystumdwy; a poem in hendecasyllables, 'Ad Apollinem et Musas', is a satire on the state of poverty in which a poet always finds himself. The longest Latin poem, and of later date (1755) than the *iuvenilia*, is another lyric poem in Sapphics to celebrate the birthday of George Herbert, Lord Ludlow, son of the Earl of Powys. Such poetry, although not large in volume, displays Goronwy Owen's complete command of Latin. It is also noteworthy that it was to take up the post of Professor of Latin at the College of William and Mary in Williamsburg that he sailed for Virginia in December 1756.

Goronwy Owen's classicism is also revealed in his translations from classical literature. Lewis Morris, in a letter to his brother William (18 June 1757), says with some pique that Goronwy Owen ('Gronwy gelwyddog', *'lying Goronwy'*, as he calls him) has just returned to him books which he had feared he would never see again, and then continues:

He sent along with the books a MS. of his to be returnd, which is a translation of his own out of ye Greek into Welsh, one of Lucian's dialogues. The subject is lying, lying stories and spirits, and I believe he sent it as a defence for telling lyes in some cases. It wont bear publication; it is too stiff, being too literal a translation, and the Greek hard and unconcocted names retaind, enough to break a man's teeth; such as Tychiades, Philocles, Arignotus, etc., whereas they should have been Gwrnerth, Llywelyn, Cynddelw, etc. I have taken the story in hand and wrote it over and new molded it, with new storys, where some things would not bear in a Christian country, and it really makes a very merry tale, and would bear publication, if people were so inclined. We shall return him his own MS. back.[28]

In turning to the works of Lucian, both Goronwy Owen and Lewis Morris showed interest in a writer whose prose satires had influenced the English works of Dryden and Swift, and especially of Henry Fielding. It is noteworthy that Lewis Morris's library contained the four-volume edition of *Tom Jones* (1749).

Goronwy Owen's version of Lucian has not survived. What has come down to us are some versions by him of three poems ascribed to Anacreon. One is in a *proest* form, the other two are *cywyddau deuair hirion*: all capture something of the immediate accessibility of the *Anacreontea*, whose popularity had grown and grown since the publication of Stephanus' *editio princeps* (1554).[29] Goronwy Owen sent his three translations to Richard Morris in a letter, dated 7 April 1754:[30]

> I lately took a fancy to my old acquaintance *Anacreon*, & as he had some hand in teaching me Greek, I've endeavour'd to teach him to talk a little Welsh & that in Metre too. I translated three or four of his prettiest little Odes.

The significant fact is that this exercise of translating Anacreon into Welsh was, for Goronwy Owen, an integral part of his becoming a Welsh poet. His classicism led, in large measure, to his rediscovery of Welsh poetry. Of his translation of Poem 39 (in the M. L. West edition) he says:

> Observe that there is but the very same number of Syllables in the Welsh as are in the Greek, not one more or less, & I think the Welsh *Englyn Prost* fully answers the shape & meaning of the Ode, and that in an almost verbatim Translation. The more I know of the Welsh language, the more I love and admire it; & think in my heart, if we had some men, of genius and abilities, of my way of thinking, we should have no need to dispair of seeing it in as flourishing a condition, as any other antient or modern.

Of even greater importance than Anacreon for Goronwy Owen's perception of his own literary role is the Latin poet Horace. For English writers of the eighteenth century Quintus Horatius Flaccus was the classical poet who, above all others, represented the linguistic and metrical perfection as well as the reasoned Epicureanism of the Augustan Age. 'The eighteenth century breathed Horace', as R. M. Ogilvie epigrammatically put it.[31] Goronwy Owen fully shared the devotion to Horace of the

English Augustans. He has two *cywyddau* which are based on
two poems from Horace's fourth book of *Odes*. 'Cywydd i'r
Awen' ('Cywydd to the Muse') is fashioned upon Horace's *Quem
tu, Melpomene* (*Odes* IV.3), and 'Cywydd i Lewis Morys'
('Cywydd to Lewis Morris') upon *Donarem pateras* (*Odes* IV.8).
They are not literal translations. As Saunders Lewis observed,
'Melpomene becomes the Welsh "Awen"; Rome is changed to
Anglesey; and Lewis Morris displaces Marcius Censorinus.'[32]
That their tone, however, is that of Horatian reasonableness is
unmistakable. The same may be said of others of Goronwy
Owen's poems. 'Awdl y Gofuned' ('The Wish') is a piece of
Epicurean idealism comparable to Horace's *Hoc erat in votis*
(*Satires* II.6) or *Epode* 2:[33]

> O chawn o'r nef y peth a grefwn,
> Dyma o archiad im a erchwn,
> Un rodd orwag ni ryddiriwn o ged,
>   Uniawn ofuned, hyn a fynnwn:
>
> Synhwyrfryd doeth a chorff anfoethus,
> Cael, o iawn iechyd, calon iachus,
> A pheidio yno â ffwdanus fyd
>   Direol, bawlyd. rhy helbulus.
>
> Dychwel i'r wlad lle bu fy nhadau,
> Bwrw enwog oes heb ry nac eisiau
> Ym Môn araul, a man orau yw hon,
>   Llawen ei dynion, a llawn doniau.
>
>   (Stanzas 1–3)

> Could I have what I begged for from heaven,
> What I'd ask would be after this fashion,
> Not an idle favour of fortune – no,
>   This upright choice would be my ambition:
>
> Alert good sense, unpampered body,
> To have from health a heart that's healthy,
> And to leave then the unruly, officious
>   World, over-distressed and filthy.
>
> I'd go back to my fathers' country,
> Live respected, not lavish nor meagrely,
> In sunlit Môn, a land most lovely, with
>   Cheerful men in it, full of ability.

Likewise 'Cywydd y Gem neu'r Maen Gwerthfawr' ('The Gem or Precious Stone'), in its treatment of the 'Happy Man' theme, contains echoes of Horace's *Integer vitae* (*Odes* I.6); and 'Cywydd y Gwahodd' ('The Invitation'), in which Goronwy Owen invites his friend William Parry, a senior official at the Mint, to come from London to visit him at Northolt, is an 'appreciation of the gentle and civilized pleasures of companionship in pleasant surroundings',[34] reminiscent of Horace's tone and style.

Goronwy Owen's classicism is seen not only in his poetry but also in his letters, vigorous and exuberant expressions of his thoughts and justifiably regarded as works of great literary merit in their own right. They reveal Goronwy discovering the Welsh literary tradition and beholding it in the light of ancient classical literature. Thus in May 1754, in a letter to William Morris, he compares the twelfth-century Gwalchmai ap Meilyr's poem for Owain Gwynedd, 'Arddwyreaf hael o hil Rodri', to the epic of Homer:[35]

> I protest Gwalchmai seems to me to have said as much, and as much to the purpose in this little Awdl, as Homer has done in his voluminous Iliad.

Goronwy Owen sees the relative merits of Welsh poets in the same way as he compares classical authors. For him, Dafydd ap Gwilym is not in the same class as Gwalchmai (a view which few readers would now share), just as Anacreon and Ovid do not stand comparison with Homer and Virgil:[36]

> Anacreon amongst the Greeks, and Ovid amongst the Latins give some people (of particular complexions) the most exquisite pleasure and delight. I don't condemn those people's taste; but give me Homer and Virgil, and in my poor opinion, so much does Gwalchmai excell D. ap Gwilym and his class, as Homer does Anacreon. But every man to his own taste, I claim no sovereignty over any one's judgment.

In a letter to Richard Morris, dated 7 October 1755, Goronwy Owen sees similarities between the Sapphic stanza and the Welsh metrical form known as *cywydd llosgwrn*.[37] Throughout the letters he emphasizes the classical blend of *ars* and *ingenium*; for example, to William Morris (16 October 1754) he writes:[38]

> E ddigwydd weithiau i Natur ei hunan (heb gynnorthwy dysg) wneuthur rhyfeddodau; etto nid yw hynny onid damwain tra anghyffredin: ac er mai prydferthwch dawn Duw yw naturiol athrylith, ac mai perffeithrwydd natur yw dysg, etto dewisach a fyddai (genyf i) feddu rhan gymhedrol o bob un o'r ddwy, na rhagori hyd yr eithaf yn yr un o'r ddwy'n unig, heb gyfran o'r llall.

> It sometimes happens that Nature herself (without the aid of learning) does wonders; yet that is nothing other than a very uncommon accident; and although natural genius has beauty by God's gift, and learning is the perfection of nature, yet I would prefer to possess a moderate portion of each of the two, rather than excel to the utmost only in one of the two, without having a share in the other.

In the same letter Goronwy goes on to quote the Latin dictum, *Poeta nascitur non fit* ('A poet is born, not made'), and refers to Cicero as an example of a man of outstanding intellect and training who nevertheless failed as a poet. Even so, Goronwy still believes that learning is necessary for the improvement of a poet's inborn talent. For Goronwy Owen, Longinian sublimity is to be aimed for, and training can assist towards that end.

In an early letter to William Morris (7 May 1752), in which he refers to his desire for the 'grave and *sublime*' in poetry, Goronwy Owen gives expression to one of his main wishes with regard to Welsh poetry. Inspired as he was by Homer and Virgil, and also by Milton's *Paradise Lost*, he declared:[39]

> If I had time to spare, my chief desire is to attempt something in Epic Poetry; but the shortness of the measures in our language makes me almost despair of success . . . Our language undoubtedly affords plenty of words expressive and suitable enough for the genius of a *Milton*, and had he been born in our country, we, no doubt, should have been the happy nation that could have boasted of the grandest, sublimest piece of poetry in the universe.

A little over a year later he declares:[40]

I fully intend to aim at something out of the common road, and try whether our Language will bear an Heroic poem.

Throughout all this, the impulse for Goronwy's quest for the right metre and form in which to present a Welsh epic was largely inspired by his reading of Homer and Virgil:[41]

> For our language, I'm certain, is not inferior for copiousness, pithiness, and significance, to any other, antient or modern, that I have any knowledge of . . . Was there not a time when Epic poetry, nay, all poetry, was but a new thing amongst the Greeks and Romans, especially the latter?

Goronwy Owen's vision was not, of course, confined to the classical past. One of his greatest *cywyddau* is 'Bonedd a Chyneddfau'r Awen' ('The Lineage and Qualities of the Muse'), in which he expresses his belief that, in an *aetas Christiana*, poetry must indeed look beyond the ancient classical world:[42]

> Bu gan Homer gerddber gynt
> Awenyddau, naw oeddynt,
> A gwiw res o dduwiesau,
> Tebyg i'w tad, iawn had Iau;
> Eu hachau o ganau gynt,
> Breuddwydion y beirdd ydynt.
> Un awen a adwen i,
> Da oedd, a phorth Duw iddi.

Sweet-songed Homer of old had/ his Muses, nine of them,/ and a worthy row of goddesses,/ similar to their father, the true stock of Jove;/ their lineage comes from ancient songs,/ they are the dreams of the poets./ I know only one Muse,/ a good one, and she has God's protection.

'Cywydd Dydd y Farn' ('Judgement Day') is the nearest Goronwy Owen comes to a Christian epic. In a splendid letter (dated 17 December 1753) to Richard Morris he comments on how his poem was born of a biblical vision which went beyond anything in Homer or Virgil:[43]

Meddwl yr oeddwn nad oedd neb a ddichon ysgrifennu dim

mewn Prydyddiaeth, na cheid rhyw gyffelybiaeth (neu *Parallel*) iddo yn y ddau Fardd godidog hynny; ac felly yr oeddwn yn disgwyl cael cryn fyrdd o debygleoedd o honynt, yn enwedig o Homer, i addurno fy mhapiryn; ond, och fi! erbyn rhoi tro neu ddau ymmysg penaethiaid y *Groegiaid* beilchion, a chlywed yr ymddiddanion oedd arferedig gan amlaf, ym mysg y rhai campusaf o honynt, hyd yn oed Πόδας ὠκύς ei hun ac *Agamemnon* ac *Ulysses*, a llawer Arwr Milwraidd arall, mi ddyellais yn y man, nad oedd un o honynt yn meddwl unwaith am ddim o'r fath beth a *Dydd y Farn*; ac felly na wnai ddim ar a dd'wedent harddwch yn y byd i'm Cywydd i; ac am a welais, nid oedd Hector focsachus ynteu, a Blaenoriaid a Phendefigion Troia fawr, ddim gwell. *Pius Aeneas* ynteu, er maint y glod a roe Virgil iddo am ei Ddwywolder, ni choeliaf nad y gwaethaf oedd o Genedl Troia, wrth ei waith yn diangc oddiyno yn lledradaidd heb wybod iw Wraig, ar hyder, (mae'n debyg) taro wrth ryw Globen arall i'w ganlyn. A pheth mae'r cast a wnaeth y Diffeithwr dau wynebog â *Dido* druan? Ai gwiw disgwyl ynteu, i'r ffalswr hwnnw feddwl am *Ddydd y Farn*? Ond o ddifrif, nid oedd iw gael yn y llyfrau hynny hanner yr oeddwn i'n ei ddisgwyl; ac nid rhyfedd, oblegid pan oeddwn yn gwneuthur y Cywyddau, nis gwn edrych o honof unwaith yn Homer na Virgil, ond y ddau Destament yn fynych.

I thought that there was no one who might write anything in poetry without there being some similarity (or parallel) to it in those two splendid poets. And so I expected to find myriads of similar passages in them, to adorn my papyrus. But, woe is me! after I had spent a turn or two among the leaders of the proud Greeks, and had heard the conversations which were most often practised among the most excellent of them, even 'swift-footed' [Achilles] himself and Agamemnon and Ulysses, and many another military hero, I shortly realized that not one of them thought even once about anything such as the Day of Judgement; and so nothing which they said would do anything to adorn my *cywydd*. As far as I could see, bragging Hector, and the leaders and chieftains of great Troy, were no better. *Pius Aeneas* too, for all the praise which Virgil gave him for his piety, I do not believe to have been anything but the worst of the Trojan race, in that he fled from there by stealth, without his wife's knowledge, hoping (I suppose) that he would light upon some other strapping woman to follow him. And what about the trick which the two-faced waster played on poor Dido? So is it reasonable, then, to expect that deceiver to think about Judgement Day? But seriously, there was not to be found in those books half of what I had expected. For when I was composing the *cywyddau*, I don't know that I looked once in Homer or Virgil, but frequently in the two Testaments.

In spite of his protestations, it is very noticeable that it is in relation to Homer and Virgil that Goronwy Owen finds the language to define his poetic aims in 'Cywydd Dydd y Farn'. The literature of Greece and Rome gave a huge impetus to his writing, and the classicism ultimately derived from that literature provided him with his literary standards.

Edward Richard (1714–77) was a much gentler and more amenable member of Lewis Morris's circle than Goronwy Owen. The school which was established under Richard's leadership at Ystradmeurig, in the fastnesses of Cardiganshire, is an important landmark in the history of the study of Greek and Latin in Wales, and it is not surprising that two of Lewis Morris's sons attended it. Lewis Morris was not renowned for lavishing praises on anyone, but he commends Edward Richard highly, in a letter to his brother Richard Morris (12 April 1760):[44] 'Ned Richards o Ystrad Meurig, lle mae fy mhlant i yn dysgu Lladin gyd ag ef, sydd ysgolhaig rhagorol iawn.' ('Ned Richards of Ystradmeurig, where my children are learning Latin with him, is an excellent scholar.')

Ystradmeurig was Edward Richard's home village, and it was there that he received his earliest instruction in Greek and Latin, from his brother Abraham, who himself kept a school in the village for two years before entering Jesus College, Oxford, in 1732/3. Like his brother before him, Edward Richard also attended the Queen Elizabeth Grammar School in Carmarthen, a school noted for the classical education which it offered, and it is further recorded that he received private tuition from the Reverend John Pugh, of Motigido near Llannarth, 'an elderly gentleman, who, at that time, had a high character for his learning, and particularly for his superior knowledge of Greek.'[45] Any intention which Edward Richard had of following his brother to Oxford was cut short by Abraham's death in tragic circumstances, and the twenty-year-old Edward, supported by some of the well-to-do people of the area, opened his own school at Ystradmeurig in 1734 or 1735. For eight years he provided elementary education there, while still possibly entertaining the hope that he might yet go to Oxford. His biographer John Williams graphically describes what then happened:[46]

He suddenly dismissed all his scholars, with an unreserved declaration, that his own knowledge was not such as qualified him to render them justice: and that, before he attempted to teach them more, he must diligently instruct himself. With this view he applied himself, with indefatigable industry, to the acquisition of a more perfect knowledge of the Latin and Greek classics. Two years did he devote to these studies. The place in which he pursued them was near his own house; it was the church of Ystradmeiric; where, during the whole of the above period, he was to be found at four o'clock in the morning, whether winter or summer.

Two years later he reopened the school, which was soon placed on firmer footing by gift of endowment. John Williams records the school's success:[47]

His school was thronged, and many good scholars were formed, who afterwards did credit to him and to themselves in various parts of the kingdom, and in different professions.

Edward Richard's main concern, as a teacher and scholar, was the instruction of his pupils in Latin and Greek: 'hammering Latin into children's heads' ('pwnio Lladin â morthwylion ym mhennau plant'), according to Lewis Morris.[48] He was also very anxious that a good library be set up in the school, and it is stated that the books in it 'amounted to the number of about seven hundred' at the time of his death.[49] As to Welsh literature, it is clear that, at first, the young teacher's scholarly interest in it was minimal. 'The misfortune is and a great loss to the world that you understand the ancient Greeks and Romans better than the ancient Celtae and Britons', Lewis Morris pointedly tells him.[50] Nevertheless, his close contact with Lewis Morris and his circle, and also the commitment to Welsh scholarship of one of his earliest and ablest pupils, Evan Evans, compelled Edward Richard to take a more informed interest in the Welsh literary tradition. Not that his response was an entirely positive one. On 5 August 1758 Lewis Morris wrote, in near ecstatic terms, to tell him of Evan Evans's recent discovery of a copy of the *Gododdin*:[51]

This discovery is to him and me as great as that of America by Columbus. We have found an epic Poem in the British called Gododin, equal at least to the Iliad, Aeneid or Paradise Lost. Tudfwlch and Marchlew are heroes fiercer than Achilles and Satan.

Edward Richard's reply has not been preserved, but it appears to have been lukewarm. The next day (6 August) Lewis Morris half-apologizes:[52]

> I have your's and it is extream wellcome, and am sorry the Bard [i.e. Evan Evans] and I have put you in any fear of our invading the territories of Homer and Virgil.

The letters, nearly all in English, which have survived from Edward Richard's own pen are full of classical quotations: a 'pedantic habit', according to the young Saunders Lewis,[53] but perhaps more fairly viewed as a sign of Edward Richard's sense of total commitment to classical literature. 'His letters are full of Latin and Greek quotations from the poets which are sheer gold, and no metal comes up to it for weight', as Lewis Morris records a friend saying of Richard's correspondence.[54] Edward Richard's regard for Longinus, doubtless largely inspired by John Dennis's critical writings, is seen in quotations from *De Sublimitate*[55] and in the use of Longinus' reflection (9.11–15) on the *Odyssey* as the work of Homer's old age.[56] References to Homer and Virgil and Juvenal abound, but Horace (in Saunders Lewis's words)[57] 'is Richard's hardest worked authority', especially the *Ars Poetica*. 'The authority of Horace'[58] is paramount for him. In discussing the line of a certain *englyn* (letter to Evan Evans, 21 July 1770),[59] three tags are introduced and attributed to Horace. (The first quotation, although often said to be by Horace, is not in fact from his *oeuvre*).

> It is not such a Number of Syllables that makes a verse as Horace hath observed, *Poeta nascitur*, and in the Close of an Epigram the last Line should be the most beautiful, but in this it is not only *Sermoni propiora* but downright Prose. A Man may utter a thousand such Sentences as 'Yn dlawd na bydol' adyn *stans pede in uno*, and no Ear in place discover the same to be Verses according to the Rules of Prosody.

Edward Richard's correspondence with Lewis Morris and Evan Evans show the modest classical scholar and teacher increasingly drawn into the concern with Welsh literature which dominated the Morris circle. As we have seen, he was initially taken aback at the thought that any comparison might be made between the *Gododdin* and the epic poetry of Homer and Virgil. However, the letters to his former pupil Evan Evans show Richard becoming increasingly interested in Welsh poetry, its history as well as the work of its contemporary practitioners, especially Goronwy Owen. Indeed it has been convincingly argued, by the late Aneirin Lewis, that it was the influence of his pupil which led Edward Richard to develop this interest.[60]

Edward Richard's own most notable poetic work in Welsh includes a two-verse epitaph, 'In Sepulchrum Infantile' (1770), written in the *englyn* form, and rightly described by Aneirin Lewis as a splendid piece born of Edward Richard's newly acquired mastery of the Welsh metre and of his long meditation in the Classics.[61] He also has two pastoral poems, the first (1766) in the form of thirty-four four-line stanzas spoken alternately by two shepherds, Gruffudd and Meurig, the second (1776) a longer work of sixty-four stanzas spoken by the shepherds Hywel and Iwan. The metre used is a free-verse form, popular for songs and carols, and well-known to Edward Richard from Huw Morys's poetry, with which he was very familiar.[62] It is also evident (as Saunders Lewis well shows)[63] that Richard was acquainted with the English pastoral tradition and with the theories of French and English writers – Rapin, Trapp, Addison and Pope – about the genre. However, underpinning all of Richard's devotion to pastoral was his reading of the pastoral poetry of Theocritus and Virgil. The amoebean style, the creation of a sense of landscape, the blending of the rustic idyll with the place-names of Cardiganshire to provide a setting for the poet's discussion of personal and philosophical concerns, all belong to the tradition of classical pastoral.[64] Edward Richard also defends and justifies his style and use of colloquial forms by reference to Theocritus and his use of a stylized form of the Doric dialect. In a letter to Evan Evans, who appears to have expressed some doubts about the diction of the pastorals, Richard says (18 April 1766):[65]

> I own your Remarks are just, and know what Dr. Davies and others from him have taught, but a Scholar or a Gentleman is one thing, and a Shepherd another. *Intererit multum Davusne loquatur an heros* . . . What are the ἐγώνγα [sic], τύγα . . . etc. of *Theocritus* but going out of Grammar Rules, and keeping in Character.

Likewise, in his correspondence with Lewis Morris, Edward

Richard shows his ready familiarity with the intricacies of Greek and Latin language and metrics.

That Theocritus mattered to Edward Richard, and to his pupil Evan Evans, is seen from a list of books held by Evans (see below p. 109). Five separate editions of Theocritus are listed in the catalogue. Also, in the one letter which has survived from Evan Evans to Edward Richard (21 July 1767) he tells his old teacher:[66]

> I am told there is a new translation of Theocritus in verse by Mr Fawkes, who has wrote some annotations on the Bible some years ago. It is said to be very well done. I have not seen it as yet, and therefore can give you no further account.

Such a display of interest confirms the place of Edward Richard, and of his school at Ystradmeurig, in bringing the study of the languages and literature of Greece and Rome to bear in a unique way upon the Welsh world and its literature in the eighteenth century. Ystradmeurig was to continue to exert its influence upon education, especially in Cardiganshire, for several generations.

Evan Evans (often referred to as 'Ieuan Fardd', sometimes as 'Ieuan Brydydd Hir') was – as has been already indicated – among the most colourful and most devoted of Edward Richard's pupils. Edward Richard himself, in a letter to him, touchingly addressed his protégé as 'my Pupil, the Son of my Youth and the first fruits and Beginning of my Strength'.[67] Evans was, without any doubt, Richard's most outstanding pupil. Years after his schooldays were over, any hesitations which he had about the place of pastoral within the poetic hierarchy were dispelled by his mentor's work, which he came to view as having its rightful place within the Theocritean tradition. Evans produced an English version of Edward Richard's first pastoral, and sent his translation to an unknown recipient together with a letter which contains the following appreciation of Theocritus:[68]

> We have few pastoral writers of note in English; Spenser and Philips are the best; but even they come far short of Theocritus. That writer has something inimitably sweet in his *Idyllia*, and his beauty is much heightened by the rusticity of the broad Doric dialect, which, like some Scotch songs, has something very

pleasing to the ear, and agreeable to the fancy of those who have a
true taste for nature in its simplicity.

Evan Evans's place in the history of Welsh scholarship is an
important one. Although he was frequently the victim of his
own addiction to drink and instability of temperament, and also
suffered the opposition of the Anglican hierarchy to his prefer-
ment within the Church, his devotion to the study of the Welsh
literary tradition knew no bounds. He was tireless in his pursuit
of manuscripts of Welsh poetry and single-minded in his
attempts to see their contents in print. Lewis Morris's report (in a
letter to Edward Richard) of Evans's discovery of a copy of the
Gododdin has already been quoted. Through his, often strained,
connections with the Morris brothers, by his untiring visits to
Oxford and to the homes of members of the Welsh gentry who
had Welsh manuscripts in their possession, and by sheer dogged
persistence, Evans amassed an unrivalled collection of Welsh
poetry from its early beginnings. Urged on by English *literati* like
Daines Barrington and Thomas Gray, whose interest in Celtic
literature had to some measure been kindled by James
Macpherson's 'Ossianic' forgeries, Evan Evans wrote in 1758–9 a
Latin essay, *Dissertatio de Bardis*, on the subject of Welsh poetry.[69]
This was the first attempt ever made to write a coherent
exposition of the Welsh poetic tradition, from its beginnings
down to the sixteenth century, and the level of scholarship in the
work is outstanding. Evans displays his knowledge of the
classical authorities for Celtic bardism, and also quotes Gerald of
Wales and Siôn Dafydd Rhys among his Welsh sources. The
most striking feature of the *Dissertatio* is Evans's careful
translations of early Welsh poetry into Latin. He does not aim at
Latin *elegantia*, nor is he attempting to use classical metres,
nevertheless there is a telling directness about his versions. Here,
for example, are some lines from his interpretation of Gruffudd
ab yr Ynad Coch's renowned lament for Llywelyn ap Gruffudd,
together with his edition of the Welsh original:

> Poni welwch chwi hynt y gwynt ar glaw?
> Poni welwch chwi'r deri yn ymdaraw? . . .
> Poni chredwch i Dduw ddyniadon ynfyd?
> Poni welwch chwi'r byd wedi bydiaw?

Och hyd attat di Dduw na ddaw mor tros dir.
Pa beth in gedir i ohiriaw?

Nonne videtis venti et imbris cursum?
Nonne videtis quercus in se invicem ruentes? . . .
Cur Deo non creditis homines, vesani?
Nonne videtis mundi finem adesse?
Exclamabo usque ad te, o Deus, cur terram non
    absorbet mare,
Et cur diutius relinquimur in angore languere?

Much to his annoyance, Evan Evans did not immediately find the necessary financial support for printing his *Dissertatio de Bardis*. However, informed interest in his work spread among English antiquarians, the most important of whom for Evans was Thomas Percy, later to be Bishop of Dromore in Ireland.[70] Percy persuaded Evans to translate examples of Welsh poetry into English. The outcome was a volume entitled *Some Specimens of the Poetry of the Antient Welsh Bards*, published in London in 1764. It contained not only the English translations, but also the *Dissertatio de Bardis*, followed by the Welsh originals of the poems translated in the *Specimens*. Significantly enough, two lines from Theocritus are attached to the title page of the third section.

Although Evan Evans's main concern as a scholar was to explore and preserve Welsh literature, it is important to understand that his scholarship was underpinned by his learning in the Greek and Latin classics. John Williams, part of whose account of the life of Edward Richard has already been quoted, records that when Richard closed the school at Ystradmeurig for two years and withdrew to the local church in order to perfect his knowledge of Greek and Latin, he did so 'without any other companion than the late Rev. Evan Evans, the Welsh bard and antiquarian, who had been the pupil of Mr. Richard, and who continued with him in this solitude until he went to Oxford'.[71] Later in life Evans, perhaps in jest, attributes his excessive drinking to the strain of those years:[72]

Myfi a fyfyriais yn ddifesur yn ieuanc yn yr Ystrad draw, ac ni byddaf byth fal dyn arall o'r achos.

As a youth I studied beyond measure over in Ystrad, and for that
reason I shall never be like any other man.

Among Evans's *iuvenilia* are translations into Welsh of sixteenth-
century compositions in Greek and Latin; a *cywydd*, purporting
to be a conversation between Dafydd ap Gwilym and Morfydd,
based on Horace's 'Donec gratus eram tibi' (*Odes* III.9); and a
Latin eclogue, a pastoral lament to mark the death of Frederick,
Prince of Wales. His letters constantly refer to his reading of
classical literature, and at one stage in his life he appears to have
been working on a translation of one of Lucian's *Dialogues*.[73]
The impetus which his classical training at Ystradmeurig and
Oxford gave to Evan Evans's Welsh scholarship can be gauged
from a catalogue of his books, only part of his collection, which
has been preserved among his papers.[74] Classical authors, thirty-
five Greek and twenty-seven Latin, dominate the list of 257
volumes, which he appears at some time to have deposited for
safe keeping at Ystradmeurig. The full span of classical literature, from Homer to Claudian, is represented. Significantly, in
view of Edward Richard's devotion to the pastoral form, five
separate editions of Theocritus are included in the catalogue.
One cannot but guess at the excitement with which the old
teacher and his pupil would have perused these texts. An even
clearer picture of Evan Evans in relation to classical literature
comes in a letter to Richard Morris, dated 29 November 1766. In
the midst of his troubled and peripatetic life, Evans has found
himself back in his home area in Cardiganshire, hired to act as
curate for six months to an aged and stingy vicar. And his
solace?[75]

Ir wyf yn cyrchu beunydd i Lyfrgell Ystrad Meurig, ag yn astudio
Plato fawr, a hen gyrff eraill o dir Groeg a[']r Eidal. Cymdeithion
mwynion iawn ydynt.

I make my way daily to the Library at Ystradmeurig, and study
mighty Plato, and other old bodies from the land of Greece and
Italy. They are most dear companions.

In the final analysis, Evan Evans's Welsh scholarship was
established upon a foundation of classical learning. Of course
the Welsh tradition itself, together with the benefits derived from

the English Augustan movement, contributed in a crucial way to the edifice which he, like Goronwy Owen and Edward Richard, built on that foundation. Throughout all their lives, however, the classical heritage remained fundamental for them.

Evan Evans represents, beyond his immediate writings, a very significant element in the cultural awareness of Wales in the second half of the eighteenth century. A priest of the Established Church, and acerbic opponent of Methodism, he nevertheless scourged his own church for its wilful neglect of the Welsh language and its literature. His attacks on the anti-Welsh bishops, 'Esgyb Eingl' as he scornfully called them, were not only prophetic in tone but also served to exclude their author from any settled living in Wales. Doubtless there is much truth in the view of the Anglican Church as an Anglicizing agent in Wales during the eighteenth and well into the nineteenth century. It is a view which continued in Daniel Owen's portrayal, almost to the point of caricature, of the Anglican clergyman in his novels of the later nineteenth century.

At the same time, it should not be forgotten that individual Anglicans, the cultural heirs of Goronwy Owen and Edward Richard and Evan Evans, did as much as any in Wales not only to teach the classical languages but also to protect and foster the interests of the Welsh language and its literature in the first half of the nineteenth century. Standards of general education, outside the Sunday Schools, were low, as the Blue Books of 1847 were, for all their other faults, to demonstrate in a graphic way. Even many of the old grammar schools, Tudor and Stuart foundations, fell on hard times, as the landed aristocracy in Wales sent their sons to famous English schools and the Welsh *gwerin* – for whatever reasons – did not avail itself of the educational opportunity offered by the more local schools.[76] True, some self-taught individuals, from the farmer-scholar and political radical William Jones of Llangadfan (d.1795)[77] to the idiosyncratic wanderer Richard Robert Jones, 'Dic Aberdaron' (1780–1843), learnt Latin and Greek and made translations of them.[78] But they are unusual. Another Evan Evans, 'Ieuan Glan Geirionydd' (1795–1855), presents a gloomy picture of Llanrwst Grammar School, endowed by the Wynn family of Gwydir early in the seventeenth century, closed and deserted in the 1820s:[79]

Mae sŵn y gloch yn ddistaw,
Heb dorf yn dod o'r dre,
A bolltau'th ddorau cedyrn
Yn rhydu yn eu lle;
Ystlum â'u mud ehediad
Sy'n gwau eu hwyrdrwm hynt,
Lle pyncid cerddi Homer
A Virgil geinber gynt.

Sound of the bell is silent,
No multitude leaves the town,
The bolts of your strong doors,
Unused, are rusted brown;
Weaving their way of an evening
Bats fly with silent beat,
Where rang the poems of Homer
And Virgil, elegant-sweet.

Without the continuation of a school like Ystradmeurig; without the tutoring given in country rectories; and certainly without the enlightened approach of men like Bishop Thomas Burgess of St David's, founder of St David's College in Lampeter, and Thomas Phillips, founder of Llandovery College, the flickering flame of classical awareness in Welsh-speaking Wales might have died out completely. A group of clergymen of the time, 'yr Hen Bersoniaid Llengar' ('the old literary clerics') also assumed the effective guardianship of Welsh literature and culture at a time when it was in danger of dying through neglect.[80] This sometimes led to a happy combination of interest in both classical and Welsh literature. It is noteworthy that, at a time when its pages were dominated by polemics against the Methodists, the Anglican monthly *Yr Haul* also found space to publish in 1848–9 a series of Welsh translations of the first twelve poems of Horace, *Odes* I, by William Saunders of Llandovery. Likewise the young D. Silvan Evans (1818–1903), clergyman, scholar and poet, a product of St David's College in Lampeter, included Welsh translations of Anacreon and of Ovid's *Metamorphoses* in his *Blodau Ieuainc*, a volume of verse published in 1843.

Such signs of interest in classical literature in a Welsh context were not, however, confined to Anglicans. David Davis,

Castellhywel, educated at the Carmarthen Dissenting Academy, translated Sappho's most famous poem (fr.31) in his *Telyn Dewi* (1824). John Peter, 'Ioan Pedr' (1833–77), at one time a carpenter who became a Congregationalist minister, translated from many languages – including Greek and, especially, Latin – into Welsh.[81] And it was from a Methodist leader that there came, in the middle of the nineteenth century, the most distinctive and coherent call for giving classical education and literature a proper place within a Welsh context. The Reverend Lewis Edwards (1809–87) is a towering figure in Welsh religious and cultural life of the Victorian Age. A Cardiganshire man, educated at first by a series of local tutors, he made his way to London and eventually to the University of Edinburgh. In Edinburgh he was much influenced by the Professor of Moral Philosophy, John Wilson, better known as 'Christopher North' of the *Blackwood's Magazine*. From Scotland Lewis Edwards returned to Wales and founded at Bala a school, later to become a college, for training prospective ministers of the Calvinistic Methodist Connexion. Furthermore, in 1845, in co-operation with Roger Edwards and Thomas Gee, he established *Y Traethodydd* ('The Essayist'), a Welsh periodical devoted to discussing theology and philosophy and literature. *Y Traethodydd* was largely inspired by journals such as *Blackwood's Magazine* and *The Edinburgh Review*, and Lewis Edwards used its pages to reveal to the Welsh people realms which were totally new to most of them. His own devotion to the study of Greek and Latin shines through many of his essays. He wrote on Homer, expressed great admiration for Gladstone's Homeric studies, and translated parts of the *Iliad* into a somewhat laboured Welsh verse form. More significant was the plea which he regularly made for the place of Greek and Latin in the educational reforms which were so needed in Wales. He wrote, of course, in the aftermath of the 1847 Blue Books, but in his call for the setting up of new grammar schools in Wales he was also much influenced by the educational ideas put into practice by Dr Thomas Arnold at Rugby. Only two years after the appearance of the Blue Books, Lewis Edwards wrote an essay entitled 'Ysgolion Ieithyddol i'r Cymry' ('Grammar Schools for the Welsh'), in which his purpose was to stress the need to establish in Wales schools where a thorough linguistic knowledge of Greek and Latin ('dysgeidiaeth ieithyddol drwyadl yn yr ieithoedd Groeg a Lladin') would be imparted.[82] It is an essay which was seen by Saunders Lewis as presenting a glorious vision of the ideals of Renaissance values restored.[83] Lewis Edwards's views are clearly summed up in one of his later essays, written in 1865:[84]

Y mae yn ymddangos i ni mai yr un a ddylai gael y lle blaenaf mewn addysgiaeth yw y *classics*; nid er mwyn yr ieithoedd Lladin a Groeg ynddynt eu hunain, ond er mwyn y llyfrau a ysgrifenwyd ynddynt. Y mae y llyfrau hyn yn werth eu darllen a'u deall o herwydd eu teilyngdod, gan eu bod yn gynnyrchion yr holl feddylwyr mwyaf a fu yn y byd erioed cyn dyddiau Crist, oddieithr ysgrifenwyr yr Hen Destament; ac heblaw hyny, dyma y paratoad goreu i'r neb sydd yn meddwl rhoddi gweddill ei oes i ddarllen gwaith y meddylwyr mwyaf a fu yn y byd ar ol hyny.

It seems to us that the prime place in education should be given to the classics; not for the sake of the Latin and Greek languages in themselves, but for the sake of the books which have been written in them. These books are worth reading and understanding because of their merits, inasmuch as they are the products of all the best thinkers who were ever in the world before the days of Christ, apart from the writers of the Old Testament; furthermore, this is the best preparation for anyone who wishes to devote the rest of his life to reading the work of the greatest thinkers who were subsequently in the world.

Such views owe more to Lewis Edwards's education in Edinburgh and to his study of Thomas Arnold's educational ideals than they do to his Welsh background. He is not renowned for any deep concern about the continuation of the Welsh language itself, and his study of Welsh literature – perceptive though it is – is mainly confined to religious writers such as Morgan Llwyd. In order, however, to widen the cultural as well as the intellectual horizons of his fellow countrymen, he effectively used on the pages of *Y Traethodydd* the one language with which most of them felt at ease. He wrote about Coleridge and Milton, about Goethe and Kant. He also informed his Welsh readers about Homer, and from his position of prestige within Welsh Nonconformity presented Wales with a vision of an educational structure which included the ordered study of Greek and Latin.[85] As will be seen in the final chapter, the seed of his ideas bore some modest fruit in the educational changes of the later nineteenth century. It is not uninteresting to note that Lewis Edwards's children played their part in those changes: one of his sons was headmaster of a school which was adopted as a 'county' school under the terms of the 1889 Intermediate Education Act, another son became the first principal of the University College established at Aberystwyth in 1872.

V

The University Movement and its Impact: The Classical Heritage since the Mid-Nineteenth Century

> Those who care for the preservation, the extension and the advancement of our culture cannot fail to interest themselves, however unqualified they may be to pass judgement, in our classical heritage.
>
> T. S. Eliot[1]

> Gallai Catwlws fod yn llawn cymaint o gyffro i fardd Cymraeg â W. H. Auden.
> (Catullus could be as great a thrill for a Welsh poet as W. H. Auden.)
>
> Saunders Lewis[2]

The second half of the nineteenth century witnessed not only an invigorating reform of the study of Classics in places of learning but also a great widening of interest in the classical world on the part of the cultured public. In England the two ancient universities set about rigorously revising the classical syllabus. In 1850 Oxford established its highly regarded course in Literae Humaniores, leading to the final examination in 'Greats', and later in the century Cambridge reviewed its Classical Tripos. The reform of school curricula, inspired especially by the work of headmasters like Samuel Butler and B. H. Kennedy (of *Latin Primer* fame) at Shrewsbury and Thomas Arnold at Rugby, also began to bear fruit.[3] Of great importance in this reform was the emphasis laid on Greek studies, and the recapturing of that rounded approach to classical study which gave Greek equality of place with Latin. The interest in the Greek world was also fuelled by recent and contemporary events. The struggle for Greek independence from Turkey, a cause for which Lord Byron was perceived to have died in 1824 at Missolonghi, had kindled the imagination of many a romantic and radically disposed spirit. Moreover, the increasing appeal in Europe of the ideals of democracy and of republicanism was supported by reference to Athens of the fifth century BC. Some Greek authors, Thucydides and Plato in particular, were especially popular and were explained in terms of the ideals and purposes of the nineteenth century. Some bolder souls – for example, a latter-day Byron like Swinburne – saw in the Greek world an escape from the grip of a Christianity which was rooted in the Roman world. Also, throughout the century, an awareness of the artistic and architectural aspects of Greek culture was ever on the increase.[4]

What impact did this wider, and deeper, interest in the Classics have in Wales? The removal of the bar against non-Anglicans going to Oxford and Cambridge meant that a number of Nonconformist Welshmen were able to go to the two ancient English universities from the 1850s onwards. Thomas Charles Edwards (1837–1900), the eldest son of Lewis Edwards of Bala, graduated in 1866 with a 'First' in Greats from Lincoln College, Oxford. Meanwhile, the demand for greater educational opportunities within Wales itself hugely increased in the second half of the nineteenth century. In the wake of far-reaching developments at the elementary level, a committee was established in 1880 under the chairmanship of Lord Aberdare to enquire into secondary provision. This led to the Welsh Intermediate Education Act of 1889 and the setting up of a network of 'county' schools throughout Wales. Latin was a required subject at these schools. Greek was to be optional, along with Welsh![5]

Parallel to the demand for more secondary schools in Wales was the call for establishing a Welsh university to which the products of the schools might aspire. The theological colleges of the different denominations, although they were restricted by their homiletic aims, were certainly providing their students with a sound grounding in the ancient languages.[6] Lewis Edwards's college at Bala, for all the humour of Daniel Owen's description of Thomas Bartley's reaction to 'learning the languages of dead people',[7] raised some very fine scholars of a classical bent. Among them were R. Llugwy Owen (1836–1906), who went on to the University of London and eventually to the University of Tübingen, and wrote in Welsh a 350-page history of Greek philosophy,[8] and Hugh Williams (1843–1911), editor of

Gildas and author of *Christanity in Early Britain* (1912).[9] Such successes notwithstanding, and despite some measured reservations, Lewis Edwards put his weight behind the call for providing, in a Welsh university setting, the kind of training which would encourage scholarship 'in those things which lie hidden, at the root of all learning'.[10] The first step in the realization of the dream of the advocates of a Welsh university was the opening of the first College at Aberystwyth in 1872, with Thomas Charles Edwards as its principal.

T. C. Edwards was not only principal at Aberystwyth, but also Professor of Greek. The small complement of staff also included, from the beginning, a Professor of Latin.[11] Aberystwyth in its first years produced some very notable scholars, including Thomas Francis Roberts, John Edward Lloyd and Owen M. Edwards. When the colleges at Cardiff and Bangor opened in the early 1880s, they too displayed a similar commitment to the study of Classics, each having Chairs both in Greek and in Latin.[12] The first Professor of Greek at Cardiff was T. F. Roberts, who had gone from Aberystwyth as a scholar to St. John's College, Oxford, and who was to succeed Thomas Charles Edwards as the second principal of Aberystwyth.[13] Bangor's first two professors were a contrasting pair. The Chair of Greek was held by W. Rhys Roberts, of whom it was said (on his departure for Leeds in 1904) that 'to know him was a liberal education'. The first Professor of Latin was E. V. Arnold, author of a major study of *Roman Stoicism* (1911) and viewed by his students as an unyielding martinet.[14] The Classical departments within the Colleges (which were federated as the University of Wales in 1893) made a contribution not only to the education of their students but also to the cultural life of their communities. In Cardiff, for example, a lively society, known as the Frogs Classical Society, was established in 1899. Among its many activities was the staging of performances of Greek plays in Cardiff's New Theatre and elsewhere, a practice which reached its peak during Gilbert Norwood's tenure (1908–26) of the Chair of Greek. Meanwhile the University of Wales Press, established in 1922, published works in Welsh which brought the results of classical scholarship to the attention of a cultured lay readership. Two volumes of importance published in 'Cyfres y Brifysgol a'r Werin' ('The University and the People Series') were *Y Groegiaid*

Gynt (1932) by T. Hudson-Williams, and *Hanes Athroniaeth, Y Cyfnod Groegaidd* (1939) by D. James Jones. Both authors were professors, one of Greek, the other of Philosophy, at Bangor.

The county schools also provided, as has been noted, instruction in Latin and, to a lesser extent, in Greek. By 1912 Latin was on the curriculum of nearly every one of the 110 secondary schools in Wales. (By 1925 the number of schools had increased to 140, and Latin was compulsory, at least for part of a pupil's time, at each of them; Greek was on the curriculum of thirty-one schools.)[15] It is difficult to estimate the extent to which such an education alienated pupils from their own culture. It has sometimes been maintained that the intermediate schools were instruments for the Anglicization of Welsh-speaking areas, that their sole aims were to provide for the abler children of those areas the kind of education which was given in English grammar schools, and that such children were therefore lost to their native communities.[16] Doubtless many teachers of Latin, false imitators of the traditions of the English public schools, behaved in a contemptuous way towards Welsh. D. Tecwyn Lloyd drew a brilliant portrait of his Latin master in Bala in the 1920s, always 'stubbornly English', without a word of Welsh heard from his lips, although he was brought up a Welsh-speaker in Penllyn.[17] Without doubt Wales also had its share of those who saw a supposedly privileged classical education as nothing more than a step to worldly advancement, the Welsh heirs of Dean Gaisford. He, it is recorded, once ended a sermon in the Cathedral at Christ Church, Oxford, with the memorable words: 'Nor can I do better, in conclusion, than impress upon you the study of Greek literature, which not only elevates above the vulgar herd but leads not infrequently to positions of considerable emolument'![18] On the other hand, for every teacher like the one in Bala, there were many who were hugely supportive of their pupils' talents. And however much truth there may be in some of the criticisms of the intermediate schools, it behoves us to remember that those schools, and the university too, played a vital part in creating the Welsh literary renascence of the twentieth century.

What impact did the more extensive awareness of the Greek and

Latin Classics have on Welsh literature? Throughout the nineteenth century, dominated as it was by the eisteddfod movement in various forms, the work of some popular poets did display faint classical dimensions. Thus the *awdl* on the fall of Jerusalem, 'Dinistr Jerusalem' (1824), by Ebenezer Thomas ('Eben Fardd'), in its attempt at epic, may owe something to an insecure awareness of Virgil's account of the fall of Troy.[19] Also the highly prolific and popular poet William Thomas, 'Islwyn', in a famous passage in the second of his lengthy works entitled 'Y Storm' ('The Storm'), acknowledges the classical heritage, only to deny any particular need of the ancient Muses:[20]

> Mae'r oll yn gysegredig, mae barddoniaeth
> Nefolaidd oddi ar y bannau hyn . . .
>   . . . Mae y byd
> I gyd yn gysegredig, a phob ban
> Yn dwyn ei gerub a'i dragwyddol gainc.
> Ac nid yw glannau yr Aegean bell, –
> Penrhynion tragwyddolwawr Groeg, y sydd
> Yn codi gyda moroedd amser fyth,
> Ac ar bob craig oleuni llawer oes, –
> Ond rhannau bychain o farddonol fyd.

> Everything is sacred, all these mountains
> Have in them heavenly music . . .
>   . . . All the world
> Is sacred, not a mountain but doth bear
> A cherub on it, and eternal song.
> And even the remote Aegean shores –
> Those headlands of the eternal dawn of Greece
> Rising for ever from the seas of time
> And on each rock the light of many ages –
> They're but small parts of the poetic world.

The National Eisteddfod itself went through a time of reform in the later nineteenth century, and it is of some importance that during the 1880s competitions were regularly set for translating from Latin, and especially Greek, into Welsh. Thus, in the 1885 National Eisteddfod at Aberdare, eighteen competitors submitted translations of Euripides' *Alcestis*; the Greek text and the two successful translations were lavishly printed by the Oxford University Press at the expense of the Marquess of Bute.[21]

Likewise, in 1889, the twenty-second book of the *Iliad* was set for translation, and the prize awarded to R. Morris Lewis. His translation, together with other parts of the *Iliad*, was published posthumously in 1928.[22]

From the turn of the century onwards the classical heritage exerted a more recognizable influence on Welsh literature than perhaps at any time since the days of William Salesbury and Maurice Kyffin. It has already been observed that Welsh literature of the early twentieth century underwent a remarkable awakening. The poems of R. Silyn Roberts and the young W. J. Gruffydd, in their joint volume of lyrics, *Telynegion*,[23] symbolized a new force which had been gaining momentum in Welsh poetry since the 1890s. The National Eisteddfod held in Bangor in 1902 was further evidence that change was afoot, when T. Gwynn Jones won the chair for his *awdl* 'Ymadawiad Arthur' ('The Departure of Arthur'), and R. Silyn Roberts the crown (with W. J. Gruffydd the runner-up) for a *pryddest* on 'Trystan ac Esyllt' ('Tristan and Iseult'). The new movement was a consciously romantic one, often finding its subject-matter in the medieval world and in Celtic mythology, and giving free rein to imaginative self-expression. It also allowed invigorating blasts of fresh air to blow through Welsh literature. One must, however, beware of falling into the trap of creating an over-convenient contrast between romanticism and classicism. The individual who gave expression to the philosophy of the renascence was Professor (later Sir) John Morris-Jones, Professor of Welsh at Bangor. Morris-Jones was himself the author of tender lyrics and the translator of Heine and of Omar Khayyám into Welsh. He was also the main upholder of linguistic and metrical correctness, and in his critical writings he regularly emphasized literary canons associated with Aristotle's *Poetics*. He expressed his Aristotelian viewpoint in an important essay, 'Swydd y Bardd' ('The Poet's Function'), written in the wake of the 1902 Eisteddfod and published in *Y Traethodydd* for that year. Towards the end of his life he repeated and developed his views in his influential volume on Welsh poetic art, *Cerdd Dafod* (1925). In that work Sir John makes Aristotle's discussion the starting-point of his treatment, claiming that the essentials emphasized by Aristotle in treating epic and drama can be applied to Welsh lyric poetry:[24]

Fe ddywaid Aristoteles mai swydd y bardd ydyw efelychu gweithredoedd a theimladau dynion. Nid adrodd yr hyn a *fu* – gwaith yr hanesydd yw hynny; ond traethu'r hyn a *allai* fod – dychmygu cymeriadau, a pheri iddynt deimlo a gweithredu yn y modd sy'n naturiol iddynt.

Aristotle says that the function of the poet is to imitate the deeds and feelings of men. Not the recounting of what *has* happened – that is the task of the historian; but to express that which *might* be – imagining characters and causing them to feel and act in the way which is natural to them.

A few sentences later he writes:[25]

Am yr arwrgerdd a'r ddrama'n unig y traetha ef . . . Ond â'r delyneg y mae a wnelom ni, canys i'r dosbarth telynegol y perthyn holl hen farddoniaeth Cymru . . . A oes gennym hawl i gymhwyso at y delyneg bur y diffiniad a seiliodd Aristoteles ar ystyriaeth o'r arwrgerdd a'r ddrama'n unig? Er nad yw priodoldeb hynny'n amlwg ar yr olwg gyntaf, eto y mae barddoniaeth yn ei hanfod yn un, ac fe geir bod y diffiniad yn wir mewn ystyr ddofn am y delyneg hefyd.

He (i.e.Aristotle) writes about epic and drama only . . . We are dealing with lyric, as all old Welsh poetry belongs to the lyric category . . . Are we entitled to apply to pure lyric the definition which Aristotle based on consideration of epic and drama only? Although the appropriateness of so doing is not immediately apparent, yet poetry is in its essence one, and it is found that the definition is true, in a deep sense, about the lyric also.

Later Sir John makes further observations, based on the *Poetics*, which are extremely interesting in relation to the poetry of the nineteenth century:[26]

Beth bynnag fo'r testun fe ddylai'r gân fod yn un peth, cyfan a chyflawn. Rhaid bod i ddrama neu arwrgerdd, medd Aristoteles, ddechreuad a chanol a diweddiad, pob rhan yn angenrheidiol i'w gilydd. Nid cyfres o rannau digyswllt, ond aelodau o'r un cyfanwaith, ag undeb organaidd creadur byw. Y mae'r un egwyddor i'w chymhwyso at bob math ar gân; yn wir, rhaid i bob darn gorffenedig o waith celfyddyd feddu ar yr unoliaeth organaidd hwn.

Yn hyn y mae holl awdlau eisteddfodol y ganrif o'r blaen yn colli, yn bennaf am na wyddai'r pwyllgorau amgen na rhoi haniaethau i'r beirdd i ganu arnynt, ac na wyddent hwythau pa fodd yn y byd i'w diriaethu ond trwy gymryd rhes o esiamplau digyswllt ohonynt. Ond unoliaeth corff byw ydyw unoliaeth cerdd i fod, nid unoliaeth casgliad o *fossils* mewn amgueddfa.

Whatever the subject, the song should be one thing, whole and complete. A drama or an epic, according to Aristotle, must have a beginning, a middle and an end, all parts being necessary for one another. Not a series of unconnected parts, but members of one complete composition, with the organic unity of a living creature. The same principle is to be applied to every kind of song; indeed, every finished piece of artistic work must possess this organic unity. It is in this respect that all the eisteddfodic *awdlau* of the last century fail, mainly because the committees did not know better than to give the poets abstract subjects about which to sing, while the poets themselves did not know how to make those abstractions concrete other than by giving a series of unconnected examples of them. But the unity of a poem should be the unity of a living body, not the unity of a collection of fossils in a museum.

These early paragraphs from *Cerdd Dafod* have been extensively quoted because they show that classical literary canons, extending back to Aristotle, were integrally part of John Morris-Jones's understanding of the standard which Welsh poetry should set before itself. However 'romantic' the themes which the poets of the renascence of the early twentieth century chose, it is unquestionable that the discipline of form and unity, which they valued so highly, came to them from the heart of the classical literary tradition. That is hardly surprising. John Morris-Jones himself was educated in Greek and Latin at Friars School, Bangor, and Christ College, Brecon; W. J. Gruffydd was one of the first pupils to attend Caernarfon County School, and studied Classics, followed by English, at Oxford; and that self-taught genius, T. Gwynn Jones, steeped himself in the literature of the classical tradition in Europe.[27]

It cannot, of course, be claimed that classical subjects ranked high in T. Gwynn Jones's mind. He usually turned to Celtic mythology for his subject-matter, and Rome in particular represented threat and danger to the old life of the Celts.

'Argoed', a poem about Gaulish reactions to the Roman invasions of the first century BC, is particularly memorable for the picture it presents of a Celtic poet who finds himself rejected by some of his own people:[28]

> Yn ofer aethai ei lafur weithion,
> O dynnu Gâl dan wadnau ei gelyn,
> A dyfod ystryw a defod estron
> I ddofi ei hynni, i ddifa heniaith
> A hen arferion ei chynnar fore:
> Na'i ddull na'i iaith ni ddeallen' weithion,
> Am ei ganiad ni chaffai amgenach
> Na thaeog wen wrth ei chwith oganu
> â di-raen lediaith o druan Ladin –
> Yn ofer aethai ei lafur weithion!

> And now, at last, vain was the labour,
> For Gaul was pulled down under heel of her enemies
> With coming of trickery, foreigner's ways,
> To tame her vigour, waste an old language
> And custom as old as her earliest dawn;
> Now they could grasp neither metre nor meaning,
> Nor would his singing earn him aught better
> Than the sneer of a slave, awkwardly mocking him
> In a patois malformed from wretched Latin –
> Ah now, at last, how vain was his labour!

In such a context the Roman world is a curse, not a blessing.

One of the most outstanding sons of the county schools was T. H. Parry-Williams, who graduated in Latin as well as in Welsh from Aberystwyth. Parry-Williams proceeded to scale further heights at the universities of Oxford, Freiburg and Paris, before returning to Aberystwyth where he was Professor of Welsh from 1920 to 1952. He was also one of the most perceptive and influential of Welsh men of letters in the mid-twentieth century. In a sonnet entitled 'Madrondod' ('Stupefaction'), written on remembering reading, as a young man, a collection of new Welsh lyric poetry (which, it has been shown, was the *Telynegion* of R. Silyn Roberts and W. J. Gruffydd),[29] Parry-Williams relives his youthful experience:[30]

Lladin oedd llef a llyfrau gwyliau haf
  Y flwyddyn honno, ac o'r awyr lefn
Dôi haul Rhufeinig i ddwnedu'n braf
  I heddwch astud yr ystafell gefn;
A'r llencyn o fyfyriwr bach â'i bwys
  Ar fin y ford, heb fod yn gaeth na rhydd,
Gan hen hen naws y clasuroldeb dwys
  Yn sobri'n swrth yn nhrymder nawn y dydd;
Nes dyfod sbel, a drachtio rhin di-ail
  Grawn awen y Gymraeg, gan lwyr gyffroi
Astudiaeth sad ei sobrwydd hyd y sail
  A'i sionci drwyddo wedi'r hir ymroi, –
Ei Horas a'i Gatwlws ar y llawr,
Yntau ar newydd win yn feddw fawr.

It was Latin in speech and books during the summer holidays/
that year, and from the calm air/ a Roman sun came to chatter
pleasantly/ in the studious quiet of the back room;/ And the
student lad, with his elbows/ on the table's edge, being neither
bound nor free,/ under the old, old ethos of solemn classicism/
was drowsily sober in the heaviness of the afternoon;/ Until there
came a respite, and he drank deep of the matchless vintage/ of the
Welsh muse's fruit, which completely stirred/ his sober, wise
study to its foundations/ and enlivened him through and through
after his long exertion, –/ His Horace and Catullus on the floor,/
he totally drunk on new wine.

The choice of the word *dwnedu* (line 3), ultimately derived
from the name of the fourth-century Latin grammarian Donatus,
to describe the companionable chatter of the 'Roman sun', is
typical of Parry-Williams's genius for choosing the exact word.
But his stance is essentially anti-classical. It is, perhaps,
surprising that he should name Catullus, the most sensitive of
Latin poets, as a representative of *clasuroldeb dwys* ('solemn
classicism'), especially when one recalls that the volume
Telynegion contains a translation by W. J. Gruffydd of Catullus'
eighth poem, 'Miser Catulle, desinas ineptire'. But it is certainly
the case that T. H. Parry-Williams's work, for all his study of
Latin literature, does not contain much overt reference to the
Greek and Roman worlds.[31]
    That lyrical translation of Catullus 8 reminds us of the classical
education which a scholar like W. J. Gruffydd had enjoyed. It has

already been stressed that an over-harsh division between classicism and romanticism is to be avoided, and it is significant that the young Gruffydd repeatedly makes romantic use of classical references and subject-matter to challenge the conventions of his day. In so doing he follows the example of English poets like Byron, Shelley and Swinburne. Gruffydd was a precocious nineteen year old when *Telynegion* appeared, and he includes a youthful lyric entitled 'Endymion'. He was, not surprisingly, influenced by John Keats's *Endymion* (1818). The romantic in W. J. Gruffydd found excellent material for treating the theme of love's agony in the myth of Endymion and his love for Diana (or Artemis). Another – and, in my view, better – 'classical' poem is 'Circe', about Homer's enchantress who by her song would attract mortal seafarers to her lonely island and turn them into animals. She features in one of the *Odyssey*'s best-known adventures, and Gruffydd's poem opens with an idyllic presentation of her island, the kind of remote paradise which appealed to many writers at the turn of the century. But however sweet and attractive the island may be, destruction is what really awaits the man who goes there, coupled with the loss of his family, his home, and his own identity.[32]

It is in the original version of his *pryddest*, 'Trystan ac Esyllt', that Gruffydd makes his boldest use of classical references, references which were used against what he regarded as a false religious puritanism. He particularly strikes such a note in the second part of the poem, entitled 'Lacrimae Musarum' ('Tears of the Muses'): a part which was omitted when Gruffydd published a revised version of the *pryddest* in his collection *Caneuon a Cherddi* (1906).[33] Gruffydd is much influenced by Swinburne, but the point which is particularly significant now is that Gruffydd, as he laments the loss of the innocent paradise which he believed puritanical Christianity had destroyed, turns to the gods of classical antiquity as symbols of that innocence. Here are some of his lines:[34]

> Mae'r goleu a'r gwirionedd wedi mynd.
> Ble mae'r holl dduwiau a'r duwiesau fu
> Yn crwydro'r goedwig las mewn dyddiau gwell?
> Ai ofer ydoedd Groeg? A gollodd Zeus
> Am byth ei folltau tân o flaen ein Crist?

Lle gynt y dawnsiai'r gwiddan dan y coed
A thorf o'i gylch yn nhemel lân y wig,
– Ac aml nos, ac ust yr hwyr yn drwm
Ar fron y ddaear, fe ddôi Pan ei hun,
Ardderchog Ban, brif-deyrn yn llys y dail,
I gyfarch gwell i'w mysg, ac hyd nes dôi'r
Rosynog wawr i spïo dros y bryniau
'Roedd siffrwd gan y ddawns, a'r pibau main
Yn chwythu cainc llawenydd.

The light and the truth have gone./ Where are all the gods and
goddesses who/ roamed the green forest in better days?/ Was
Greece in vain? Has Zeus lost/ for ever his thunderbolt before our
Christ?/ Whereas before, the wizard used to dance under the
trees,/surrounded by a crowd in the holy temple of the wood, – /
and many a night, when the silence of evening was heavy/ on the
breast of earth, Pan himself would come,/ Glorious Pan, chief-
ruler in the court of the leaves,/ into their midst to greet them , and
until there came/ the rosy dawn to spy over the hills/ there was
the rustling of the dance, and the slender pipes/ would blow a
tune of joy.

The poem's lament for the surrender of ancient religion to
Christianity reflects a tradition which extends back to Schiller's
The Gods of Greece.[35] Gruffydd also knows Elizabeth Barrett
Browning's 'The Dead Pan',[36] and his anti-puritanical stance
reflects something of the tone of Swinburne's 'Hymn to
Proserpine' and its 'Thou hast conquered, o pale Galilean'.[37]
However, what is here underlined is that W. J. Gruffydd uses
classical references to express his protest, in a poem whose
subject-matter, the story of Trystan and Esyllt, did not belong to
the classical world at all. The ancient Greek world was part of
the way in which this young poet saw and expressed his vision.
Essential to that were, first, the education which he had received,
and, second, his Welsh literary perspective. This was the new
world of Wales's *poetae novi*.

Such, then, was the context within which many Welsh poets
treated classical subjects at the beginning of the twentieth
century. The young W. J. Gruffydd is already a figure of
towering significance, just as in later years he was destined,
through his editorship of *Y Llenor*, to impose his stamp on

subsequent developments in Welsh literature.[38] Nor should it be thought that interest in the classical world remained exclusively confined to those who had received the benefits of a broader education. The most poignant story in the history of Welsh literature in the twentieth century is the story of 'Y Gadair Ddu' ('the Black Chair'), of the 1917 National Eisteddfod at Birkenhead. Ellis Evans ('Hedd Wyn'), a young farmer from Trawsfynydd in Merionethshire, had been killed in action in France only weeks before the *awdl* which he had submitted on 'Yr Arwr' ('The Hero') was judged the prize-winning poem of the year. Of interest now is that the figure of Prometheus, as a symbol of the heroic and unyielding element in human nature, is central to Hedd Wyn's poem. Hedd Wyn did not know the Greek of Aeschylus' *Prometheus Vinctus*. He was inspired (as many studies, especially a penetrating analysis of the poem by Alan Llwyd, have shown) by Shelley's *Prometheus Unbound* and *The Revolt of Islam*.[39] Nevertheless, the classical myth is meaningfully used by Hedd Wyn to express his confidence that a successful new world, replete with possibilities, is about to dawn:[40]

> Er maith sen Prometheus wyf,
> Awdur pob deffro ydwyf,
> A'r oes well wrth wawrio sydd
> Ar dân o'm bri dihenydd.

Despite long rebuke I am Prometheus,/ I am the author of every awakening,/ And the better age dawns and is/ ablaze from my ancient glory.

We turn now to consider the interplay between the Greek and Latin Classics and literature written in Welsh during the rest of the twentieth century. A strictly chronological pattern will not be followed. Rather, different ways of treating classical material will be looked at in turn.

It is fitting to begin with translation from Greek and Latin, and especially appropriate to do so after mentioning T. Gwynn Jones and W. J. Gruffydd, two of the most successful translators of classical literature into Welsh. There is a brightness about the young Gruffydd's version of Catullus, Poem 8, a foreshadowing of his skilful rendering (although in a different style) of

Sophocles' *Antigone* in the days of his maturity.[41] And the great genius of T. Gwynn Jones, also a young man, translated parts of Homer, Aeschylus and especially Horace into Welsh. His versions of some of Horace's *Odes* in the *cywydd* metre are among the most sensitive translations of the century.[42] Also very successful are renderings which he made, together with H. J. Rose, of epigrams from the Greek Anthology, and published as a volume, *Blodau o Hen Ardd*.[43] For his translations of the epigrams Gwynn Jones took hold of the idea, advanced by Sir John Rhŷs, that there was a connection between the classical epigram and the *englyn* form in Welsh.[44] Gwynn Jones has done away with the rhyme-pattern of the *englyn*, and produced two-line units as in the epigram, with an interesting attempt to represent within the accented patterns of Welsh something of the rise and fall of quantitative classical verse.[45] The resultant pattern is inevitably heavier than in the Greek epigram and is more suited to Gwynn Jones's quasi-epic 'Madog'. Nevertheless, the control of language and of medium in *Blodau o Hen Ardd* is remarkable.

W. J. Gruffydd and T. Gwynn Jones were joined by a considerable number of other accomplished translators throughout the century, nearly all of them beneficiaries of the increased opportunities offered by the educational reforms of the late nineteenth century. Henry Parry-Jones, like W. J. Gruffydd, attended Caernarfon County School and proceeded at the same time as Gruffydd as an Open Scholar to Jesus College, Oxford, to study Classics. He became a schoolmaster, and was from 1920 until 1946 Headmaster of Llanrwst County School. A cousin of Sir John Morris-Jones, he too was a master of the intricacies of *cynghanedd* and a most skilful translator of Greek and Latin poetry into Welsh, often in the *cywydd* form. Many of his earlier translations were of Horace's *Odes* and appeared in *Y Llenor*, edited by Gruffydd. In his retirement he produced some remarkably fine renderings of some of the *Anacreontea* and of poems in the Greek Anthology.[46] He also turned to Greek drama, and wrote accomplished versions of Euripides, *Alcestis*, and (for broadcast by the BBC) of Aristophanes, *Clouds*. An equally skilled translator from many languages was John Henry Jones, for a short time a lecturer in Classics at the University College of Swansea and subsequently Director of Education in Cardiganshire. His translation of Aeschylus, *Agamemnon*, was originally made for broadcasting, and was published in 1991, together with H. Parry-Jones's *Alcestis*.[47]

The most notable translator of classical Greek prose into Welsh from the mid–1930s until the late 1950s was Sir D. Emrys Evans, the first holder of the Chair of Classics at the University College of Swansea and subsequently principal, for over thirty years, of the University College of North Wales, Bangor. Emrys Evans turned six of Plato's dialogues into highly polished works in Welsh, beginning with the *Apology* (1936) and culminating in the *Republic*, published in 1956.[48] The style is dignified and the idiom often that of the Welsh Bible, and in some of the earlier translations the tenor of the work may appear over-formal, more comparable to the English versions of Benjamin Jowett than to those of Evans's closer contemporaries, F. M. Cornford and Desmond Lee. The more, however, one considers Emrys Evans's work, the more one admires his achievement, especially in his version of the *Republic*. The task of translating such a monumental work, with its many stylistic registers and nuances, not to mention the problem of consistently conveying the colour of a precise philosophical vocabulary, was a daunting one. Emrys Evans clearly wrestled with these issues, and there is an unmistakable greatness about his *Republic*.

An important milestone in the history of translating classical literature into Welsh was the establishment of the Classical Section of the Guild of Graduates of the University of Wales in 1951, with J. Gwyn Griffiths as its very active secretary. The publication of several translations was sponsored by the section. In 1954 a selection of stories from Herodotus was published by that extraordinary linguist, Emeritus Professor T. Hudson-Williams, doyen of Welsh classicists.[49] In 1975, Tacitus' *Agricola* appeared in a fine translation by A. O. Morris, together with a full introduction and notes by J. Ellis Jones and D. Ellis Evans.[50] J. Gwyn Griffiths, in 1962, edited a collection of translations of Latin poems by several translators, *Cerddi o'r Lladin*, and followed it in 1989 with a similar anthology of translations from Greek, *Cerddi Groeg Clasurol*.[51] Since his undergraduate days J. Gwyn Griffiths had been publishing occasional classical translations of his own. His greatest achievement is a rendering of Aristotle's *Poetics*, coupled with a highly enlightening introduction.[52] It was not without good reason that a reviewer said at the time of J. Gwyn Griffiths's *Poetics*, 'one's only regret is that there is nothing to compare with it as an introduction for English students to the classical text which has been the most influential in Western European literature, albeit also the most misunderstood'.[53] The *Poetics* has been followed by Aristotle's *Nicomachean Ethics*, translated by John FitzGerald.[54] The work of other translators first appeared in journals: for example, Saunders Lewis's verse translations of two stories from Ovid's *Metamorphoses*, those of Pyramus and Thisbe (IV.55–166) and of Baucis and Philemon (VIII.618–720).[55] The Welsh Arts Council sponsored A. O. Morris's translation of Terence, *Adelphi*,[56] while A. Maximilian Thomas's rendering of Theophrastus' *Characters* appeared in the journal first established by Lewis Edwards, *Y Traethodydd*.[57]

The most prolific and successful of all twentieth-century translators of classical literature into Welsh was Euros Bowen (1904–88). His translations are mainly from Virgil and Sophocles,[58] and his use of a free form of *cynghanedd* gives to his versions a distinctive and remarkably compelling feel. A translation of Virgil's first *Eclogue* appeared in the first number of the journal *Taliesin* (1961), and in 1975 all ten poems were published as a volume, *Bugeilgerddi Fyrsil*.[59] In an introduction to the translations Euros Bowen states that he was inspired by an essay of Paul Valéry to attempt to render the poems 'in his own way', and Bowen's own poetic genius has made out of the *Eclogues* ten remarkably engaging poems in Welsh. He is not so impressive in the distinctly Roman parts of the poems, and the same criticism holds for his highly experimental presentation of the first book of the *Aeneid*.[60] Euros Bowen's really great successes are four of Sophocles' tragedies in Welsh: *Oedipus Tyrannus* (1972), *Oedipus Coloneus* (1979), *Electra* (1984) and – posthumously – *Philoctetes* (1991).[61] His command of Welsh idiom accurately conveys the linguistic and stylistic registers of Sophocles' dialogue. In the choral odes – the second stasimon (863–910) of *Oedipus Tyrannus*, for example – his sensitivity to the strophic pattern, coupled with his own free form of *cynghanedd*, results in poetry where Welsh literature, let alone Greek, reaches a very high level. Euros Bowen's versions, and those of many other twentieth-century translators of Greek and Latin classics into Welsh, are a substantial contribution to Wales's literary heritage. They are to be cherished, not only for their intrinsic worth, but also because in the modern period they give Welsh literature a direct link with one of the main sources of European culture.

Translations apart, in what other ways has Welsh literature of the twentieth century displayed an awareness of the classical heritage? John Morris-Jones's emphasis on formal canons, based on Aristotle's *Poetics*, has already been mentioned. It was in Greek drama, especially tragedy, that Aristotle saw perfection of form expressed, and it is no accident that the main Welsh dramatist of the century, Saunders Lewis, steeped himself in the creative techniques of the Greek dramatists. Saunders Lewis was in Athens in 1918, working in the British Legation, and his rapture with Greek literature is encapsulated in a letter of that period: 'I want to steep myself in the study of Greek thought and art, I am going to read its history, its drama, its philosophy and religion, and it is only by regarding it as the crowning gesture of this great activity that I shall ever understand the Parthenon.'[62] Thus Saunders Lewis's *Siwan*, in the play which bears her name, is an Euripidean figure, likened to Helen of Troy and to Cassandra.[63] The sense of tragedy which hangs over her, and the all-too-late recognition (*anagnorisis*, in Aristotle's language) of the truth both by Llywelyn and by her, make her one of the greatest characters in Welsh drama. Saunders Lewis was not the only playwright to be influenced, to some degree at least, by the Greek dramatists and by Aristotle's reflections on them. John Gwilym Jones, as dramatist and especially as critic, frequently turned to the *Poetics*.[64] And to a greater or lesser extent Huw Lloyd Edwards's *Y Llyffantod*,[65] Tom Parri Jones's metrical play *Y Gwybed*,[66] together with Sir Thomas Parry's *Llywelyn Fawr*,[67] are all witnesses to the contemporary possibilities of using individual actors and a chorus, and that sometimes set within a context which is classical in nature.

In addition to drama there are other lengthy compositions in which the ancient world has an essential bearing on the work. In poetry, the *awdl* 'I'r Duw Nid Adwaenir' ('To the Unknown God'), which won Albert Evans Jones ('Cynan') the chair at the National Eisteddfod for 1924, perhaps stands out.[68] In the field of creative prose, Gweneth Lilly's attractive novel, *Orpheus*, has fourth-century Roman Britain as its background.[69] It is also worth noting that one of Wales's most prolific and thought-provoking bilingual writers, Emyr Humphreys, in his English novel, *A Man's Estate* (1955), has used the ancient myth of Electra and Orestes as a thematic leitmotiv in his study of a Welsh family. Among writers of short stories in Welsh none was more fascinated by classical literature than R. G. Berry, as is shown especially by his story 'Llaw y Llifwr' ('The Dyer's Hand') and its awareness of the poems of Horace.[70] There have also been many successful literary presentations of ancient myths, especially for children.[71]

We turn now to the other extreme, the short poem or the reference in passing: small matters in themselves, perhaps, yet full of significance as part of the total sense of classical awareness during this century. For example, the title of a poem may call for some response to the ancient world, even if the classical reference is not developed in the body of the poem. Thus two of Robert Williams Parry's sonnets are entitled 'Taw, Socrates' ('Quiet, Socrates') and 'Hen Gychwr Afon Angau' ('Styx's Old Boatman'),[72] and two poems by his friend William Jones, Tremadog, are headed 'Carpe Diem' and 'Summum Bonum'.[73]

Similarly, the practice of quoting classical literature, sometimes in the original, sometimes in translation, should be noted. Saunders Lewis, like his friend David Jones, was very fond of introducing such quotations, especially from Virgil, into his poetry, his plays and his prose writing. In 'Marwnad Syr John Edward Lloyd' ('Elegy for Sir John Edward Lloyd'), for example, he very effectively quotes from the sixth book of the *Aeneid* some of the words which epitomize the imperial mission of the Romans, *Tu . . . regere populos* (VI.851), and sees that mission realized in Agricola's victory in Anglesey.[74] In *Amlyn ac Amig*, when the leper Amig reaches the castle and is given hospitality by Amlyn, Amig responds:[75]

> Duw a dalo it, arglwydd;
> Yma hefyd mae dagrau am bethau dyn
> A throeon dynion yn cyffwrdd y galon ddynol.

> God reward you, lord;
> Here too there are tears for the things of man
> And the turns of men's fortunes touch the human heart.

The last two lines are a free translation of the well-known line (*Aeneid* I.462) spoken by Aeneas to Achates, in response to the depiction of Troy's suffering in Juno's temple in Carthage, *Sunt lacrimae rerum et mentem mortalia tangunt*. Saunders Lewis did likewise in his prose-writing. For a tribute to a young student who died of tuberculosis Saunders Lewis gives the title 'Rhowch Lili â Dwylo Llawn', 'Give Lilies from Full Hands', a translation of one of Virgil's most sensitive lines (*Aeneid* VI.883) in memory of the young Marcellus, and the tribute ends with a quotation of the Latin words.[76]

Saunders Lewis is not alone among twentieth-century Welsh writers for whom such direct contact with classical literature is an inseparable part of their literary make-up. A similar detailed awareness of, and quotation from, classical texts is found in the work of many of the poets known as the Cadwgan Circle ('Cylch Cadwgan'), a group of like-minded poets and intellectuals whose association began in the Rhondda Valley during the Second World War. Their commitment to classical literature is not surprising, as at least two of their number, J. Gwyn Griffiths and Pennar Davies, were classicists of the first order. Thus Pennar Davies, in a poem in memory of Yvette Cauchon, places those words from Virgil's tribute to Marcellus, *manibus date lilia plenis*, as the title of his meditation and quotes them in the course of the poem.[77] Likewise, J. Gwyn Griffiths, in his poem 'Ataracsïa', quotes in Latin the words of Horace (*Odes* II.iii.1–2), *Aequam memento rebus in arduis servare mentem*, and 'Hecate' opens with yet another quotation from *Aeneid* VI (line 126), *Facilis descensus Averno*.[78]

In a slightly different vein, many writers make use of classical references as points of comparison in their work, in the 'dyfalu' manner of medieval *cywyddwyr*. Thus Saunders Lewis, in one of the greatest of all Welsh poems, sees Mary Magdalen as 'Christ's Niobe', recalling Tantalus' weeping daughter who was turned into stone by Zeus:[79]

> Gwelwch hi, Niobe'r Crist, yn tynnu tua'r fron
> Graig ei phoen i'w chanlyn o'r Pasg plwm
> Drwy'r pylgain du, drwy'r llwch trwm,
> I'r man y mae maen trymach na'i chalon don.

See her, Christ's Niobe, dragging to the hillside
The rock of her pain behind her from the leaden Pasch
Through the dark dawn, the cold dew, the heavy dust,
To the place with a stone heavier than her broken heart.

In the same poem Mary is likened in her lamenting to Orpheus:

Mor unsain â cholomen yw ei chwyn,
Fel Orphews am Ewridice'n galaru
Saif rhwng y rhos a chrio heb alaru.

As monotoned as a dove, her lament,
Like Orpheus mourning for Eurydice
She stands among the roses crying insatiably.

It is the poetry of D. Gwenallt Jones which most abounds with
the use of this kind of reference. For example, in the poem 'Y
Sipsi' ('The Gipsy'), he sees the old fortune-teller as 'a swoonless
Pythia sitting on her tripod' ('Pythia ddilesmair yn eistedd ar ei
thrybedd') and as a Sibyl for a disorientated generation.
Similarly, he likens the efforts of philosophers and scientists to
lift the burden of Time from the backs of their contemporaries to
the futile struggle of Tantalus in Hell. The picture of the
Minotaur is one which appeals greatly to Gwenallt. In *Cnoi Cil*,
as he thinks of elements which are threatening Wales's survival,
he sees them as 'y Minotawros totalitaraidd', 'the totalitarian
Minotaur'. And in the poem 'Rhydcymerau', the darkness which
has overtaken his family's original heartland is seen as 'ffau'r
Minotawros Seisnig', 'the den of the English Minotaur'. From an
associated myth, in the remarkable poem 'Yr Awyren Fôr' ('The
Seaplane') the plane is seen, in the central stanza, as

Y peiriant â'i ddeudod yn undod gloyw:
Icarws a Neifion ynghyd.

The machine whose duality was a shining unity:/ Icarus and
Neptune together.

That is not the only reference to Icarus in Gwenallt's work. There
is a reference to him also in the last stanza of the poem 'Cip' ('A
Glimpse').[80]

Such classical allusions in Gwenallt's work verge on being far more than passing references or fleeting images. They are central to what he has to say. The remainder of this chapter will concentrate on that element in twentieth-century literature where a classical text, or a thread of classical mythology, is thematically central in the work of Welsh poets. And it is mildly surprising to observe how much sustained use of classical reference does occur in Welsh poetry of the century. This is, of course, one with much of what was happening in English, in the work of poets like W. H. Auden and Louis MacNeice. But there was also a reaction against such classicism in England. Philip Larkin, for instance, pronounced that 'classical references are a liability nowadays'.[81] That is not a sentiment which seems to have been shared by some of Wales's most eminent writers. There is, for example, a considerable amount of direct writing on classical subjects. Thus, among the poets already mentioned, Gwenallt has a series of *englynion* on 'Homer' and 'Hesiod' and 'Heracleitos' (the last based on Callimachus' epigram, *Anthologia Palatina* VII.80, famously put into English by William Cory) and gives a poet's sensitive response to the Homeric world in a sonnet on the *Iliad*. William Jones writes of 'Elen Troea' ('Helen of Troy'), 'Socrates' and 'Antigone'. Pennar Davies has a poem to 'Nice Adeiniog Samothracia' ('The Winged Nike of Samothrace'), and J. Gwyn Griffiths to 'Cassandra mewn Cariad' ('Cassandra in Love') and 'I Pindaros Roegwr' ('To Pindar the Greek').[82] These are only examples, but they suffice to show that contemporary Wales has had its learned poets whose classicism is part of their cultural patrimony and whose writing on classical subjects arises naturally from that patrimony.

One poem, Saunders Lewis's 'Marwnad Syr John Edward Lloyd' (Elegy for Sir John Edward Lloyd'), stands out for the notably precise use which it makes of a classical text. J. Edward Lloyd was Professor of History at the University College of North Wales, Bangor, from 1899 until 1930. His study of the history of early and medieval Wales, especially in his two-volume *A History of Wales to the Edwardian Conquest* (1911) and *Owen Glendower* (1931), was nothing short of epoch-making. Thus we have in Saunders Lewis's poem an elegy for the father of Welsh historical study in the twentieth century, written after his death in 1947. However, it is to the classical world, to the

Sixth Book of Virgil's *Aeneid*, that Saunders Lewis takes his reader in the first two stanzas of the poem:[83]

> Darllenais fel yr aeth Eneas gynt
> Drwy'r ogof gyda'r Sibil, ac i wlad
> Dis a'r cysgodion, megis gŵr ar hynt
> Liw nos mewn fforest dan y lloer an-sad,
> Ac yno'n y gwyll claear
> Tu draw i'r afon ac i Faes Wylofain
> Gwelodd hen arwyr Tro, hynafiaid Rhufain,
> Deiffobos dan ei glwyfau, drudion daear,
>
> Meibion Antenor ac Adrastos lwyd;
> A'i hebrwng ef a wnaent, a glynu'n daer
> Nes dyfod lle'r oedd croesffordd, lle'r oedd clwyd,
> A golchi wyneb, traddodi'r gangen aur,
> Ac agor dôl a llwyni'n
> Hyfryd dan sêr ac awyr borffor glir,
> Lle y gorffwysai mewn gweirgloddiau ir
> Dardan ac Ilos a'r meirwon diallwynin.
>
> I read how, long ago, Aeneas went
> Through the cavern with the Sibyl, and to the land
> Of Dis and the shades, like a man wayfaring
> In a wood by night beneath the inconstant moon,
> And there in the mild dusk
> Beyond the river and the Field of Wailing,
> He saw Troy's ancient heroes, ancestors of Rome,
> Deiphobus with his wounds, earth's daring men,
>
> The sons of Antenor and pale Adrastus;
> And they guided him, and crowded close beside him,
> Till he came to a crossroads, to a gate,
> Where his face was washed, the golden bough presented,
> And a field opened and groves
> Delightful under stars and a clear purple sky,
> Where lay in green meadows, at their ease,
> Dardanus and Ilus and the undejected dead.

Saunders Lewis here adheres closely to Virgil's own words to describe Aeneas' journey to the Underworld in the company of the Sibyl. The first four lines are virtually a translation of *Aeneid* VI.268–71:

Ibant obscuri sola sub nocte per umbram
perque domos Ditis uacuas et inania regna:
quale per incertam lunam sub luce maligna
est iter in siluis.

Equally precise are the details of the journey through the *Lugentes Campi*, where Aeneas and the Sibyl saw the old Trojan heroes, *Deiphobum, lacerum crudeliter ora* (*Aeneid* VI.495), *tris Antenoridas* (484), *Adrasti pallentis imago* (480). These dead Trojans led Aeneas to where the road parted in two (540), one way leading to Tartarus, the other to Elysium. Here Aeneas caught a glimpse of Tartarus, and the Sibyl gives a long description of the punishments suffered there (548–627). At this point Saunders Lewis significantly passes over that part of Aeneas' experience in the Underworld. Rather, he goes on to describe Aeneas' entry into Elysium, with which compare *Aeneid* VI.635–6:

occupat Aeneas aditum corpusque recenti
spargit aqua ramumque aduerso in limine figit.

Aeneas leapt on the threshold, sprinkled his body with fresh water and fixed the bough full in the doorway.[84]

The account of the entry into the Fortunata Nemora is a summary of *Aeneid* VI.638–41, where were 'Dardanus and Ilus' (see *Aeneid* VI.650) and 'the undejected dead' ('meirwon diallwynin') 'at their ease in green meadows'.

It is important to notice that Saunders Lewis ends his summary of this part of *Aeneid* VI with 'the undejected dead'. *Allwynin* ('dejected') and its opposite *diallwynin* ('undejected') are unusual words, but (as will be demonstrated presently) the negative form here is very significant as the word chosen to sum up the panoramic view, not of the sufferers in Tartarus, but of Troy's old heroes and of the blessed dead in Elysium.

In the third stanza the poet turns to J. E. Lloyd, 'hen ddewin Bangor' ('the old seer of Bangor'). He is the poet's Sibyl, who led him into the mysteries of Welsh history. Classical imagery is maintained here:

Minnau, un hwyr, yn llaw hen ddewin Bangor
Euthum i lawr i'r afon, mentro'r cwch,

Gadael beisdon yr heddiw lle nid oes angor
A chroesi'r dŵr, sy ym mhwll y nos fel llwch,
I wyll yr ogofâu
Lle rhwng y coed y rhythai rhithiau geirwon
Gan sisial gwangri farw helwyr meirwon
Nas clywn; nid ŷnt ond llun ar furiau ffau.

So I, one evening, led by Bangor's ancient seer,
I went down to the river, ventured the boat,
Left the shoals of today where there is no anchor
And crossed the water, like ashes in night's pit,
To the darkness of the caves
Where among the trees stern phantoms peered
Whispering dead hunters' faint dead cry
I could not hear; a mere shape on a den's wall.

And then the poet's vision, in the company of the historian, begins. The pageant of Roman heroes is paralleled by a pageant of people in Welsh history, beginning with the time of the Roman occupation of Wales. The symbol of what the occupation meant for Wales is Agricola and his campaign in Anglesey. Saunders Lewis adheres to *Aeneid* VI by seeing Agricola as the personification of the ideals expressed in Anchises' prophetic words to Aeneas, and by quoting in Latin (as has already been seen) some of Anchises' words:

Yna daeth golau a ffurf fel gwawr a wenai,
Helm a llurig yn pefrio ac eryr pres
A chwympo coed, merlod dan lif ym Menai,
Palmantu bryniau a rhaffu caerau'n rhes:
Tu . . . regere populos,
Mi welwn lun Agricola yn sefyll
Ar draeth ym Môn, murmurai frudiau Fferyll,
A'r heli ar odre'r toga'n lluwch fin nos.

Then light came, and a form like a smiling dawn,
Helmet and cuirass sparkling and a brazen eagle
And trees were felled, ponies in the tides of Menai,
Hills were paved and fortresses roped in a row:
Tu . . . regere populos,
I saw the image of Agricola standing
On a beach in Môn, he was murmuring Virgil's prophecies,
The brine on the toga's hem like a snowdrift at nightfall.

Following the Romans, the next stanza goes on to the beginnings of Christianity in Wales in the Age of the Saints, leading (in the sixth stanza) to an expression of Saunders Lewis's vision of the European unity of Christianity and the classical tradition, 'ymerodraethau'r Groes a'r Eryr' ('the Empires of the Cross and the Eagle'). But then, in the sixth stanza, the poet turns to the historian and asks after those Welshmen, 'the lineage of Cunedda', whose lot in the world is that of Sisyphus:

> Ond yma ym mro'r cysgodion y mae hil
> Gondemniwyd i boen Sisiffos yn y byd,
> I wthio o oes i oes drwy flynyddoedd fil
> Genedl garreg i ben bryn Rhyddid, a'r pryd –
> O linach chwerw Cunedda, –
> Y gwelir copa'r bryn, trwy frad neu drais
> Teflir y graig i'r pant a methu'r cais,
> A chwardd Adar y Pwll ar eu hing diwedda'.

> But here in the region of shades is a race
> Condemned to the pain of Sisyphus in the world,
> To push from age to age through a thousand years
> A stone nation to Freedom's hill-crest, and when –
> Oh bitter lineage of Cunedda –
> The hill's summit is in sight, through treachery or violence
> The rock is hurled to the valley and the effort fails,
> And the Birds of the Pit laugh at their latest pangs.

The significance of the Sisyphus imagery is that Sisyphus belongs to Tartarus, that part of the Virgilian Underworld which Saunders Lewis chose to omit from his recounting of Aeneas' journey in the first two stanzas. Virgil does not in fact name Sisyphus, but he is there:[85]

> saxum ingens uoluunt alii, radiisque rotarum
> districti pendent.

> Some are rolling huge rocks, or hang spreadeagled on the spokes of wheels.

Those frustrated fighters for the freedom of Wales belong to the race of Sisyphus. But where are they? 'Pa le mae'r rhain?' And there opens up before the poet's eyes a wide panorama, corresponding to the Virgilian panorama in *Aeneid* VI. The characters mentioned were discussed and illumined in J. E. Lloyd's studies. Most of them belonged to the heroic age of the Princes who defended Wales against the Normans. The culmination of the panorama is Owain Glyndŵr himself. The hopes of the nation were pinned on him, and for a brief moment, at the beginning of the fifteenth century, it looked as if those hopes would be realized. Owain, 'heir of the two houses of Wales' ('etifedd deudy Cymru'), Powys and Deheubarth, took Harlech and Aberystwyth castles. Is the nation's stone at last safely to reach the top of the hill of freedom?

> Yna ger Glyn y Groes
> Rhoes ail Teiresias ym mhylgain Berwyn
> Ddedfryd oracl tynged, a bu terfyn:
> Toddodd ei gysgod yn y niwl a'i toes.

> Then near Glyn y Groes
> A second Teiresias in the dawn of Berwyn gave
> The verdict of fate's oracle, and there was an end:
> His shade melted in the mist that covered him.

The story goes that Owain Glyndŵr was walking early one morning near Valle Crucis Abbey, *Glyn y Groes*, and that he met the abbot. Owain greeted the abbot: 'Ah, Sir Abbot, you have risen too early.' 'No', replied the abbot, 'it is you who have risen too early, by a hundred years.' Such was 'the sentence of fate's oracle', that Owain was a century ahead of his time. But for Saunders Lewis, the abbot is a Sophoclean figure, a 'second Tiresias'. There remains with us a picture of failure and of hopelessness. After so much suffering, dejection is what characterizes the Welsh panorama.

It will be recalled that, in the first two stanzas, Saunders Lewis selected characters from Elysium for his Virgilian section. These were 'the undejected dead', 'meirwon diallwynin', of *Aeneid* VI, not Tartarean sufferers like Sisyphus. It was suggested that the choice of the unusual word *diallwynin* was important. The reason is now clear. The panorama of those who tried to safeguard the freedom of Wales is full of failures. It stands in contrast to that from the *Aeneid*. Furthermore, when Saunders Lewis calls the dead in Elysium 'undejected', *diallwynin*, he is surely echoing one of the most famous and poignant of Welsh medieval poems, the Elegy of Gruffudd ab yr Ynad Coch after the death of Llywelyn ap Gruffudd, 'the Last Prince', in 1282:[86]

> Oer calon dan fron o fraw – allwynin
> Am frenin, dderwin ddôr, Aberffraw.
>
> Cold heart under a breast of fear – dejected
> For a king, oak door of Aberffraw.

Llywelyn and his brother Dafydd feature in Saunders Lewis's Welsh panorama, in the ninth stanza:

> A dacw ben ar bicell, a rhawn meirch
> Yn llusgo yn llwch Amwythig tu ôl i'w seirch
> Gorff anafus yr ola' eiddila' o'i lin.
>
> And there, a head upon a spear, and horses' hair
> Dragging in Shrewsbury's dust behind their harness
> The battered body of the feeblest last of his line.

Unlike the Elysian picture, however, the Welsh panorama is one of sadness and dejection. Saunders Lewis not only imitates the Virgilian underworld, but also uses motifs and references from *Aeneid* VI in order to contrast them as well as to compare them with the Welsh material.

Such is Virgil's importance for the interpretation of the poem that it is no accident that Saunders Lewis has chosen to end his elegy by comparing J. E. Lloyd, not with the Sibyl any more, but with Virgil himself:

> Fel hwnnw a ddringodd sblennydd gwlad anobaith
> Trois innau at fy mlaenor.
>
> Like him who climbed the cliffs of the land of despair
> I turned to my leader.

This is now not only Virgil, the author of the *Aeneid*, but also Dante's guide, that other Sibyl-like figure, who vanished at the appearance of Beatrice. And when the poet questions him whether he sees any grounds for hope, especially for the survival of the Welsh language, 'the last relic of Cunedda', there is silence. Like Dante's Virgil, the historian has disappeared without giving an answer:

> Ond ef, lusernwr y canrifoedd coll,
> Nid oedd ef yno mwy, na'i lamp na'i air.

> But he, the lantern-bearer of lost centuries,
> He was there no longer, neither his lamp nor his word.

Saunders Lewis's 'Elegy for Sir John Edward Lloyd' stands out as a poem which not only has a classical dimension to it but also maintains an extraordinary intertextual relationship with the *Aeneid*. As the titles of poems by William Jones and by members of the Cadwgan Circle show, and also some of the short quotations given from Gwenallt's work, most twentieth-century poets have turned to classical mythology without of necessity evoking a specific literary working of the myth. Sometimes the use of classical mythology is veiled, as in Waldo Williams's poignant poem, 'Oherwydd Ein Dyfod' ('Because of Our Coming'), a short poem which teems with suggestive echoes of some of the main Greek myths: Theseus and Ariadne, Demeter and Persephone, Orpheus and Eurydice.[87] Other poems are written directly about characters who belong to classical mythology: for example, 'Icarus' by Tom Parri Jones,[88] 'Tantalus' by Caradog Prichard,[89] 'Alcestis' by Rhydwen Williams[90] and 'Antaios' by J. Gwyn Griffiths.[91] The mythological character is frequently used for symbolic or allegorical ends. Thus, for Caradog Prichard Tantalus symbolizes man's pride and arrogance, whereas the dangers of nuclear power underlie Rhydwen Williams's poem. For J. Gwyn Griffiths the myth of Antaios, son of Poseidon and Gaia (Earth), represents the force of the poet's attachment to the land of Wales.

The same fertile use of the possibilities of myth is found in the poetry of Gwenallt. His use of brief allusions to mythological characters has already been mentioned. There are also poems by Gwenallt in which powerful use is made of the extended treatment of ancient myths and of the suggestions which are implicit in them. His poems 'Narcisws' ('Narcissus'), 'Arachne' and 'Promethews' are fine examples, and also his use of the myth of Zeus and Leda in 'Yr Alarch' ('The Swan'), where the classical literary tradition and the Welsh tradition are combined in a masterly way.[92] These poems by Gwenallt not only present characters from classical mythology as symbols which carry the poet's meaning. The juxtaposition within them of modern world and ancient myth also creates a highly effective contrapuntal medium for the meditative presentation of a message, a style which is so much part of Gwenallt's mature writing. The poem which best displays this is the poem from *Eples* entitled 'Cymru' ('Wales'):[93]

> Gwlad grefyddol gysurus oedd hi,
> A dyn yn feistr ar ddaear a nef,
> Pan ddaeth dwy sarff anferth eu maint,
> A'u boliau yn gosod y tonnau ar dân,
> Ac yn bwrw eu gwenwyn ar ei thraethau yn lli.
>
> Edmygai'r bechgyn eu cyntefigrwydd garw,
> A'u parlysu fel adar gan eu llygaid slic;
> Ac ymddolennai eu cyrff yn araf bach
> Am droed a choes a chanol a gwddf,
> A'u gwasgfeuon yn dychrynu'r bustach marw.
>
> Yn gynt na'r gwynt ac yn welw ei liw
> Y rhedodd Laocôn yn ei phylacterau llaes,
> Ac wrth geisio datrys eu clymau tyn
> Clymasant ei draed a'i forddwydydd ef:
> Nid oes a'i gwaredo ond ei ddwylo a'i Dduw.

It was a religious, comfortable country,/ and man was master of earth and heaven,/ when two serpents came, huge in size,/ their bellies setting the waves ablaze,/ and casting their poison on the beaches in floods.

The boys admired their rough primitiveness,/ and were paralysed like birds by their slick eyes;/ and their bodies slowly entwined themselves/ around foot and leg and middle and neck,/ and their constrictions frightened the dead bullock.

Faster than the wind and his complexion pale,/ Laocoon ran in his loose phylacteries,/ and as he tried to undo their tight knots/ they bound his feet and thighs:/ nothing can save him but his hands and his God.

The picture comes from the second book of the *Aeneid*, where
Aeneas tells Dido the story of the fall of Troy, and how the
Trojans were convinced by the fate of the priest Laocoon and his
two sons that the Wooden Horse should be brought into the city
(lines 199–234). Virgil gives a marvellous description of the two
serpents coiling themselves about the three men, a scene which
is captured in the Hellenistic-style sculpture (now in the Vatican)
which was rediscovered in the sixteenth century and became the
starting-point of Lessing's discussion of the relationship between
literature and the visual arts.[94] Gwenallt may not engage as
closely with Virgil's text as Saunders Lewis does in 'Marwnad
Syr John Edward Lloyd', but he captures Virgil's tone and uses
the detail of the story skilfully to create a sense of the
independent 'world' of the Trojan War. But the title of the poem
is 'Cymru'. Wales, as much as ancient Troy, is the 'religious,
comfortable country'. And the message of the last line is directed
as much towards Wales as towards Laocoon and his sons in the
grip of the serpents, namely that, without God's aid in the
business of working out the salvation of both man and nation,
little hope remains.[95]

Several Welsh poets of the mid-twentieth century have been
mentioned and an attempt made at discussing their use of
various aspects of the classical heritage. One important name
remains. As in the account of translating Greek and Latin
literature into Welsh, so too in recording the relationship
between creative writing in Welsh in the second half of the
twentieth century and the classical tradition, Euros Bowen is a
singular figure. No poet has been more consistently committed
to classical themes. Some hints of his awareness of the
possibilities of classical imagery are found in his first volume,
Cerddi (1957): for example, in the poem entitled 'Y Gangen Aur'
('The Golden Bough'), where the story of Aeneas' descent to the
Underworld, the golden bough in hand, is an integral part of the
poet's portrayal of experience; or, similarly, in 'Nant Sibil', where
the same myth, together with the tradition about the Sibyl at
Delphi, is closely woven into the fabric of the poem.

From 1970 onwards, however, and the publication of *Cylch o
Gerddi*, classical themes came to play an extraordinarily

important part in Euros Bowen's work. I estimate that, in some twelve volumes, about one hundred and fifty of his poems are on classical subjects, or contain sustained classical references. Euros Bowen was an inveterate traveller to classical lands, and many of his poems derive from his journeys. Thus, in *Cylch o Gerddi*, a cycle of poems (with titles like 'Olympos', 'Delffi', 'Omphalos', 'Micenai') arise from a visit to Greece. In *Elfennau* (1972) Italy, and especially Sicily, provide him with his subject-matter – for example 'Pompeii', 'Gwynt ar Etna' ('Wind on Etna'), 'Ffynnon Arethwsa' ('Arethusa's Spring'), 'Affrodite Siracwsa' ('Syracusan Aphrodite'), 'Latomïa', and so forth. In *Cynullion* (1976) many of the poems are about the Middle East, but here too classical subjects have their place: 'Y Cnu Aur' ('The Golden Fleece'), 'Sawdl Achil' ('Achilles' Heel'), 'Aigina', 'Alecsander wrth Byrth Thebai' ('Alexander at the Gates of Thebes'). The following year (1977) *O'r Corn Aur* appeared, a volume entirely devoted to Asia Minor. 'Y Corn Aur', 'the Golden Horn', refers to the long bay near Istanbul, an area which offers the poet all manner of classical possibilities, especially the legends connected with the fall of Troy. In the same volume there are poems to 'Ynys Lesbos' ('The Island of Lesbos'), 'Fforest Ortyga' ('Ortyga's Forest'), 'Medwsa' and 'Bosfforos', and a long poem on Orpheus, whose end was connected with Lesbos. In *Amrywion* (1980) the classical material is again evident: a poem on Narcissus, for example, and another on Icarus. In *Masg Minos* ('Minos' Mask', 1981), a visit to Crete provides the stimulus, and the poetry encapsulates his sense of that island's *genius loci*. The volume also includes a cycle of fourteen poems which aim to reflect the Minoan culture of Knossos. In *Gwynt yn y Canghennau* (1982) Euros Bowen has some of his most important poems on classical themes: 'Afalau Aur yr Haul' ('The Sun's Golden Apples'), whose imagery reflects the apples of the Hesperides; 'Cwmwl Helen' ('Helen's Cloud'), arising from part of the mythology surrounding Helen of Troy; and 'Y Gwaed yw'r Bywyd' ('The Blood is the Life'), where the Welsh poets Taliesin and Aneirin are linked to the myths about Odysseus and Aeneas. The same volume also contains two of his longest and most important poems – 'Phaëthon' and 'Cerdd Ofydd' ('Ovid's Song'). *Gwynt yn y Canghennau* was followed by *O Bridd i Bridd* (1983), containing some six poems on classical subjects; then

Buarth Bywyd (1986), in which eight poems belong to the Greek world; also in 1986, *Goleuni'r Eithin*, where 'Affrodite' and 'Y Caryatides' are on classical subjects, and two others, 'Cydwybod' ('Conscience') and 'Grym yr Atgyfodiad' ('Resurrection Power') make fertile use of Greek mythology. The last volume to appear before Euros Bowen's death was *Oes y Medwsa* (1987), containing eight poems on classical themes. Since his death in 1988 two further volumes have appeared: *Lleidr Tân* (1989) contains at least eleven classical poems, for example 'Thalasa, Thalasa!', 'Cimeriaid', 'Danäe', 'Ewropa', and a poem about Prometheus, 'Lleidr Tân' ('Stealer of Fire'), which gives its name to the volume. Finally, in 1990, a collection entitled *Dathlu Bywyd* ('Celebration of Life') appeared, a volume which is also rich in classical material, and where many of the poems – 'Leda', for example, and 'Laocoon' – are based on the literature and mythology of the ancient world. Other material still awaits publication, including 'Tarian Achil', a poem – like W. H. Auden's 'The Shield of Achilles' (1952) – based on *Iliad*, Book XVIII.

Such a list shows clearly not only that Euros Bowen was an exceptionally prolific poet but also that classical themes were central to his work. The poems which have been mentioned are the work of one who had detailed knowledge of classical mythology and was well-read in many of the main classical authors. There is also a consistency between the work of translating Sophocles and writing these poems. Take, for example, two poems in *Buarth Bywyd*: 'Henaint Soffocles' ('Sophocles' Old Age') and 'Philoctetes yn ffarwelio ag Ynys Lemnos' ('Philoctetes' farewell to Lemnos').[96] In the first the poet gives his reaction to Cephalus' quotation (at the beginning of Plato's *Republic*) of the words of Sophocles about the blessings of old age; in the second the inspiration comes from some of Philoctetes' words in Sophocles' play about him (*Philoctetes* 1453–9). Sometimes places in the classical world inspire the imagery of his poems; at other times, a statue, or part of a legend or tradition, will provide a stimulus; and, as might be expected, characters from Greek mythology, especially those connected with Greek religion, appeal greatly to him. He frequently returns to the same place, or the same myth, in more than one poem, and the first poem is extended or deepened by the later work. So, for example, there are two poems which treat the story of Laocoon, one in *Cylch o Gerddi*, the other in *Dathlu Bywyd*; two poems are on the Medusa, in *O'r Corn Aur* and *Oes y Medwsa*; three poems are given to Prometheus, in *Elfennau*, *Buarth Bywyd* and *Lleidr Tân*.

Three particular uses which Euros Bowen makes of classical material call for special mention. First, there is the reaction in his work to a place or event or object – a statue, for example – which belonged to the ancient world. The poems which were stimulated by his travels in classical lands provide good examples of this feature. The poet visits a place in Greece or Italy or Crete. His technique is not to take his camera out of his pocket, but rather to let his imagination work on the scene. The images which present themselves to him serve to re-create the feel of the place for his readers, and we see it through the poet's eyes. In the manner of the French Symbolists (who were a major influence upon him)[97] an intricate web of images is built up, frequently enriched by mythological associations. So, in the area of Troy, the poet sees Turkish women labouring in the fields, and relates their suffering to that of Andromache and Hecuba.[98] In Pompeii the heat and the dust, along with the museum's plaster images of the victims of the Vesuvius eruption, speak of death and decay, until a lizard's sudden dash out of a crack in a temple wall gives life to the whole of ancient Pompeii in his imagination. At Mycenae, too, the midday sun oppresses him, but then he recalls that this is Homer's *poluchrusos Mukene*, 'Mycenae rich in gold', the place which witnessed also the shedding of the blood of Agamemnon and Clytemnestra:[99]

> Lle na ddena wair,
>> ac felly'n ddi-nwyd,
> oddieithr am aur
>> ar daen
>> yn asur y dydd
> heddiw
>> a thramwy ei waed
> hyd drum
>> yn batrymau
> trwm eu hanes
>> hyd dir y meini,

Aur a'i waed
yn hŷn
        nag elïau'r esgyrnog olewydd,

Aur a'i waed
yn iau nag angau
                yn niwyg ango,

Aur a'i waed
yn fwy bygylus
nag arfau bugeiliol
holl wae
        crynhous
        y carn noeth
ym Mhorth y Llewod,

Aur a'i waed
                yn fwy ei rym
na'r masgiau wyneb
yn rhwymo esgyniad
ffosil araith
                cyrff y selerydd,

Aur a'i waed
yn fwy newynog
                        yn y fan honno
na'i gam a'i amnaid
                        yn awr hiraeth
Agamemnon,

Aur a'i waed
yn fwy sychedig
                na'r dig
                        yn mwydo ei egin
yn nhwymyn astrus Clytemnestra,

Aur yn waed
o dynged angerdd,
lle na ddaw un nwyd,
lle
  na ddena wair.

No grass allured,
                no passion there,
except for the gold of the sun
                        spreading now
in the azure of day
and the passage of its blood
along the crest
          heavily
patterned with history
                  over the stony ground,

Gold and blood
older
       than the oils of the gnarled olive-trees,

Gold and blood
younger than death
              in the guise of oblivion,

Gold and blood
more fearsome
than the guardian arms
of all the compact woe
              of the bare cairn
within the Lion Gate,

Gold and blood
          of greater power
than the face-masks
binding the ascent
of the fossil speech
          of cellared bodies,

Gold and blood
more famished
          in that place
than the step and gesture
of Agamemnon's nostalgic hour,

Gold and blood
a greater thirst
than the wrath
            that quickens the seed
of Clytemnestra's dark fever,

Gold and blood
of violent destiny
in a place
where no passion stirs,
where no grass is allured.

Secondly, Euros Bowen makes striking use of Greek and Roman mythology in his work. These myths are often interwoven with the reaction to place, as in the poem on Mycenae. At other times the image arises directly from some legend or piece of mythology, and the myth turns into a vessel for conveying the poet's grasp of some mystery or other. In a poem entitled 'Edefyn' ('A Thread'), Ariadne's gift to Theseus symbolizes the hope, however tenuous, which links mankind with all that makes for its freedom:[100]

Gwell y fenter hwyrach
na charchar diantur.

Rhoes Ariadne bellen o edafedd
i einioes Thesews gynt
rhag ei ddifetha yn nryswch y labrinth
gan Finotawros tynged y lle,
a dad-ddirwyniad yr edefyn
yn ei dywys allan wedyn
i olau dydd.

Better the venture, it would seem,
than a prison without adventure.

Ariadne of old gave Theseus
a ball of thread
to escape in the confusion of the labyrinth
the fate of destruction
by the Minotaur there,

> and the unwound thread
> brought him out
> into the light of day.

Likewise, the lengthy poem on Phaëthon is a spectacularly rich reworking of the details of Phaëthon's flight, and his disregard for the instructions of his father Helios. This poem, one of Euros Bowen's longest works, contains – unusually for him – a propagandist note: Phaëthon clearly suggests man's folly as he runs the risk of overreaching himself in his hold on nuclear weapons.

Thirdly, Euros Bowen made use of the classical world to express much of what he had to say about the place and power of poetry. His own devotion to the symbolic use of images may owe something not only to the French Symbolists but also to his understanding of Plato's Theory of Ideas.[101] Certainly Euros Bowen was a writer who thought deeply about the nature of a poet's calling. What lies behind the creative impulse intrigued him, and his sympathy with other poets was total. This emerges in his long poem, 'Cerdd Ofydd', inspired by seeing Ovid's statue at Constanţa on the shores of the Black Sea. The poem is a fellow-writer's exploration of the plight of a poet exiled from all that gave meaning to his work:[102]

> Cosb yw cau
> dyn oddi wrth wlad ei eni,-
> hynt oer mewn tir
> na ŵyr Ladin iaith.

It is punishment to shut/ a man away from the country of his birth, –/ a cold sojourn in a land/ that knows not the Latin tongue.

He draws his references from the classical world: Laodameia, Sappho, Medea, Iocasta, Deianira, Dido. But not the classical world only. The title of the poem is a quotation from Dafydd ap Gwilym's *cywydd* to the song-thrush,[103] and throughout the work the experience of the Latin love poet is linked to the Welsh tradition: the work of Hywel ap Owain Gwynedd, Gruffudd ap Maredudd, Cynddelw Brydydd Mawr, Tudur Aled and Dafydd ap Gwilym himself. That is part of Euros Bowen's achievement, time and time again: that he links the classical world to Wales, and places it all in the context of his continual interest in the power of song and in the function of a poet.

Even more striking than Euros Bowen's reaction to Ovid is his presentation of Orpheus: poet, musician and cultic figure, the enchantment of whose lyre was such that wild animals, trees and rocks were charmed by his song. The story of Orpheus' quest for his wife Eurydice was immortalized in Virgil, *Georgics* IV, and in Ovid, *Metamorphoses* XI; and in his poem 'Ar Lan Afon Alaw' ('On the Bank of the River Alaw') Euros Bowen relates that part of the Orpheus myth to the story of Branwen.[104] However, the aspect of the Orpheus story which particularly caught Euros Bowen's imagination was the account of the singer torn apart by the jealous Maenads and his severed head, still singing to the accompaniment of his lyre, carried down the River Hebrus towards Lesbos. The mystic, quasi-sacramental, side of Orpheus, the poet who still communicates, even in death, is what appeals particularly to Euros Bowen, and he returns to it frequently. In 'Y Corff a Dorrir' ('The Body is Broken'), for example, he sees a resemblance between Orpheus and Christ, and their broken bodies as sources of rebirth. Likewise, in the opening poems of *Lleidr Tân* and *Dathlu Bywyd*, Euros Bowen views the calling of a poet as part of the same creative instinct as was represented and celebrated by Orpheus.[105]

The poets and other writers who have been the main subject of this chapter were nearly all the beneficiaries of the wider educational opportunities which, since the late nineteenth century, were available to far more Welsh pupils and students than previously. Euros Bowen's death in 1988 occurred in the same year as the publication of a new translation of the Bible into Welsh, *Y Beibl Cymraeg Newydd*. That work was the result of co-operation, over a period of twenty-five years, between theologians and biblical scholars, experts in the Semitic and classical languages, and a panel of scholars of the Welsh language. A large number of those who were engaged in the work of producing the new translation had received, to some degree or other, a classical education. The year which saw *Y Beibl Cymraeg Newydd* appear was also the quatercentenary of the first complete translation of the Bible into Welsh, by Bishop William Morgan. His work was the greatest achievement of Renaissance scholarship in Wales. *Y Beibl Cymraeg Newydd*, completed while there were still in Wales those who were equipped for undertaking the task, in many ways marked the climax of classical achievement in twentieth-century Wales.

It would be easy to succumb to the temptation of thinking that, after the modest fruitfulness of the relation between Welsh literature and the Greek and Latin Classics for much of the twentieth century, the end of the century is witness to sudden and terminal decline. Gwenallt, in an elegy for E. D. T. Jenkins, formerly Professor of Classics at Aberystwyth, tells of the wounding of Greek and Latin in the citadels of learning:[106]

> Yr oedd y Roeg yn cael ei chlwyfo hyd angau yn y
>   ceyrydd addysg . . .
> Yr oedd y Lladin yn llesgáu; y clasuron yn clafychu.

If that was true by the time of E. D. T. Jenkins's death in 1960, how much more true is it in the 1990s. Many of the Welsh-medium secondary schools gave an honourable place, for some twenty years, to the study of Latin, and a Latin–Welsh diction-ary, the result of enthusiastic co-operation between teachers and others, was produced for their use.[107] In the last decade of the century, however, the secondary schools which offer Latin (not to mention Greek) have become so few that the Welsh Joint Education Committee has felt compelled to abandon its classical syllabuses and examinations. Meanwhile, three out of five constituent Colleges of the University of Wales have seen fit to close their departments of Classics and to discontinue the teaching of the classical languages. Such developments are consistent with the picture throughout the United Kingdom, but the decline appears to be more pronounced in Wales. It is beyond the purpose of this work to seek to explain such a situation. It may be that, even after the educational advances of the twentieth century, the study of Classics in Wales, and especially within a Welsh-speaking context, has been too much confined to individuals or small groups.

It would, however, be as wrong as it would be inappropriate to end on such a note. Even if the study of the classical languages has declined, interest in the classical world and its heritage thrives. As has often been the case over the centuries, it is some of Wales's poets who have been most open in recent years to the influence of the classical past. In the context of the National Eisteddfod, the chair in 1980 was won by Donald Evans for an *awdl* entitled 'Y Ffwrnais' ('The Furnace'), in which – as for Hedd Wyn in 1917 – the myth of Prometheus is central to the poet's vision.[108] Bobi Jones, an astonishingly prolific and versatile writer, in 'Hunllef Arthur' ('Arthur's Nightmare') produced a quasi-epic poem of over 20,000 lines, and, although classical themes do not loom large in the rest of his vast *oeuvre*, he can make pointed use of ancient mythology, such as the story of Orpheus and Eurydice.[109] Likewise Alan Llwyd, a brilliant master of the traditional craft of Welsh poetry, finds in the myth of Orpheus a means of expressing an aspect of his vision of the artist's role.[110] Gwyn Thomas, one of the most refreshing of contemporary voices, has turned to the *Iliad* for some of his most sustained imagery, and has echoes of Sophocles and Catullus resonating through other poems.[111] Notable also is the vigour with which Welsh drama companies have captured the power of some of the works of the Greek tragedians. The performance by Cwmni Dalier Sylw of a version of Euripides' *Bacchae*, prepared by Gareth Miles,[112] remains a vivid memory for all who experienced it in 1991.

One of the most evocative of modern poetic responses to the classical world, not only its antiquity but also its cultural potential for the present, is 'Y Parthenon', by Bryan Martin Davies.[113] The poem recalls a visit to Athens in October 1971, and its descriptive qualities remind the reader of Euros Bowen's sense of scene and atmosphere. In the concluding lines the Parthenon is viewed as a symbol of the culture which created it. For us too, at the end of this study of the relationship between the classical world and a literature composed in a minority language in a far-flung outpost of Rome's old Empire, the poet's words are both an encouragement and a challenge:

> Ar chwâl heddiw
> > chwedlau Athena,
> ond ynot,
> > chwiliwn ei choel,

a cheisiwn ei chred,
nes gwawrio o'th gelfyddyd di
olau ei hystyr hen
i'n dyneiddio drachefn.

Scattered today
Athena's tales,
but in you,
we search her conviction,
we seek her creed,
till from your art there dawns
the light of her ancient meaning
to humanize us once more.

Notes

Notes to Introduction

1. Quoted by J. Gwyn Griffiths, in D. Eirug Davies (ed.), *Pennar Davies, Cyfrol Deyrnged* (Abertawe, 1981), p.41.

2. 'Cyn y ganrif hon, anodd yw dod o hyd er y chweched ganrif i un llenor Cymraeg na fyddai'n arddel y label "Cristion" pe bai galw am hynny.' R. M. Jones, *Llên Cymru a Chrefydd* (Llandybïe, 1977), p.13.

3. *Annals* XIV.29–30.

4. Text edited by Ifor Williams (Bangor, 1908); English translation by Gwyn Jones and Thomas Jones, *The Mabinogion* (London, 1949), pp.79–88.

5. See also Gwynfor Evans, *Macsen Wledig a Geni'r Genedl Gymreig/ Magnus Maximus and the Birth of Wales the Nation* (Swansea, 1983).

6. V. E. Nash-Williams, *The Early Christian Monuments of Wales* (Cardiff, 1950), pp.55–7, and Plate VII (13).

7. Gwyn A. Williams, *The Welsh in their History* (London, 1982), p.191.

8. In, for example, 'The Boundary Line of Cymru' (Sir John Rhŷs Memorial Lecture, 1940), *PBA* XXVI (1940), 275–300; *The Personality of Britain*, 4th edition (Cardiff, 1943), passim.

9. *Agricola* 21.

10. *Language and History in Early Britain* (Edinburgh, 1953), p.112. For a critique, see A. S. Gratwick, 'Latinitas Britannica: was British Latin archaic?' in N. Brooks (ed.), *Latin and the Vernacular Languages in Early Medieval Britain* (Leicester, 1982), pp.1–79.

11. For succinct studies of the Latin element in the Welsh language, see Henry Lewis, *Datblygiad yr Iaith Gymraeg* (Caerdydd, 1931), esp. Chapter 5; id., *Yr Elfen Ladin yn yr Iaith Gymraeg* (Caerdydd, 1943).

12. See J. J. Tierney, 'The Celtic Ethnography of Posidonius', *PRIA* LX, Section C (1959–60), 189–275; id., 'The Celts and the Classical Authors', in J. Raftery (ed.), *The Celts* (Cork, 1964), pp.23–33; H. D. Rankin, *Celts and the Classical World* (London and Sydney, 1987).

Notes to Chapter I

1. *The Classical Heritage and its Beneficiaries* (Cambridge, 1958), p.94.

2. *Canu Taliesin* (ed. Ifor Williams, Caerdydd, 1960) VI, Gweith Argoet Llwyfein, lines 25–28. Translation by Anthony Conran, *PBWV*, p.73; *OBWVE*, p.1. The same refrain recurs, with small textual variations, in six other poems to Urien.

3. For a judicious and lucid discussion of a subject of alarming complexity for the non-expert, see D. Ellis Evans, 'Insular Celtic and the Emergence of the Welsh Language', in A. Bammersberger and A. Wollmann (eds.), *Britain 400–600, Language and History* (Heidelberg, 1990), pp.149–77.

4. A. O. H. Jarman, *The Cynfeirdd: Early Welsh Poets and Poetry* (Cardiff, 1981), p.26.

5. H. Idris Bell, *The Nature of Poetry as Conceived by the Welsh Bards*, Taylorian Lecture, 1955 (Oxford, 1955), p.7.

6. On the dating of Gildas, see especially T. D. O'Sullivan, *The 'De Excidio' of Gildas: Its Authenticity and Date* (Ph.D. thesis, Columbia University, 1973), Facsimile copy (Michigan and London, 1981), passim; D. Dumville, 'Gildas and Maelgwn: problems of dating', in M. Lapidge and D. Dumville, *Gildas: New Approaches* (Woodbridge, 1984), pp.51–9; M. W. Herren, 'Gildas and Early British Monasticism', in Bammersberger and Wollmann (eds.), *Britain 400–600* (see n.3 above), pp.65–78; Nicholas J. Higham, *Rome, Britain and the Anglo-Saxons* (London, 1992), esp. pp.153–68.

7. See Nicholas J. Higham, *CMCS* 22 (1991), 1–14.

8. *De Excidio Britanniae* 34.6. Text edited and translated by Michael Winterbottom, *Gildas: The Ruin of Britain and Other Documents* (London and Chichester, 1978). For a stylistic analysis, and a slightly different interpretation of this paragraph, see P. Sims-Williams, 'Vernacular Poetry', in M. Lapidge and D. Dumville (eds.), *Gildas: New Approaches*, pp.174–5.

9. Anthony Conran, *PBWV*, Introduction, p.13.

10. Margaret Deanesly, 'The implications of the term *Sapiens* as applied to Gildas', in D. J. Gordon (ed.), *Fritz Saxl, 1890–1948: A Volume of Memorial Essays from his friends in England* (London, 1957), p.54.

11. See F. Kerlouégan, 'Le latin du *De excidio Britanniae* de Gildas', in M. W. Barley and R. P. C. Hanson (eds.), *Christianity in Britain, 300–700* (Leicester, 1968), pp.151–76; id., *Le 'De Excidio Britanniae' de Gildas: Les Destinées de la Culture Latine dans l'Ile de Bretagne au VIe Siècle* (Paris, 1987), passim; and (all in Lapidge and Dumville, *Gildas: New Approaches*) M. Lapidge, 'Gildas's education and the Latin culture of sub-Roman Britain', pp.27–50; Neil Wright, 'Gildas's prose style and its origins', pp.107–28; Giovanni Orlandi, '*Clausulae* in Gildas's *De Excidio Britanniae*', pp.129–49.

12. See Michael Winterbottom, *Gildas: The Ruin of Britain*, p.10, n.8.

13. The definitive treatment is F. Kerlouégan, *Le 'De Excidio Britanniae' de Gildas*: see n.11 above.

14. See J. E. Caerwyn Williams, 'Gildas, Maelgwn and the Bards', in R. R. Davies and others (eds.), *Welsh Society and Nationhood* (Cardiff, 1984), pp.19–34.

15. *Vita Gildae auctore monacho Ruiensi* 3 (ed. Hugh Williams, London, 1899, p.326).

16. Ibid., p.328f.

17. M. Lapidge and D. Dumville (eds.), *Gildas: New Approaches*, p.50.

18. *Vita Sancti Samsonis* 7. Text in R. Fawtier, *La Vie de Saint Samson* (Paris, 1912), p.105f.; translation by T. Taylor (London, 1925), p.14. On the dating of the *Life of Samson*, see L. Fleuriot, *Les Origines de la Bretagne* (Paris, 1980), p.284; also Norah Chadwick, *Early Brittany* (Cardiff, 1969), on Fawtier's scepticism about the early dating of the Vita Prima.

19. For surveys of the extant material, see Kenneth Jackson, *Language and History in Early Britain* (Edinburgh, 1953), pp.42–58; D. Simon Evans, *Llafar a Llyfr yn yr Hen Gyfnod* (Caerdydd, 1982); Michael Lapidge, 'Latin Learning in Dark Age Wales: Some Prolegomena', in D. Ellis Evans, John G. Griffith and E. M. Jope (eds.), *Proceedings of the Seventh International Congress of Celtic Studies, Oxford 1983* (Oxford, 1986), pp.91–107.

20. See George Henderson, *From Durrow to Kells, The Insular Gospel-Books 650–800* (London, 1987) pp.122–9; D. Jenkins and M. E. Owen, 'The Welsh Marginalia in the Lichfield Gospels', *CMCS* 5 (1983), 37–65; 7 (1984), 91–120.

21. See John Morris (ed.), *Nennius: British History and The Welsh Annals*, (London and Chichester, 1980); also David N. Dumville's epoch-making studies on the *Historia Brittonum*, now conveniently brought together in his *Histories and Pseudo-histories of the Insular Middle Ages* (Aldershot, 1990), Studies II–VII.

22. Cambridge, Corpus Christi College MS 153, part i. See W. M. Lindsay, *Early Welsh Script* (Oxford, 1912), pp.19–22 and Plates IX, X; T. A. M. Bishop, 'The Corpus Martianus Capella', *Transactions of the Cambridge Bibliographical Society* 4 (1964–8), pp.257–75.

23. Cambridge University Library MS Ff.4.42. See W. M. Lindsay, *Early Welsh Script*, pp.16–18, Plates VI, VII.

24. Oxford, Bodleian Library MS Auct.F.4.32. Facsimile, with introduction, in R. W. Hunt (ed.), *St Dunstan's Class Book from Glastonbury* (Umbrae Codicum Occidentalium, 1961). See also W. M. Lindsay, *Early Welsh Script*, pp.7–10.

25. For the Latin text, see W. H. Stevenson (ed.), *Asser's Life of King Alfred* (Oxford, 1904); translation by S. Keynes and M. Lapidge (Harmondsworth, 1983). See also James Campbell, 'Asser's *Life of Alfred*', in C. Holdsworth and T. P. Wiseman (eds.), *The Inheritance of Historiography, 350–900* (Exeter, 1986), pp.115–35.

26. See Norah K. Chadwick, 'Early culture and learning in North Wales', in Norah K. Chadwick *et al.*, *Studies in the Early British Church* (Cambridge, 1958), pp.29–120; D. Simon Evans, 'The Welsh and the Irish before the Normans – Contact or Impact', Sir John Rhŷs Memorial Lecture, *PBA* LXXV (1989), 143–61. For a succinct discussion of Europe's cultural debt to Ireland in the early Middle Ages, see Padráig A. Breatnach, 'Bernhard Bischoff (d.1991), the Munich School of Medieval Latin Philology and Irish Medieval Studies', *CMCS* 26 (1993), 7–14.

27. Text (of BL Cotton MS Vespasian A xiv), and translation, in A. W. Wade-Evans (ed.), *Vitae Sanctorum Britanniae et Genealogiae* (Cardiff, 1944), pp.24–141. Definitive text in H. D. Emanuel, 'The Latin Life of St Cadoc: a textual and lexicographical study' (University of Wales, MA thesis, 1950). See also Karen Gail Borst, 'A Reconsideration of the *Vita Sancti Cadoci*', in Patrick K. Ford (ed.), *Celtic Folklore and Christianity* (Santa Barbara, 1983), pp.1–15; J. K. Knight, 'Sources for the Early History of Morgannwg', Chapter 9 in H. N. Savory (ed.), *Glamorgan County History*, vol.II (Cardiff, 1984), esp. pp.385–9.

28. See J. Gwenogvryn Evans, *The Text of the Book of Llan Dav* (Oxford, 1893), pp.271, 273, 274.

29. 'Llancarfan and St Cadoc', in Stewart Williams (ed.), *The Garden of Wales* (Cowbridge, 1961) pp.61–9.

30. See B. Bischoff, *Latin Palaeography, Antiquity and the Middle Ages*, English edition (Cambridge, 1990), pp.109–11.

31. 'Beneventana Civitas', *Journal of the Historical Society of the Church in Wales* 3 (1953), 62. See also G. Goetinck, 'Lifris and the Italian connection', *BBCS* 35 (1988), 10–13.

32. See N. K. Chadwick, 'Intellectual Life in West Wales in the Last Days of the Celtic Church', *Studies in the Early British Church*, pp.121–82; E. G. Bowen, *A History of Llanbadarn Fawr* (Llanbadarn Fawr, 1979), chapter 4.

33. Thomas Jones (trans.), *Brut y Tywysogion, or The Chronicle of the Princes: Peniarth MS 20 Version* (Cardiff, 1952), p.18.

34. See Michael Lapidge, 'The Welsh-Latin Poetry of Sulien's Family', *SC* 8–9 (1973/4), 68–106.

35. J. W. James (ed.), *Rhigyfarch's Life of St David* (Cardiff, 1967).

36. BL MS Cotton Faustina C.1, fols 66–93. See A. Peden, *CMCS* 2 (1981), pp.21–45, and B. C. Barker-Benfield, in L. D. Reynolds (ed.), *Texts and Transmission: A Survey of the Latin Classics* (Oxford, 1983), pp.224–32.

37. Cambridge, Corpus Christi College MS 199.

38. Text and translation by M. Lapidge, loc.cit. (n.34), 80–89.

39. For text of the *englynion*, and commentary, see Ifor Williams, *BBCS* 6 (1932), 101–10, 205–24.

40. Text in Ifor Williams, *Canu Aneirin* (Caerdydd, 1938); translation, together with an invaluable modern introduction, in A. O. H. Jarman, *Aneirin: The Gododdin* (Llandysul, 1988). Professor Jarman cogently argues (pp.lxviii–lxxv) for *c.*AD 600 as the date for the composition of *Y Gododdin* in its original form, but that additions and interpolations were later made to an orally preserved text. See also B. F. Roberts (ed.), *Early Welsh Poetry: Studies in the Book of Aneirin* (Aberystwyth, 1988), where some dissident views are expressed on the early dating of *Y Gododdin*; but see J. E. Caerwyn Williams, *Book News from Wales*, Winter 1989, 9–10, and Gwyn Thomas, *LlC* XVII (1992), 153–6. On the manuscript of the work, see Daniel Huws (ed.), *Llyfr Aneirin: Ffacsimile* (Aberystwyth, 1989).

41. P. Sims-Williams, in Lapidge and Dumville, *Gildas: New Approaches*, p.181.

42. Ibid., p.182.

43. *THSC*, 1968, 293–8; also in Alun R. Jones and Gwyn Thomas (eds.), *Presenting Saunders Lewis* (Cardiff, 1973), pp.145–53.

44. Ibid., p.179.

45. NLW MS Peniarth 2 (=*BT*): reproduced, with diplomatic text, in J. Gwenogvryn Evans, *Facsimile and Text of the Book of Taliesin* (Llanbedrog, 1910).

46. *CMCS* 13 (1987), 7–38.

47. See George Cary, *The Medieval Alexander* (Cambridge, 1956), Part A; Ian Michael, *Alexander's Flying Machine: the History of a Legend* (Southampton, 1974).

48. Text edited and translated by Marged Haycock, loc.cit. (n.46), 26–7.

49. Text edited and translated by Marged Haycock, ibid., 28–9.

Notes to Chapter II

1. *European Literature and the Latin Middle Ages* (New York, 1953), p.19.

2. Thomas Jones (transl.), *Brut y Tywysogion, Peniarth MS 20 Version* (Cardiff, 1952), p.17.

3. *SC* 8–9 (1973–4), 104.

4. Ibid., 88–91.

5. Ibid., 86–7.

6. Alison Peden, 'Science and Philosophy in Wales at the time of the Norman Conquest: a Macrobius Manuscript from Llanbadarn', *CMCS* 2 (1981), 21–45.

7. Cambridge, Corpus Christi College, MS 199; Dublin, Trinity College, MS 50 (A.4.20). See W. M. Lindsay, *Early Welsh Script* (Oxford, 1912), pp.32–3, Plates XVI and XVII; H. J. Lawlor (ed.), *The Psalter and Martyrology of Ricemarch*, 2 vols., Henry Bradshaw Society, 47 and 48 (London, 1914).

8. NLW, Peniarth MS 540. See Daniel Huws, 'A Welsh Manuscript of Bede's *De natura rerum*', *BBCS* XXVII, Part 4 (1978), 491–504.

9. Jac L. Williams and Gwilym R. Hughes (ed.), *The History of Education in Wales: I*, (Swansea, 1978), p.13. On the monastic contribution, see F. G. Cowley, *The Monastic Order in South Wales, 1066–1349* (Cardiff, 1977), chapter 6.

10. See R. W. Southern, *Medieval Humanism and Other Studies* (Oxford, 1970), pp.37–41.

11. For introductions to such functional prose in the twelfth and following centuries, see T. M. Charles-Edwards, *The Welsh Laws*: Writers of Wales (Cardiff, 1989); D. Simon Evans, *Medieval Religious Literature*: Writers of Wales (Cardiff, 1986); Wendy Davies, *The Llandaff Charters* (Aberystwyth, 1979); Thomas Jones, 'Historical Writing in Medieval Welsh', in *Scottish Studies* 12 (1968), 15–27; J. Beverley Smith, *The Sense of History in Medieval Wales* (Aberystwyth, 1989).

12. References to the text of *Historia Regum Britanniae* are given in accordance with the book and chapter numbers used in Commelin's edition (1587) and followed in Lewis Thorpe's Penguin translation (1966). For a conversion table to the chapter numbers used by Faral and Wright, see N. Wright, *Historia Regum Britannie I: Bern, Burgerbibliothek, MS 568* (Cambridge, 1985), pp.172–4.

13. *Geoffrey of Monmouth: History of the Kings of Britain* (Harmondsworth, 1966), pp.226–7. The Latin text is that of Bern MS 568 (ed. Wright).

14. See C. N. L. Brooke, 'The Archbishops of St David's, Llandaff and Caerleon-on-Usk', in Nora K. Chadwick (ed.), *Studies in the Early British Church*, (Cambridge, 1958), pp.201–42; reprinted in C. N. L. Brooke, *The Church and the Welsh Border in the Central Middle Ages* (Woodbridge, 1986), pp.16–49.

15. See M. Dominica Legge, 'Master Geoffrey Arthur', in K. Varty (ed.), *An Arthurian Tapestry: Essays in Memory of Lewis Thorpe* (Glasgow, 1981), pp.22–7.

16. *Brut y Brenhinedd: Llanstephan MS 1 Version* (Dublin, 1971), Introduction, pp.xiv–xv.

17. See Basil Clarke (ed.), *Geoffrey of Monmouth: Life of Merlin / Vita Merlini* (Cardiff, 1973).

18. G. W. S. Barrow, in 'Wales and Scotland in the Middle Ages', *WHR* X (1980–81), 303. On this aspect of *Historia Regum Britanniae*, see also J. Gillingham, 'The Context and Purposes of Geoffrey of Monmouth's *History of the Kings of Britain*', in *Anglo-Norman Studies XII*, Proceedings of the Battle Conference, 1990 (Woodbridge, 1991), 99–118.

19. *Historia Brittonum*, pp.7–18.

20. See J. Conway Davies, *Episcopal Acts and Cognate Documents relating to Welsh Dioceses, 1066–1272*, vol.I (Cardiff: Historical Society of the Church in Wales, 1946), p.308 (D.307), quoted by R. R. Davies, *Conquest, Coexistence and Change*, p.79.

21. On the names used in the *Historia*, see especially J. S. P. Tatlock, *The Legendary History of Britain: Geoffrey of Monmouth's 'Historia Regum Britanniae' and its Early Vernacular Versions* (California, 1950), pp.116–70.

22. See especially H. Tausendfreund, *Vergil und Gottfried von Monmouth* (Halle, 1913), passim; E. Faral, *La Legende Arthurienne: Études et Documents* (Paris, 1929) vol.2, pp.69–92; J. Hammer, 'Remarks on the sources and textual history of Geoffrey of Monmouth's *Historia Regum Britanniae*', *Quarterly Bulletin of the Polish Institute of Arts and Sciences in America*, January 1944, 509–21.

23. N. Wright, op.cit., p.9; translation by Lewis Thorpe, with some alterations.

24. 'Remarks on the sources' (see n.22), 521.

25. Modern authoritative studies of Gerald are Robert Bartlett, *Gerald of Wales, 1146–1223* (Oxford, 1982) and Brynley F. Roberts, *Gerald of Wales: Writers of Wales* (Cardiff, 1982). Very readable also is Charles Kightly and others, *A Mirror of Medieval Wales: Gerald of Wales and his Journey of 1188* (Cardiff, 1988).

26. *Itinerarium Kambriae* I.12 (*Giraldi Cambrensis Opera*, Rolls Series,

vol.VI, ed. J. F. Dimock, p.93); L. Thorpe (transl.), *Gerald of Wales: The Journey through Wales and the Description of Wales*, p.151.

27. *uterque populus me sibi tanquam alienum reputans et non suum*: from the *Symbolum Electorum* (see *Giraldi Cambrensis Opera*, Rolls series, vol.VIII, ed. G. F. Warner, 1891, p.lviii), quoted by Bartlett, *Gerald of Wales, 1146–1223*, p.17.

28. *Speculum Ecclesiae* (R.S. IV, p.104). See also H. E. Butler, *The Autobiography of Giraldus Cambrensis* (London, 1937), p.79.

29. *De Rebus a Se Gestis* I.2 (*Giraldi Cambrensis Opera*, Rolls Series, vol.I, ed. J. S. Brewer, 1861, p.23); H. E. Butler, op.cit., p.37.

30. *Gerald of Wales, 1146–1223*, p.3.

31. Ibid., p.3.

32. Text in *Giraldi Cambrensis Opera*, Rolls Series, vol.V, ed. J. F. Dimock (London, 1867). Translation of *Topographia Hibernica* by J. J. O'Meara, *History and Topography of Ireland* (Harmondsworth, 1982).

33. Text in *Giraldi Cambrensis Opera*, Rolls Series, vol.VI, ed. J. F. Dimock (London, 1868). Translation by Lewis Thorpe, *The Journey through Wales and the Description of Wales* (Harmondsworth, 1978). The text and translation are quoted from these two works.

34. *Itinerarium Kambriae*, Praefatio Prima (Rolls Series, vol.VI, p.4); *Descriptio Kambriae* (Rolls Series, vol.VI, p.163).

35. *Itinerarium Kambriae* I.8; *Descriptio Kambriae* I.15.

36. *Itinerarium Kambriae* I.5; cf. II.7.

37. *Itinerarium Kambriae* I.5. Translation by L. Thorpe (see n.33), pp.114–15.

38. *De Rebus a Se Gestis* II.16 (*Giraldi Cambrensis Opera*, Rolls Series, vol.I, p.72); H. E. Butler, op.cit., p.97.

39. See R. W. Hays, 'Welsh Students at Oxford and Cambridge Universities in the Middle Ages', *WHR* 4 (1968–9), 325–61.

40. See J. Swanson, *John of Wales* (Cambridge, 1989).

41. See L. D. Reynolds (ed.), *Texts and Transmission: a Survey of the Latin Classics* (Oxford, 1983), p.xxxvi, n.180; pp.120, 124.

42. See R. A. B. Mynors, R. H. Rouse and M. A. Rouse (eds.), *Registrum Anglie de Libris Doctorum et Auctorum Veterum* (London, 1991), p.291. I am grateful to Mr Daniel Huws for drawing my attention to this important edition of the *Registrum* and especially to the Margam entry.

43. *A Guide to Welsh Literature*, volume 2, ed. A. O. H. Jarman and Gwilym R. Hughes, p.74. See also J. E. Caerwyn Williams, *The Poets of the Welsh Princes* (Cardiff, 1978).

44. The definitive edition of the bardic grammars is by G. J. Williams and E. J. Jones, *Gramadegau'r Penceirddiaid* (Cardiff, 1934). See also Thomas Parry, 'The Welsh Metrical Treatise attributed to Einion Offeiriad', *PBA* XLVII (1961), 179–95; Ceri W. Lewis, 'Einion Offeiriad and the Bardic Grammar', in A. O. H. Jarman and Gwilym R. Hughes, *A Guide to Welsh Literature*, Volume 2, pp.58–87; A. T. E. Matonis, 'The Welsh Bardic Grammars and the Western Grammatical Tradition', *Modern Philology* LXXIX (1981–2), 121–45. On Dafydd Ddu of Hiraddug, see R. Geraint Gruffydd, *LlC* XVIII (1995), 205–20.

45. *Gwaith Llywarch ap Llywelyn, 'Prydydd y Moch'* (Cyfres Beirdd y Tywysogion V), ed. Elin M. Jones and Nerys Ann Jones (Caerdydd, 1991), p.44; Rachel Bromwich, *TYP*, p.123. See also D. Myrddin Lloyd, *Rhai Agweddau ar Ddysg y Gogynfeirdd* (Caerdydd, 1977), esp. pp.12–14.

46. Ceri W. Lewis, in *A Guide to Welsh Literature*, Volume 2, p.93.

47. *TYP* 47, p.122.

48. *TYP* 47b, p.122f.

49. *TYP* 48, p.127.

50. *TYP* 50, p.129.

51. Welsh text in Thomas Jones (ed.), *Brut y Tywysogyon, Peniarth MS 20* (Caerdydd, 1941), also quoted in Professor Jones's Aberystwyth Inaugural Lecture, *Brut y Tywysogion* (Caerdydd, 1953), p.17; translation from Thomas Jones, *Brut y Tywysogyon, or the Chronicle of the Princes, Peniarth MS 20 Version* (Cardiff, 1952), p.77.

52. Latin text in: *Daretis Phrygii de Excidio Troiae Historia*, ed. F. Meister (Leipzig: Teubner, 1873).

53. For Welsh text, see J. Gwenogvryn Evans and J. Rhys (eds.), *The Text of the Bruts from the Red Book of Hergest*, pp.1–39. Detailed discussion in B. G. Owens, 'Y Fersiynau Cymraeg o Dares Phrygius (*Ystorya Dared*) – Eu Tarddiad, Eu Nodweddion a'u Cydberthynas' (M.A. thesis, University of Wales, 1951).

54. Thomas Jones (transl.), *Brut y Tywysogyon: Peniarth MS 20 Version* (Cardiff, 1952), p.1.

55. Standard texts and introductions are in the monumental editions of Thomas Jones. In addition to those referred to in n.51 above, see *Brut y Tywysogyon, or the Chronicle of the Princes. Red Book of Hergest Version* (Cardiff, 1955).

56. See Daniel Huws, 'Llyfrau Cymraeg 1250–1400', *NLWJ* XXVIII (1993), 1–21.

57. *GDG* 14.22; 20.60.

58. *GDG* 24.29; 50.1; 58.19–20.

59. See L. P. Wilkinson, *Ovid Recalled* (Cambridge, 1958), esp. Chapter 11 (pp.366–98). On the Ovidian tradition in literature, esp. English literature, see Charles Martindale (ed.), *Ovid Renewed* (Cambridge, 1988). On continental influences on Dafydd, especially the use of rhetorical *topoi* derived by Medieval Latin poets from classical authors, see A. T. E. Matonis, *BBCS* XXVIII (1980), 47–72. For the wider dimension, see Helen Fulton, *Dafydd ap Gwilym and the European Context* (Cardiff, 1989).

60. See especially *Tradition and Innovation in the Poetry of Dafydd ap Gwilym* (Cardiff, 1967), included also in *Aspects of the Poetry of Dafydd ap Gwilym: Collected Papers* (Cardiff, 1986).

61. Latin text from Ovid, *Amores, Ars Amatoria, Remedia Amoris*, ed. E. J. Kenney (Oxford Classical Texts, 1961); English translation by Guy Lee, *Ovid's Amores* (London, 1968), p.139.

62. *GDG*, p.194; translation by Rachel Bromwich, *Dafydd ap Gwilym: A Selection of Poems* (Llandysul, 1982), p.112.

63. op.cit. (n.60), pp.26–7.

64. *BBCS* XXV (1974), 24–6.

65. *GDG* 5.14, 25, 41.

66. *GDG* 51. Translation by R. M. Loomis, *Dafydd ap Gwilym: The Poems* (New York, 1982), p.130.

67. *TYP* 50. For a discussion of Dafydd's use of the triadic material, see R. Geraint Gruffydd, 'Cywyddau Triawdaidd Dafydd ap Gwilym', in *Ysgrifau Beirniadol* XIII (Dinbych, 1985), pp.167–77.

68. The standard study is still Domenico Comparetti, *Vergil in the Middle Ages* (English translation by E. F. M. Benecke, New York, 1895). See also T. S. Pattie, 'The Popular Traditions', in R. D. Williams and T. S. Pattie, *Virgil: His Poetry through the Ages* (London, 1982), pp.84–93.

69. *GDG* 32.32.

70. *GDG* 84.57–8. Translation by Rachel Bromwich, *Dafydd ap Gwilym: A Selection of Poems*, pp.36–8.

71. See *Hanes Taliesin* (from Peniarth MS 111) in Patrick K. Ford, *Ystoria Taliesin* (Cardiff, 1992), p.133; *The Book of Taliesin*, ed. J. Gwenogvryn Evans (Llanbedrog, 1910), 27.12. Cf. also, Juliette Wood, 'Virgil and Taliesin: the Concept of the Magician in Medieval Folklore', in *Folklore* 94 (1983), 91–104.

72. *GGG* XLIX.22 (p.132); *GTA* LXIII.64 (p.255).

73. *GGG* LXX.25–30 (pp.186–7); LXVII.55–8 (p.180).

74. *PWDN* XVI.57–62 (p.45).

75. See E. Meinir James,'Secretum Secretorum: Astudiaeth feirniadol o ddetholiadau Cymraeg a Lladin o'r llythyr ffug-Aristotelaidd at Alecsander Fawr', Ph.D. (Wales) thesis, 1986.

76. See D. R. Johnston (ed.), *GIG*, Rhagymadrodd, p.xxi.

77. *GIG* XV.1, XXX.1–5, XXVIII.37–40. A Welsh translation of substantial parts of the *Elucidarium* is contained in the fourteenth-century *Book of the Anchorite*: see J. Morris-Jones and J. Rhŷs, *The Elucidarium and other tracts in Welsh from Llyvyr Agkyr Llandewivrevi* (Oxford, 1894); Idris Foster, *PBA* XXXVI (1950), 197–226.

78. *GIG* I.28, III.71, XXII.43; VI.73–8; XXVIII.41–62, XII, XIII.

79. *IGE* LXXXVIII, especially lines 29–62 (p.266).

80. *Braslun o Hanes Llenyddiaeth Gymraeg: I*, pp.104–13. Saunders Lewis repeated the same view in a later essay, published in *Meistri a'u Crefft* (Caerdydd, 1981), pp.148–60. For a critique, see Thomas Parry in *Taliesin* XLIII (1981), 12–15. See also G. E. Ruddock, in *A Guide to Welsh Literature*, Volume 2, pp.169–88.

81. *The Welsh Church, From Conquest to Reformation* (Cardiff, 1976), p.239.

82. See E. J. Dobson, 'The Hymn to the Virgin', in *THSC* 1954, 70–124.

83. *IGE* LXXVII. See E. J. Jones, *Education in Wales during the Middle Ages*: Inaugural Lecture (Swansea, 1947), pp.38–42.

84. *Braslun o Hanes Llenyddiaeth Gymraeg: I*, chapter 7.

85. *Gwaith Tudur Aled*, ed. T. Gwynn Jones (Caerdydd, 1926), XLIX.66. See Saunders Lewis, *Meistri'r Canrifoedd*, p.109.

86. See Glanmor Williams, *Welsh Reformation Essays* (Cardiff, 1967), pp.67–75, 85–7.

Notes to Chapter III

1. From 'The Dialogue of the Government of Wales', George Owen, *The Description of Pembrokeshire*, Part III, ed. H. Owen (London, 1906), p.56. (Modernized orthography.)

2. Dafydd Johnston (gol.), *Gwaith Lewis Glyn Cothi*. (Caerdydd, 1995), 14 (pp.42–4, 'Awdl Foliant Harri VII'), 89–92.

3. Quoted in V. J. Scattergood, *Politics and Poetry in the Fifteenth Century* (London, 1971), p.214. I am indebted to Glanmor Williams, *Recovery, Reorientation and Reformation: Wales c.1415–1642*, p.237, for this reference.

4. See Glanmor Williams, *Harri Tudur a Chymru: Henry Tudor and Wales* (Cardiff, 1985).

5. M. M. Phillips, *Erasmus and the Northern Renaissance* (London, 1949), p.xii.

6. Reprinted, ed. Heinz-Dieter Leidig, *Renaissance Latin Drama in England*, First Series, 13 (Hildesheim/New York, 1983).

7. See W. P. Griffith, 'Addysg Brifysgol i'r Cymry yn y Cyfnod Modern Cynnar', *Cof Cenedl* VI (Llandysul, 1991), p.39f.

8. See A. Breeze, 'Leonard Cox, a Welsh Humanist in Poland and Hungary', *NLWJ* XXV (1988), 399–410. During his time in Poland Cox published an important essay on education and the study of the classical languages; see A. Breeze and J. Glomski, *Humanistica Lovaniensia* XL (1991), 112–67. On its title page, however, he terms himself *Anglus*, and can hardly be regarded as typical of the Welsh humanists! On Cox, see further Henryk Zins, 'A British humanist and the University of Kraków at the beginning of the sixteenth century: a chapter in Anglo-Polish relations in the age of the Renaissance', *Renaissance Studies* VIII (1994), 13–39.

9. London, 1573. Re-issued 1586, 1607.

10. William Vaughan: Ἐρωτοπαίγνιον *pium* (1597), *Erotopainion pium, pars II* (1598), *Poematum libellus* (1598), *The Golden-Grove* (1st ed., 1600, 2nd ed., 1608), *Cambrensium Caroleia* (1625); see J. W. Binns, *Intellectual Culture in Elizabethan and Jacobean England: The Latin Writings of the Age* (Leeds, 1990), passim. John Stradling: *Epigrammatum Libri Quatuor* (1607), *Beati Pacifici: a Divine Poem* (1623), *Divine Poems* (1625); see C. Davies, *Latin Writers of the Renaissance*, pp.39–46.

11. See John Cule, *THSC* 1979, 105–28; Emyr Wyn Jones, *Ymgiprys am y Goron* (Dinbych, 1992), pp.119–50.

12. A modern edition of John Owen's epigrams is available in two volumes, ed. J. R. C. Martyn (Leiden, 1976, 1978). On Owen's work, see three articles by J. Henry Jones: *Y Llenor* XVII (1938), 215–20; *THSC*, 1940, 130–43; *Greece and Rome* X (1941), 65–73; also, C. Davies, *Latin Writers of the Renaissance*, pp.46–53.

13. J. Henry Jones, *Greece and Rome* X (1941), 73.

14. III.37. Translation by Thomas Harvey (London, 1677).

15. G. Williams and R. O. Jones (eds.), *The Celts and the Renaissance: Tradition and Innovation* (Cardiff, 1990), p.32.

16. See C. Davies, *Ceredigion* XI (1988–9), 1–18; id., *LlC* XVI (1989), 7–22.

17. *The descripcion of the sphere or the frame of the worlde . . . Englysshed by W. Salysbury* (London, 1550); on William Morgan's Latin epigram, to greet Maurice Kyffin's translation of Terence's *Andria*, see C. Davies, *Ceredigion* XI (1988–9), 13–14, *LlC* XVI (1989), 17–18; Edmwnd Prys's hexameter poem appears at the beginning of John Davies's Grammar (1621); Parry's preface to the 1620 translation of the Bible, and John Davies's introductions to his Grammar (1621) and Dictionary (1632), fine examples of clear Latinity, are translated in C. Davies, *RhChLl*, pp.101–56.

18. Saunders Lewis, 'Damcaniaeth Eglwysig Brotestannaidd', *Meistri'r Canrifoedd*, pp.116–39; G. J. Williams, 'Hanes Ysgolheictod Cymraeg yng Nghyfnod y Dadeni, 1550–1700', in *Agweddau ar Hanes Dysg Gymraeg*, pp.31–81; id., 'The History of Welsh Scholarship', *SC* VIII/IX (1973–4), 195–219.

19. *SC* VIII/IX (1973–4), 198.

20. Denys Hay, *Annalists and Historians: Western Historiography from the VIIIth to the XVIIIth Century* (London, 1977), p.119.

21. See T. D. Kendrick, *British Antiquity* (London, 1950), p.85f.

22. Printed by Henry Bynneman, published by Humphrey Toy (*STC* 20309).

23. See further in C. Davies, *Latin Writers of the Renaissance*, pp.17–20.

24. Ibid., pp.20–8.

25. See further in J. W. Binns, *Intellectual Culture*, p.271. For a Welsh translation of the whole of Price's letter to William Herbert, see *RhChLl*, pp.35–40.

26. See C. Davies, 'Erasmus and Welsh Renaissance Learning', *THSC*, 1983, 48–55.

27. Preface to *Oll Synnwyr Pen Kembero Ygyd: Rhagymadroddion*, p.14.

28. W. Salesbury, *A Briefe and a Playne Introduction* (1550).

29. Erasmus, *Adagia* I.ix.4 (LB 335B); I.v.27 (LB 191F); Virgil, *Aeneid* IX.548.

30. *Pontici Virunnii Viri Doctissimi Britannicae Historiae Libri Sex* (1585), A2v; *RhChLl*, p.49.

31. *RhChLl*, p.94.

32. *Rhagymadroddion*, p.120.

33. *RhChLl*, pp.169–84.

34. Henry Lewis (ed.), *Hen Gyflwyniadau* (Cardiff, 1948), p.8.

35. See, for example, David Powel's addresses to Henry and Philip Sidney, 1585 (*RhChLl*, pp.48–57) and Siôn Dafydd Rhys's address to Edward Stradling, 1592 (*RhChLl*, pp.71–8).

36. R. R. Bolgar, *The Classical Heritage* (1954), pp.526–9.

37. Text edited and discussed by E. J. Jones, *BBCS* III (1927), 286–92.

38. Text edited and discussed by Bedwyr Lewis Jones, *LlC* VI (1961), 208–18.

39. Text edited and discussed by Nesta Lloyd, *BBCS* XXIV (1972), 450–58.

40. Printed by Thomas East, published by Thomas Woodcock.

41. First published 1587, reissued (with additions) 1588. The work was reprinted in 1885 by the London printers Whiting & Co., for the Honourable Society of Cymmrodorion.

42. Printed in London by Richard Field. A new printing, with introduction, was edited by W. Pritchard Williams (Bangor, 1908).

43. See especially Glanmor Williams, *Bywyd ac Amserau'r Esgob Richard Davies* (Cardiff, 1953); id., 'Bishop Richard Davies (?1501–1581)', in *Welsh Reformation Essays* (Cardiff, 1967), pp.155–90; id., 'Richard Davies, Esgob Tyddewi, a'r Traddodiad Protestannaidd', *LlC* XVI (1989), 88–96.

44. Preface to *Cambrobrytannicae Cymraecaeve Linguae Institutiones* (1592). See *RhChLl*, p.74.

45. On Llwyd, see especially R. Geraint Gruffydd, 'Humphrey Llwyd of Denbigh: Some Documents and a Catalogue', *Denbighshire Historical Society Transactions* XVII (1968), 54–107; id., 'Humphrey Llwyd: Dyneiddiwr', *EA* XXXIII (1970), 57–74.

46. See the magisterial introduction and meticulous edition by G. J. Williams, *Gramadeg Cymraeg gan Gruffydd Robert, yn ôl yr argraffiad y dechreuwyd ei gyhoeddi ym Milan yn 1567* (Cardiff, 1939).

47. T. Gwynfor Griffith, *Avventure Linguistiche del Cinquecento* (Firenze, 1961), p.40; id., *THSC*, 1966, 287; Heledd Hayes, *Cymru a'r Dadeni* (Caernarfon, 1987) p.10f.; id.,'Claudio Tolomei: a major influence on Gruffydd Robert', *Modern Language Review* LXXXIII (1988), 55–66.

48. *Dosparth ar yr ail rann i ramadeg*, p.3.

49. *Dosparth Byrr ar y rhann gyntaf i ramadeg cymraeg*, p.5.

50. *Y Rhann Diwaethaf i ramadeg a elwir Tonyddiaeth*, p.3.

51. On the early history of the printed text, see J. G. F. Powell (ed.), *Cicero: Cato Maior de Senectute* (Cambridge, 1988), p.49; translations, see R. R. Bolgar, *The Classical Heritage*, p.526f.

52. Saunders Lewis, *Ysgrifau Dydd Mercher* (Llandysul, 1945), p.56; transl., T. G. Griffith, *THSC*, 1966, 288.

53. Preface to *Deffynniad Ffydd Eglwys Loegr*. See *Rhagymadroddion*, p.92.

54. *Dosparth Byrr ar y rhann gyntaf*, p.1f.; transl., *THSC*, 1966, 286.

55. *THSC*, 1966, 281.

56. T. G. Griffith, ibid., 281–5.

57. See Thomas Parry, *Y Llenor* IX (1930), 157–65, 234–41; X (1931), 35–46; R. Geraint Gruffydd, *THSC*, 1971, 175–90; id., *Archaeologia Cambrensis* CXLI (1992), 1–13.

58. *Cambrobrytannicae Cymraecaeve Linguae Institutiones* (1592), Epistola Dedicatoria, p.*3v; *RhChLl*, p.76. The title *Philosophiae professor* probably refers to Gruffydd Robert's position as Canon Theologian in Milan: see G. J. Williams in *Gruffydd Robert: Gramadeg Cymraeg*, pp.xxxiii–iv.

59. Siena MS 6439, fol.78v. See A. B. Melchior, 'Siôn Dafydd Rhys, M.D.(Siena)', *Sudhoffs Archiv*, Band 60, Heft 3 (1976), 289–94.

60. Facsimile reprint of *De Italica Pronunciatione* in Nicoletta

Maraschio (ed.), *Trattati di Fonetica del Cinquecento* (Firenze, 1992).

61. See W. P. Griffith, 'Some passing thoughts on the early history of Friars School, Bangor', *Transactions of the Caernarvonshire Historical Society* XLIX (1988), 117–49.

62. Sir John Wynn, *The History of the Gwydir Family* and *Memoirs*, ed. J. Gwynfor Jones (Llandysul, 1990), pp.61–2.

63. *Cambrobrytannicae Cymraecaeve Linguae Institutiones* (1592), Epistola Dedicatoria, p.*3v; *RhChLl*, p.77. The translation, now lost, 'is said to have once belonged to Jesus College, Oxford, and to have been in the custody of Henry Vaughan' (R. Geraint Gruffydd, *THSC*, 1971, 187). Cf. Bodleian Library MS Aubrey 8, f.11. On Edward Stradling, see especially Ceri W. Lewis, in *Ysgrifau Beirniadol* XIX (Dinbych, 1993), pp.139–207.

64. Printed by Thomas Orwin (*STC* 20966).

65. NLW MS 5276D, pp.50b–55a; see Thomas Jones, *BBCS* X (1939–41), 284–97; XI (1941–4), 21–30, 85–90; also *Rhyddiaith Gymraeg, Cyfrol I, Detholion o Lawysgrifau 1488–1609* (Caerdydd, 1954), pp.23–31.

66. See R. Telfryn Pritchard, *NLWJ* XXIV (1985–6), 295–308.

67. *Recovery, Reorientation and Reformation: Wales, c.1415–1642*, p.441.

68. *Rhagymadroddion*, p.66.

69. *Rhyddiaith Gymraeg, Cyfrol II. Detholion o Lawysgrifau a Llyfrau Printiedig 1547–1618* (Caerdydd, 1956), p.158 ('Llythyr Siôn Dafydd Rhys at y Beirdd'). See Branwen Jarvis, *LlC* XII (1972), 45–56.

70. Text and introduction in Gruffydd Aled Williams (ed.), *Ymryson Edmwnd Prys a Wiliam Cynwal* (Cardiff, 1986); id., 'Golwg ar Ymryson Edmwnd Prys a Wiliam Cynwal', *Ysgrifau Beirniadol* VIII (Denbigh, 1974), pp.70–109.

71. *Rerum Memorandarum Libri* I.19.4 (quoted by R. Pfeiffer, *History of Classical Scholarship, 1300–1850*, p.4).

72. *GGH* 19; 23; 28. Also D. J. Bowen, 'Cywyddau Gruffudd Hiraethog i Dri o Awduron y Dadeni', *THSC*, 1974/5, 103–31.

73. *GGH* 1.16–17; 7.9; 68.84.

74. *GGH* 59.37–52.

75. *GGH* 112.27–34.

76. *GGH* 71.67–8.

77. *Rhagymadroddion*, p.14.

78. *GST* 14.20 (cf. *GGH* 113.6); 8.7–12; 12.11–16, 23.11–16, 36.83–4; 177.53–60.

79. *GST* 14.73–6.

80. *GST* 17.1–4; 12.43–4.

81. *GST* 118, esp. lines 67–96.

82. *GST* 151.1–4 ; translation by Anthony Conran, *PBWV*, p.197.

83. Cardiff MS 84.541; NLW MS 18; Cardiff MS 23.309 (among many). See W. Ll. Davies, 'Phylipiaid Ardudwy', MA thesis, University of Wales, 1912.

84. *Cefn Coch MSS*, ed. J. Fisher (1899), pp.51–4. Cf. D. Gwenallt Jones, *EA* XXVI (1963), 4. (This *cywydd* was at one time ascribed to Dafydd Nanmor, but its ascription to Tomos Prys is now generally accepted. See W. J. Gruffydd, *Llenyddiaeth Cymru, 1450–1600*, pp.22–4, 117.)

Notes to Chapter IV

1. *A History of Welsh Literature* (Oxford, 1955), p.237.

2. G. Williams and R. O. Jones (eds.), *The Celts and the Renaissance: Tradition and Innovation* (Cardiff, 1990), p.36.

3. A royalist supporter who made a great name for himself on the Continent as a scholar was another John Price (*c.*1600–76), a man of Welsh parentage, although born in London. Pricaeus (as he Latinized his name) became Professor of Greek in Pisa and subsequently a protégé of Francesco Barberini in Rome. As a classical scholar Price is particularly remembered for his editions of the works of Apuleius: *Apologia* (Paris, 1635), *Metamorphoses* (Gouda, 1650).

4. 'Ad Posteros', lines 3–4, prefixed to *Olor Iscanus*. Text and translation from Henry Vaughan, *The Complete Poems*, ed. Alan Rudrum (Harmondsworth, 1976), p.63. See Roland Mathias, 'In Search of the Silurist', *Poetry Wales* II.2 (1975), 6–35. For a more positive view of Vaughan as a Welsh writer, see M. Wynn Thomas, *Morgan Llwyd: ei gyfeillion a'i gyfnod* (Caerdydd, 1991), pp.34–50.

5. H. Vaughan, *The Complete Poems*, ed. Rudrum, pp.46–60 (Juvenal), pp.97–107 (Ovid).

6. Ibid., p.355 (*Consolation of Philosophy* III.xii). For all eighteen poems, see pp.111–22, 353–60.

7. Hugh Hughes (ed.), *Barddoniaeth Edward Morris, Perthi Llwydion* (Liverpool, 1902), pp.60–65.

8. Mostyn MS 96 (NLW MS 3027E). The poems are printed in T. Gwynn Jones (ed.), *Llên Cymru. Detholiad o Ryddiaith a Phrydyddiaeth*, Rhan III (Aberystwyth, 1926), pp.21–7.

9. See G. Bullough (ed.), *Philosophical Poems of Henry More* (Manchester, 1931), 'Resolution' (pp.127–30), lines 85–96. Cf. M.-S. Roestvig, *The Happy Man. Studies in the Metamorphoses of a Classical Ideal, 1600–1700* (Oslo, 1954), p.200f.

10. R. Burton, *The Anatomy of Melancholy*, II.ii.5: Everyman's Library, vol.2 (London, 1932), p.102.

11. See p.67 above.

12. Abraham Cowley, *Essays, Plays and Sundry Verses*, ed. A. R. Waller (Cambridge, 1906), pp.399–400 (Seneca), 412–13 (Horace, *Epode* 2).

13. Op.cit. (n.9), p.71.

14. John Dryden, *Preface to Ovid's Epistles* (1680), in W. P. Ker (ed.), *Essays of John Dryden*, vol.1 (Oxford, 1900), p.237.

15. William Baxter (1650–1723) was a fine classical scholar and author of popular editions of Anacreon (1695) and of Horace (1701). On him, and on Moses Williams, see John Davies, *Bywyd a Gwaith Moses Williams* (Caerdydd, 1937). On Lhuyd, see Frank Emery, *Edward Lhuyd, F.R.S., 1660–1709* (Caerdydd, 1971), and on Iaco ap Dewi (James Davies), see Garfield H. Hughes, *Iaco ap Dewi, 1648–1722* (Caerdydd, 1953). For a very useful overview, see G. J. Williams, *Agweddau ar Hanes Dysg Gymraeg*, ed. A. Lewis (Caerdydd, 1969), pp.82–147.

16. See R. I. Aaron, 'Dylanwad Plotinus ar Feddwl Cymru', *Y Llenor*

VII (1928), 115–26; E. Lewis Evans, *Morgan Llwyd* (Lerpwl, 1930), pp.126–7.

17. See Saunders Lewis, *Ysgrifau Dydd Mercher* (Llandysul, 1945), pp.60–64; id., *Meistri'r Canrifoedd*, ed. R. Geraint Gruffydd, pp.172–82; D. Llwyd Morgan, *Ysgrifau Beirniadol* IV (Dinbych, 1969), pp.47–74; id., *Charles Edwards* (Caernarfon, 1994).

18. See Saunders Lewis, *Meistri'r Canrifoedd*, pp.217–24; Gwyn Thomas, *Y Bardd Cwsg a'i Gefndir* (Caerdydd, 1971), pp.175–8.

19. See David Thomas (ed.), introduction to Theophilus Evans, *Drych y Prif Oesoedd, Y Rhan Gyntaf* (Caerdydd, 1955), pp.xxviii–xxxii; Saunders Lewis, *Meistri'r Canrifoedd*, pp.234–6.

20. *Meistri'r Canrifoedd*, p.255, in an important essay on Jeremy Owen. A modern edition of *Golwg ar y Beiau*, with introduction, was prepared by R. T. Jenkins (Caerdydd, 1950).

21. See G. J. Williams, *Traddodiad Llenyddol Morgannwg* (Caerdydd, 1948), pp.241–3.

22. Wrexham and London (1924); reprinted, Bath (1969).

23. D. Gwenallt Jones (ed.), *Blodeugerdd o'r Ddeunawfed Ganrif* (Caerdydd, 1936), pp.5–12.

24. See Saunders Lewis, *Meistri'r Canrifoedd*, pp.225–31; A. D. Carr, *Journal of the Merioneth Historical and Record Society* V (1965/68), 127–32. For some of John Morgan's translations of lines of Latin poetry into Welsh, see NLW Llanstephan MS 15.

25. See *ALMA*, pp.794–807, 'A Catalogue of the Books at Penbryn' (drawn up 1764–5).

26. *A New History of Wales: The Eighteenth Century Renaissance* (Llandybïe, 1981), p.77.

27. Text in Robert Jones (ed.), *The Poetical Works of the Rev. Goronwy Owen (Goronwy Ddu o Fôn), with his Life and Correspondence*. 2 vols. (London, 1876).

28. J. H. Davies (ed.), *The Morris Letters*, vol.1 (Aberystwyth, 1907), p.488f. The version by Lewis Morris is, it is supposed, the 'Lucian's Dialogues by L.M.' which appears in the list of books at L.M.'s home at Penbryn, *ALMA*, p.107 (see n.25 above). On the literary connections between Lewis Morris and Goronwy Owen, see Bedwyr L. Jones, *Ysgrifau Beirniadol* X (1977), pp.290–308.

29. The three poems are numbers 21, 24 and 39 in M. L. West (ed.), *Carmina Anacreontea* (Leipzig, 1984). On the popularity of the *Anacreontea*, see Patricia A. Rosenmeyer, *The Poetics of Imitation: Anacreon and the Anacreontic tradition* (Cambridge, 1992).

30. J. H. Davies (ed.), *The Letters of Goronwy Owen* (Cardiff, 1924), pp.102–5.

31. *Latin and Greek: A History of the Influence of the Classics on English Life from 1600 to 1918* (London, 1964), p.45.

32. *A School of Welsh Augustans*, p.91.

33. D. Gwenallt Jones (ed.), *Blodeugerdd o'r Ddeunawfed Ganrif*, pp.36–8. Translation by Anthony Conran: *PBWV*, pp.213–14; *OBWVE*, pp.134–5.

34. Branwen Jarvis, *Goronwy Owen* (Cardiff, 1986), p.38.

35. J. H. Davies (ed.), *The Letters of Goronwy Owen*, p.112. For the text of Gwalchmai's poem, see *OBWV*, p.24f.

36. J. H. Davies (ed.), *The Letters of Goronwy Owen*, p.116.

37. Ibid., p.155.

38. Ibid., p.130.

39. Ibid., p.7.

40. Ibid., p.61.

41. Ibid., p.74f.

42. D. Gwenallt Jones (ed.), *Blodeugerdd o'r Ddeunawfed Ganrif*, pp.44–9.

43. J. H. Davies (ed.), *The Letters of Goronwy Owen*, p.79f. On this letter, see also Branwen Jarvis, op.cit. (n.34), p.52f.

44. J. H. Davies (ed.), *The Morris Letters*, vol.2 (Aberystwyth, 1909), p.189.

45. John Williams, 'Yr Hen Syr', Edward Richard's successor at Ystradmeurig, in 'A Short Account of the Life of Edward Richard', printed in *The Poetical Works of the late Mr Edward Richard* (London, 1811), p.8. See Aneirin Lewis, *Ysgrifau Beirniadol* X (Dinbych, 1977), pp.267–89; *Dysg a Dawn* [see n.60 below], pp.170–85.

46. Ibid., p.11.

47. Ibid., p.16.

48. *ALMA* 188, p.373.

49. John Williams, op.cit. (n.45), p.21.

50. *ALMA* 287, p.546.

51. *ALMA* 174, p.349.

52. *ALMA* 175, p.350.

53. *A School of Welsh Augustans*, p.82.

54. *ALMA* 335, p.649.

55. See, for example, *ALMA* 204, p.408; 291, p.557.

56. Letter to Lewis Morris, 28 December 1759: *ALMA* 218, p.435.

57. *A School of Welsh Augustans*, p.82.

58. Edward Richard to Lewis Morris, 12 May 1762: *ALMA* 289, p.551.

59. NLW Panton MS 74.142. Transcript by the late Aneirin Lewis. I am most grateful to Mrs Mary Lewis for permission to use Aneirin Lewis's unpublished transcript of letters between Edward Richard and Evan Evans.

60. 'Edward Richard ac Ieuan Fardd', see n.45 above; also ' "Hen Gyrff o Dir Groeg a'r Eidal": Ieuan Fardd a'i Gymdeithion', *Dysg a Dawn: Cyfrol Goffa Aneirin Lewis*, ed. W. A. Mathias and E. W. James (Caerdydd, 1992), pp.186–201.

61. *Dysg a Dawn*, p.185. For the text, see D. Gwenallt Jones (ed.), *Blodeugerdd o'r Ddeunawfed Ganrif*, p.35.

62. See Aneirin Lewis, *Dysg a Dawn*, p.179. The text of the first pastoral is in *OBWV*, pp.286–93, and in D. Gwenallt Jones (ed.), op.cit. (n.61), pp.28–35. For both pastorals, see O. M. Edwards (ed.), *Gwaith Edward Richard o Ystrad Meurig* (Llanuwchllyn, 1912), pp.5–23.

63. *A School of Welsh Augustans*, pp.64ff. See also Tecwyn Ellis, *Y Llenor* XXVII (1948), 173–82.

64. See D. Emrys Evans, *Y Beirniad* (gol. J. Morris-Jones), VII (1917), 252–62.

65. NLW Panton MS 74.141. Transcript by Aneirin Lewis.

66. NLW MS 11729E. Transcript by Aneirin Lewis.

67. 23 July 1764, NLW Panton MS 74.134. Transcript by Aneirin Lewis.

68. 20 June 1768. See D. Silvan Evans (ed.), *Gwaith y Parchedig Evan Evans (Ieuan Brydydd Hir)* (Caernarfon, 1876), p.242.

69. For a discussion of the *Dissertatio de Bardis*, together with an English translation of the text, see Charlotte Johnston, *NLWJ* XXII (1981–2), 64–91.

70. The correspondence of Thomas Percy and Evan Evans, together with an introduction in English, is published in Aneirin Lewis (ed.), *The Percy Letters* (Louisiana, 1957).

71. Op.cit. (n.45), pp.11–12.

72. Letter to Richard Morris, 28 September 1767: *ALMA*, p.724.

73. Letter to Richard Morris, 4 February 1767: *ALMA*, p.683.

74. NLW Panton MS 74.164/5/6. See especially Aneirin Lewis, *Dysg a Dawn*, pp.186–201.

75. *ALMA* 348, p.678.

76. See J. R. Webster, 'Dyheadau'r Bedwaredd Ganrif ar Bymtheg', in Jac L. Williams (gol.), *Addysg i Gymru (Ysgrifau Hanesyddol)*, (Caerdydd, 1966), pp.45–75.

77. See Tecwyn Ellis, *LlC* I (1950–51), 174–84; Geraint H. Jenkins, *Y Chwyldro Ffrengig a Voltaire Cymru* (Darlith Eisteddfodol y Brifysgol, Eisteddfod Genedlaethol Cymru, Llanrwst, 1989).

78. Some of Dic Aberdaron's translations (all into English) from Greek and Latin are preserved in NLW MSS 503–8.

79. Text in Saunders Lewis, *Detholion o Waith Ieuan Glan Geirionydd* (Caerdydd, 1931), pp.60–1. Translation by Anthony Conran: *PBWV*, p.219.

80. See Bedwyr Lewis Jones, '*Yr Hen Bersoniaid Llengar*' (Yr Eglwys yng Nghymru, 1963).

81. See R. T. Jenkins, 'John Peter (Ioan Pedr), 1833–1877', *JWBS* IV (1934), 137–68. On the study of the classical languages and their literature in nineteenth-century Nonconformist colleges, see R. Tudur Jones, 'Diwylliant Colegau Ymneilltuol y Bedwaredd Ganrif ar Bymtheg', in *Ysgrifau Beirniadol* V (1970), pp.112–49.

82. *Y Traethodydd* V (1849), 347; *Traethodau Llenyddol* (Wrexham, 1867), p.20.

83. *Meistri a'u Crefft* (Caerdydd, 1981), pp.97–101.

84. *Y Traethodydd* XX (1865), 136; *Traethodau Llenyddol*, pp.180–81.

85. Works of a classical nature by other authors, published in early issues of *Y Traethodydd*, include a translation into Welsh of Sophocles' *Antigone* (by Owen Jones: XXI, 1866, 171–202) and essays, with translation of selected passages, on Virgil (by John Peter: XXII, 1867, 309–22; XXIII, 1868, 23–36). For a more detailed discussion of Lewis Edwards and Classics, see Ceri Davies, *Y Traethodydd* CXLII (1987), 115–30. More generally, see Trebor Lloyd Evans, *Lewis Edwards, Ei Fywyd a'i Waith* (Abertawe, 1967).

Notes to Chapter V

1. From 'The Classics and the Man of Letters' (Classical Association Presidential Address, 1942). Reprinted in T. S. Eliot, *Selected Prose*, ed. J. Hayward (Harmondsworth, 1953), p.224f.

2. *Y Faner*, 7 Mehefin 1950. Reprinted in *Meistri a'u Crefft* (Caerdydd, 1981), p.189.

3. See M. L. Clarke, *Classical Education in Britain, 1500–1900* (Cambridge, 1959), pp.74–127.

4. See especially Richard Jenkyns, *The Victorians and Ancient Greece* (Oxford, 1980) and Frank M. Turner, *The Greek Heritage in Victorian Britain* (New Haven and London, 1981).

5. See Wynford Davies, *The Curriculum and Organization of the County Intermediate Schools, 1880–1926* (Cardiff, 1989), p.60.

6. See R. Tudur Jones, in *Ysgrifau Beirniadol* V (Dinbych, 1970), pp.126–30.

7. 'Wel be ar affeth hon y ddaear sy eisio dysgu iaith pobol wedi marw?': *Rhys Lewis* (1885), ed. E. G. Millward (Caerdydd, 1993), p.342.

8. *Hanes Athroniaeth y Groegiaid* (Conwy, 1899).

9. Gildas, *De Excidio Britanniae, Fragmenta, Liber de Paenitentia, etc.* (London, Hon. Society of Cymmrodorion, two volumes, 1899–1901); *Christianity in Early Britain* (Oxford, 1912).

10. 'Y pethau hyny sydd o'r golwg wrth wraidd pob celfyddyd': *Traethodau Llenyddol* (Wrexham, 1867), p.189. See also J. Gwynn Williams, *The University Movement in Wales* (A History of the University of Wales, Volume 1: Cardiff, 1993), p.34f.

11. See E. L. Ellis, *The University College of Wales, Aberystwyth, 1872–1972* (Cardiff, 1972), pp.36–41.

12. For details, see D. Emrys Evans, *The University of Wales, A Historical Sketch* (Cardiff, 1953), pp.156, 162.

13. For a fine appreciation of T. F. Roberts, see David Williams, *Thomas Francis Roberts, 1860–1919: A Centenary Lecture* (Cardiff, 1961).

14. See J. Gwynn Williams, *The University College of North Wales: Foundations, 1884–1927* (Cardiff, 1985), pp.130–32. E. V. Arnold, together with R. S. Conway, Professor of Latin in Cardiff, produced – partly on the basis of experience of teaching in Wales – an important document on the pronunciation of the classical languages: *The Restored Pronunciation of Greek and Latin: with Tables and Practical Explanations* (Cambridge University Press, 1895). The obvious folly of trying to teach Welsh students to adopt the pronunciation used in Victorian England provided the impetus for their scheme.

15. See A. G. Geen, 'The Teaching of Classics in the Schools of England and Wales in the Twentieth Century': M.Ed. (Wales) thesis (Cardiff, 1974); Wynford Davies, op.cit. (n.5), pp.84–6.

16. For a trenchant expression of such a view by one of the greatest scholars produced by the system, see G. J. Williams, *JWBS* IX (1958–65), 152–61.

17. *Cymysgadw* (Dinbych, 1986), pp.55–60.

18. Jan Morris (ed.), *The Oxford Book of Oxford* (Oxford, 1978), p.237.

19. See R. Telfryn Pritchard, 'Dinistr Caerdroea a Dinistr Jerusalem', in *Ysgrifau Beirniadol* IX (Dinbych, 1976), pp.13–32. On the cultural background, see Hywel Teifi Edwards, *The Eisteddfod* (Cardiff, 1990).

20. Text from M. Walters (ed.), *Yr Ail 'Storm' gan Islwyn* (Caerdydd, 1990), p.5f. Translation by Anthony Conran, *PBWV* p.224.

21. *Yr Alcestis gan Euripides: Chwareugerdd Roegaidd wedi ei throi i'r Gymraeg* gan (a) Proffeswr D. Rowlands, BA (Dewi Môn) a'r (b) Parch. D. E. Edwardes, MA (Llundain, 1887). One of the unsuccessful entries was by Daniel Rees, later to become well known as translator of selections from Dante's *Divine Comedy* (*Dwyfol Gân Dante*, 1903): his translation of *Alcestis* was also privately published (Trübner and Son, London [1887]).

22. *Iliad Homer.* Cyfieithiadau gan R. Morris Lewis, gyda Chwanegiadau, Rhagair a Nodiadau gan T. Gwynn Jones (Wrecsam, 1928).

23. Bangor, Jarvis and Foster, 1900.

24. *Cerdd Dafod, sef Celfyddyd Barddoniaeth Gymraeg* (Oxford, 1925), p.4.

25. Ibid., p.5.

26. Ibid., pp.13–14.

27. On John Morris-Jones's classical education, see J. E. Caerwyn Williams, *THSC*, 1965, 194–204; on W. J. Gruffydd's classical schooling, see J. Ifor Davies, *The Caernarvon County School: A History* (Caernarfon, 1989), pp.86–8; on T. Gwynn Jones and classical literature, see D. Jenkins, *Thomas Gwynn Jones, Cofiant* (Dinbych, 1973), pp.131f., 187.

28. *Caniadau* (1934), p.111; translation by Anthony Conran, *PBWV*, p.234; *OBWVE*, p.150.

29. Dyfnallt Morgan, *Rhyw Hanner Ieuenctid* (Abertawe, 1971), pp.23, 153 (n.8).

30. *Lloffion* (1942), p.89.

31. Neither 'Y Rhufeiniaid', *Synfyfyrion* (1937), p.82 nor 'Cesar', *Myfyrdodau* (1957), p.117 presents an admiring view of Roman imperial achievement.

32. *Telynegion*, pp.42–5 ('Endymion'), pp.79–80 ('Circe'). See Alun Llywelyn-Williams, *Y Nos, Y Niwl a'r Ynys* (Caerdydd, 1960), esp. pp.118–28.

33. Alafon, W. J. Gruffydd, Eifion Wyn, *Eisteddfod Genedlaethol Bangor, 1902: Yr Awdl, Y Bryddest a'r Telynegion (ail-oreu)* (Caernarfon), pp.56–92; revised version, *Caneuon a Cherddi* (Bangor, 1906), pp.75–100. See also Alun Llywelyn-Williams, op.cit. (n.32), pp.35–9.

34. Op.cit. (n.33) (1902), p.62.

35. See R. Jenkyns, *The Victorians and Ancient Greece*, p.175.

36. E. B. Browning, *Poems* (4th edition), vol.1 (London, 1856), pp.150–63.

37. Algernon Charles Swinburne, *Poems* (London: J. M. Dent, 1940), pp.30–5. The words 'Vicisti Galilaee', which form the subtitle of Swinburne's poem, were supposed by some Christians to be the dying words of the Emperor Julian, 'the Apostate'.

38. See T. Robin Chapman, *W. J. Gruffydd* (Caerdydd, 1993), esp. pp.73–84.

39. Alan Llwyd, *Gwae Fi Fy Myw: Cofiant Hedd Wyn* (Barddas, 1991), pp.331–403. See also William Morris, *Hedd Wyn* (Caernarfon, 1969), esp. pp.82–92; Derwyn Jones, in *Ysgrifau Beirniadol* VI (Dinbych, 1971), pp.197–231.

40. Hedd Wyn, *Cerddi'r Bugail* (Wrecsam, 1931), p.134; new edition (Caerdydd, 1994), p.115.

41. Catullus 8, in *Telynegion* (1900), p.89f.; *Antigone* (Caerdydd, Gwasg Prifysgol Cymru, 1950).

42. *Manion* (1930), pp.115–19.

43. Cyfres y Werin, Rhif 15 (Wrecsam, 1927).

44. *The Origin of the Welsh Englyn and Kindred Metres*, *Y Cymmrodor* XVIII (1905). See also D. Emrys Evans, 'Yr Epigram a'r Englyn', in *Y Llenor* I (1922), 158–86; J. G. F. Powell, 'Yr Epigram Groeg a'r Englyn Cymraeg', in *Y Traethodydd* CXXXVIII (1983), 59–71.

45. See Stephen J.Williams, *Y Llenor* XXVIII (1949), 134–40.

46. Many of H. Parry-Jones's translations are included in *Cerddi o'r Lladin* (1962) and *Cerddi Groeg Clasurol* (1989): see n.51 below. I am indebted to John Ellis Jones, an old pupil of Llanrwst School, for providing me with information about H. Parry-Jones.

47. R. Telfryn Pritchard (ed.), *Agamemnon gan Aischulos* (Cyfieithwyd gan John Henry Jones); *Alcestis gan Ewripides* (Cyfieithwyd gan Henry Parry-Jones) (Aberystwyth: Y Ganolfan Astudiaethau Addysg). A collection of other work by John Henry Jones, including translations from Greek and Latin and some poems on classical themes, was edited by Gareth Alban Davies, *Cardi o Fôn: Detholion o Gerddi a Throsiadau John Henry Jones* (Aberystwyth, 1991).

48. *Amddiffyniad Socrates* (1936), *Phaedon* (1938), *Ewthuffron, Criton* (1943), *Gorgias* (1946), *Y Wladwriaeth* (1956) – all from University of Wales Press.

49. *Straeon Tad Hanes, sef Pigion o Waith Herodotos* (Caerdydd, 1954).

50. *Cofiant Agricola, Llywodraethwr Prydain* (Caerdydd).

51. Both works published by the University of Wales Press (acting, in the case of *Cerddi Groeg Clasurol*, on behalf of Yr Academi Gymreig).

52. *Aristoteles: Barddoneg*. Cyfieithiad gyda Rhagymadrodd a Nodiadau (Caerdydd, 1978).

53. B. R. Rees, in *Classical Review* XXX (1980), 150.

54. Caerdydd, Gwasg Prifysgol Cymru (1998).

55. Pyramus and Thisbe: *Baner ac Amserau Cymru* (22 December 1948), and subsequently in *Siwan a Cherddi Eraill*, pp.27–30. Baucis and Philemon: *Trivium* VIII (1973), 37–9. Both translations are included in R. Geraint Gruffydd (ed.), *Cerddi Saunders Lewis* (Gwasg Gregynog, 1986; Gwasg Prifysgol Cymru, 1992).

56. *Y Brodyr* (Caerdydd, 1974).

57. *Y Traethodydd* CXXXVIII (1983), 147–55, 208–15. A. M. Thomas also produced a translation of Augustine's *Confessions*, Books 1–10, *Cyffesion Awstin Sant* (Caernarfon, 1973).

58. Euros Bowen also has a prose translation of the Greek text of the treatise on the Incarnation by the fourth-century Bishop of Alexandria,

St Athanasius: *De Incarnatione (Ymgnawdoliad y Gair) Athanasios* (Caernarfon, 1976).

59. Caerdydd, Gwasg Prifysgol Cymru, 1975.

60. *Aenëis Fyrsil: Y Llyfr Cyntaf (Cyflwyniad ar Gynghanedd Rydd)* (Bala, 1983).

61. All from University of Wales Press, the first three on behalf of the Welsh Arts Council.

62. Saunders Lewis, *Letters to Margaret Gilcriest* (Cardiff, 1993), p.301.

63. *Siwan a Cherddi Eraill* (Llandybïe, 1956), pp.40, 74.

64. See J. Gwilym Jones, *Swyddogaeth Beirniadaeth* (Dinbych, 1977), pp.9–33, 50f.

65. *Y Llyffantod, Drama mewn Pedair Golygfa* (Dinbych, 1973).

66. *Eisteddfod Genedlaethol Frenhinol Cymru, Maldwyn 1965: Cyfansoddiadau a Beirniadaethau*, pp.63–80.

67. *Llywelyn Fawr, Drama mewn Tair Act ac Epilog* (Lerpwl, 1954).

68. *Cerddi Cynan, Y Casgliad Cyflawn* (1959), pp.178–84.

69. Llandysul, Gwasg Gomer, 1984.

70. *Y Llawr Dyrnu. Naw Stori Fer* (Aberystwyth, 1930), pp.33–9. See Huw Ethall, *R. G. Berry. Dramodydd, Llenor, Gweinidog* (Abertawe, 1985), pp.71–5.

71. For example, volumes by Juli Phillips (Gwasg y Dref Wen), and *Chwedlau Rhyfeddol Gwlad Groeg* (Llandysul, 1987). Notable also are Derec Llwyd Morgan's radio adaptation of the *Iliad, Iliad Homer* (Llandysul, 1976) and Hilma Lloyd Edwards's *Y Llwybr Disglair* (Llandysul, 1982), a novel for children which is set in Roman Wales.

72. *Cerddi'r Gaeaf* (1952), pp.74, 77.

73. *Sonedau a Thelynegion* (1950), pp.13, 56.

74. *Siwan a Cherddi Eraill* (1956), pp.13–15.

75. Saunders Lewis, *Amlyn ac Amig: Comedi* (Aberystwyth, 1940), p.26. Translation by Joseph P. Clancy, *The Plays of Saunders Lewis* vol.1 (Llandybïe, 1985), p.20.

76. *Baner ac Amserau Cymru*, 31 May 1939. Saunders Lewis, in a letter to Kate Roberts, 21 November 1947, says that Virgil was part of his daily reading: 'rhyw hanner awr o Ladin bob dydd yn rheolaidd rhag imi ei golli, byddaf felly'n mynd trwy Fyrsil bob blwyddyn.' (Dafydd Ifans, gol., *Annwyl Kate, Annwyl Saunders: Gohebiaeth 1923–1983* (Aberystwyth, 1992), p.137f.)

77. *Cinio'r Cythraul* (1946), p.16.

78. *Cerddi Cairo* (1969), p.12; *Cerddi'r Holl Eneidiau* (1981), p.31.

79. 'Mair Fadlen', *Siwan a Cherddi Eraill*, pp.24–6. Translation by Joseph P. Clancy, *Saunders Lewis: Selected Poems* (Cardiff, 1993), pp.23–5. For discussion of Niobe and Orpheus in the poem, see J. G. F. Powell, *LlC* XV (1984–6), 166. Two outstanding readings of the poem as a whole are R. Geraint Gruffydd, 'Mair Fadlen: Dadansoddiad', in J. E. Caerwyn Williams (ed.), *Llên Doe a Heddiw* (Dinbych, 1964), pp.44–50, and Bobi Jones, 'Cerdd Fwya'r Ganrif?', *Barddas* 142 (1989), 8–12, both included in M. Hughes (ed.), *Saunders Lewis y Bardd* (Dinbych, 1993).

80. 'Y Sipsi', *Eples* (1951), p.36; 'Amser', *Eples*, p.46; Minotaur: *Cnoi Cil*

(1942), p.18, *Eples*, p.21; Icarus: *Gwreiddiau* (1959), p.97; *Eples*, p.55.

81. Philip Larkin, *Required Writing. Miscellaneous Prose, 1955–1982* (London, 1983), p.185.

82. D. Gwenallt Jones: *Ysgubau'r Awen* (1938), pp.53, 71; William Jones: *Adar Rhiannon a Cherddi Eraill* (1947), p.59, *Sonedau a Thelynegion*, pp.49–50; Pennar Davies: *Y Tlws yn y Lotws* (1971), p.45f.; J. Gwyn Griffiths: *Yr Efengyl Dywyll a Cherddi Eraill* (1944), pp.16, 27.

83. *Siwan a Cherddi Eraill*, pp.13–15. The translation by Joseph P. Clancy (see n.75), pp.31–3, is used throughout, with some alterations (mainly from Gwyn Thomas's translation, in Alun R. Jones and Gwyn Thomas, *Presenting Saunders Lewis* (1973), pp.186–9). For discussion of this poem, see Ceri Davies, *LlC* XII (1972), 57–60; John Rowlands, in R. Geraint Gruffydd (ed.), *Bardos. Penodau . . . cyflwynedig i J. E. Caerwyn Williams* (Caerdydd, 1982), pp.111–27. On Saunders Lewis's classicism in general, see J. Gwyn Griffiths, in *Barn* (Rhif 273, Hydref 1985), 381–4.

84. Translation by D. A. West, *Virgil: The Aeneid* (Harmondsworth, 1990), p.140.

85. *Aeneid* VI.616–17. Translation by D. A. West, p.151.

86. *OBWV* 36, pp.45–9. Translation by Anthony Conran, *PBWV*, p.128, with one alteration.

87. *Dail Pren* (Aberystwyth, 1957), p.40. See R. Geraint Gruffydd in *Y Traethodydd* CXXVI (1971), 292–5.

88. *Cerddi Malltraeth* (Abertawe, 1978), pp.41–8.

89. *Cerddi Caradog Prichard, Y Casgliad Cyflawn* (1979), pp.91–4.

90. *Barddoniaeth Rhydwen Williams. Y Casgliad Cyflawn, 1941–1991* (1991), pp.71–2. Translation in R. Gerallt Jones, *Poetry of Wales 1930–1970* (Llandysul, 1974), pp.284–7. See also Alan Llwyd, *Barddoniaeth y Chwedegau* (Barddas, 1986), pp.569–72.

91. *Ffroenau'r Ddraig* (1961), p.42. Translation in R. Gerallt Jones, op.cit. (n.90), p.249.

92. *Eples*, p.39; *Gwreiddiau*, pp.94, 95, 89. For a fine study of Gwenallt's 'Promethews', see D. Llwyd Morgan in *Y Traethodydd* CXXIV (1969), 84–9. Cf. also Gwenallt's autobiographical novel *Ffwrneisiau* (Llandysul, 1982), where the fire in the furnaces of the iron and steel works is likened (p.15) to Prometheus' fire ('y tân a ddygodd Promethews oddi ar Zews a'i ddefnyddio i'w bwrpas ei hun').

93. *Eples*, p.26; *OBWV*, p.477. I follow Sir Thomas Parry in reading *a'i gwaredo* in the last line (not *a'u gwaredo*, 'save them', as in *Eples*).

94. Gotthold Ephraim Lessing, *Laokoon, oder über die Grenzen der Malerei und Poesie* (1766).

95. Gwenallt also makes use of the Laocoon story in an earlier, and more overtly religious, poem, 'Y Sarff' ('The Serpent') (*Ysgubau'r Awen*, p.99), where the initial impulse comes from Genesis, chapter 3. Professor Geraint Gruffydd has suggested to me that 'Cymru' may be open to a more allegorical interpretation than I give it: e.g., that the serpents may represent the twin forces of imperialism and materialism, and that Saunders Lewis may be implicit in the figure of Laocoon.

96. *Buarth Bywyd* (Caernarfon, 1986), pp.80, 81.

97. Euros Bowen gave an interpretation, with translations, of the work of the French Symbolists in *Beirdd Simbolaidd Ffrainc* (Caerdydd, 1980).

98. 'Gwragedd'. Two versions of this poem were published, in *O'r Corn Aur* and in *O Bridd i Bridd*.

99. 'Micenai', *Cylch o Gerddi*, p.75f. The English translation printed here is Euros Bowen's own version, from *Poems* (1974).

100. *Elfennau* (1972), p.12; Euros Bowen's translation, *Poems*, p.111.

101. Cf. Bowen's comparison of Mallarmé's approach and the Platonic doctrine of Ideas, *Beirdd Simbolaidd Ffrainc*, p.6.

102. *Gwynt yn y Canghennau*, p.80.

103. *GDG* 28.21.

104. *Buarth Bywyd*, pp.16–17.

105. For a fuller discussion of the classical dimension in Euros Bowen's work, see Ceri Davies, 'Euros Bowen a'r Clasuron Groeg a Lladin', in *Taliesin* 78/79 (1992), 87–105. Cf. also J. Gwyn Griffiths, *I Ganol y Frwydr* (Llandybïe, 1970), 124–8.

106. 'I Gofio yr Athro Emeritws E. D. T. Jenkins', *Y Coed* (1969), p.18.

107. Huw Thomas (ed.), *Geiriadur Lladin–Cymraeg* (Caerdydd, Gwasg Prifysgol Cymru, 1979). See also Huw Thomas in *Rhydfelen: Y Deng Mlynedd Cyntaf* (Llandysul, 1973), pp.76–85.

108. *Eisteddfod Genedlaethol Dyffryn Lliw, 1980: Cyfansoddiadau a Beirniadaethau*, pp.20–7; also in Donald Evans, *Eden* (Llandysul, 1981), pp.51–60. Similar striking use of classical myths is made by Donald Evans in a cycle of poems on the year's seasons as reflected in rivers, 'Drychluniau o Dymhorau'r Dŵr', *Egin* (Llandysul, 1976), pp.38–43.

109. *Hunllef Arthur* (Cyhoeddiadau Barddas, 1986); 'Portread o Athro Ysgol', *Rhwng Taf a Thaf* (Llandybïe, 1960), p.14.

110. 'Orffews', *Marwnad o Dirdeunaw, a rhai cerddi eraill* (1982), p.29.

111. *Iliad*: 'Hiliogaeth Cain', *Ysgyrion Gwaed* (Dinbych, 1968), pp.28–9, 'Arwrol', *Gwelaf Afon* (Dinbych, 1990), p.42; Sophocles: 'Cwestiwn', *Ysgyrion Gwaed*, p.47; Catullus: 'Yn y Sêr', *Croesi Traeth* (Dinbych, 1978), p.17.

112. *Bacchai, gan Ewripides. Deialog Gymraeg.* Cyfaddasiad Gareth Miles (Aberystwyth: Y Ganolfan Astudiaethau Addysg, 1991).

113. *Y Golau Caeth* (1972), pp.58–9. Translation by Joseph P. Clancy, *Twentieth Century Welsh Poems* (1982), pp.213–14.

Bibliography

References to source-material and to secondary discussions have been included in the notes to the individual chapters of this book. The purpose of this bibliography is to indicate the main works on which the author relied and also to offer suggestions for further reading on some of the book's main themes.

1 The Classical Tradition

Binns, J. W., *Intellectual Culture in Elizabethan and Jacobean England: The Latin Writings of the Age* (Leeds, 1990).

Bolgar, R. R., *The Classical Heritage and its Beneficiaries* (Cambridge, 1954).

——(ed.), *Classical Influences on European Culture, AD500–1500* (Cambridge, 1971).

——(ed.), *Classical Influences on European Culture, AD1500–1700* (Cambridge, 1976).

——(ed.), *Classical Influences on Western Thought, AD1650–1870* (Cambridge, 1979).

Bradner, L., *Musae Anglicanae: A History of Anglo-Latin Poetry, 1500–1925* (New York and London, 1940).

Brink, C. O., *English Classical Scholarship* (Cambridge, 1986).

Clarke, M. L., *Classical Education in Britain, 1500–1900* (Cambridge, 1959).

——, *Greek Studies in England, 1700–1830* (Cambridge, 1945).

Curtius, E. R., *European Literature and the Latin Middle Ages*, trans. by W. R. Trask (New York, 1953).

Erskine-Hill, H., *The Augustan Idea in English Literature* (London, 1983).

Finley, M. I. (ed.), *The Legacy of Greece. A New Appraisal* (Oxford, 1981).

Griffin, J., *The Mirror of Myth. Classical Themes and Variations* (London, 1986).

Grimal, P., *The Dictionary of Classical Mythology*, trans. by A. R. Maxwell-Hyslop (Oxford, 1985).

Highet, G., *The Classical Tradition. Greek and Roman Influences on Western Literature* (Oxford, 1949).

Howatson, M. C. (ed.), *The Oxford Companion to Classical Literature*, second edition (first edition by P. Harvey), (Oxford, 1989).

Jenkyns, R., *The Victorians and Ancient Greece* (Oxford, 1980).

——(ed.), *The Legacy of Rome. A New Appraisal* (Oxford, 1992).

Kristeller, P. O., *Renaissance Thought and its Sources* (New York, 1979).

Les Études classiques aux XIXe et XXe siècles: leur place dans l'histoire des idées (Fondation Hardt: Entretiens sur l'Antiquité Classique, Tome XXVI) (Genève, 1980).

Lloyd-Jones, H., *Blood for the Ghosts. Classical Influences in the Nineteenth and Twentieth Centuries* (London, 1982).

Martindale, J. (ed.), *English Humanism, Wyatt to Cowley* (London, 1985).

Ogilvie, R. M., *Latin and Greek. A History of the Influence of the Classics on English Life from 1600 to 1918* (London, 1964).

Pfeiffer, R., *History of Classical Scholarship, 1300–1850* (Oxford, 1976).

Reynolds, L. D. *et al.*, *Texts and Transmission. A Survey of the Latin Classics* (Oxford, 1983).

—— and Wilson, N.G., *Scribes and Scholars. A Guide to the Transmission of Greek and Latin Literature*, third edition. (Oxford, 1991).

Rigg, A. G., *A History of Anglo-Latin Literature, 1066–1422* (Cambridge, 1992).

Sandys, J. E., *A History of Classical Scholarship*, three volumes (Cambridge, 1908–21).

Stanford, W. B., *Ireland and the Classical Tradition* (Dublin, 1976).

Turner, F. M., *The Greek Heritage in Victorian Britain* (New Haven and London, 1981).

Weiss, R., *The Renaissance Discovery of Classical Antiquity*, second edition (Oxford, 1988).

2   Welsh History and Culture
(Works in English, or in both English and Welsh)

Bywgraffiadur Cymreig hyd 1940, ed. J. E. Lloyd, R. T. Jenkins, W. Ll. Davies (London, 1953). English version, *The Dictionary of Welsh Biography down to 1940* (London, 1959).

Davies, John, *Hanes Cymru* (Harmondsworth, 1990). English version, *A History of Wales* (Harmondsworth, 1993).

Davies, R. R., *Conquest, Coexistence and Change. Wales 1063–1415* (Oxford, 1987).

Davies, Wendy, *Wales in the Early Middle Ages* (Leicester, 1982).

Humphreys, Emyr, *The Taliesin Tradition. A Quest for the Welsh Identity* (London, 1983).

Jenkins, Geraint H., *The Foundations of Modern Wales. Wales 1642–1780* (Oxford, 1987).

Jenkins, Philip, *A History of Modern Wales, 1536–1990* (London, 1992).

Jones, E. J., *Education in Wales during the Middle Ages* (Swansea, 1947).

Jones, J. Graham, *The History of Wales: A Pocket Guide* (Cardiff, 1990).

Jones, J. Gwynfor, *Early Modern Wales, c.1525–1640* (London, 1994).

——, *Wales and the Tudor State. Government, Religious Change and the Social Order, 1534–1603* (Cardiff, 1989).

Jones, R. Brinley, *'Certain Scholars of Wales': The Welsh Experience in Education* (Llanwrda, 1986).

Lloyd, J. E., *A History of Wales, from the Earliest Times to the Edwardian Conquest*, two volumes (London, 1911).

Morgan, K. O., *Rebirth of a Nation. Wales 1880–1980* (Oxford, 1981).

Morgan, Prys T. J., *The Eighteenth Century Renaissance* (Llandybïe, 1981).

—— and Thomas, D., *Wales, The Shaping of a Nation* (Newton Abbott, 1984).

Morris, John, *The Age of Arthur. A History of the British Isles from 350 to 650* (London, 1973).

Roderick, A. J. (ed.), *Wales through the Ages.* 2 volumes (Llandybïe, 1959, 1960).

Walker, David, *Medieval Wales* (Cambridge, 1990).

Williams, David, *A History of Modern Wales* (London, 1950).

Williams, Glanmor, *Recovery, Reorientation and Reformation. Wales c.1415–1642* (Oxford, 1987).

——, *Religion, Language and Nationality in Wales* (Cardiff, 1979).

——, *The Welsh Church, from Conquest to Reformation* (Cardiff, 1962; revised edition, 1976).

——, *Welsh Reformation Essays* (Cardiff, 1967).

Williams, Gwyn A., *When Was Wales?* (Harmondsworth, 1985).

Williams, J. L. and Hughes, G. R. (eds.), *The History of Education in Wales* (Llandybïe, 1978).

3 Welsh Literature

a. Some modern anthologies and collections of texts

Blodeugerddi *Barddas* (*Barddas* anthologies), 'Cyfres y Canrifoedd':

Johnston, Dafydd R., *Blodeugerdd Barddas o'r Bedwaredd Ganrif ar Ddeg* (1989).

Jones, R. M., *Blodeugerdd Barddas o'r Bedwaredd Ganrif ar Bymtheg* (1988).

Lake, A. Cynfael, *Blodeugerdd Barddas o Ganu Caeth y Ddeunawfed Ganrif* (1993).

Lloyd, Nesta, *Blodeugerdd Barddas o'r Ail Ganrif ar Bymtheg*, cyfrol 1 (1993).

Millward, E. G., *Blodeugerdd Barddas o Gerddi Rhydd y Ddeunawfed Ganrif* (1991).

Ap Gwilym, Gwynn and Llwyd, Alan, *Blodeugerdd o Farddoniaeth Gymraeg yr Ugeinfed Ganrif* (Llandysul, 1987).

Davies, Ceri, *Rhagymadroddion a Chyflwyniadau Lladin, 1551–1632* (Caerdydd, 1980).

Hughes, Garfield H., *Rhagymadroddion, 1547–1659* (Caerdydd, 1951).

Jones, Bedwyr Lewis, *Blodeugerdd o'r Bedwaredd Ganrif ar Bymtheg* (Aberystwyth, 1965).

Jones, D.Gwenallt, *Blodeugerdd o'r Ddeunawfed Ganrif* (Caerdydd, 1936).

Lloyd, Nesta and Owen, Morfydd E., *Drych yr Oesoedd Canol* (Caerdydd, 1986).

Parry, Thomas, *The Oxford Book of Welsh Verse* (Oxford, 1962).
Rhyddiaith Gymraeg, three volumes (Caerdydd, 1954, 1956, 1988).

b. Some translations (relevant to this book) of Welsh literature

Bowen, Euros, *Poems* (Llandysul, 1974).
Bromwich, Rachel, *Dafydd ap Gwilym, A Selection of Poems* (Llandysul, 1982).
Clancy, Joseph P., *Medieval Welsh Lyrics* (London, 1965).
——, *Saunders Lewis, Selected Poems* (Cardiff, 1993).
——, *The Plays of Saunders Lewis*, four volumes (Llandybïe, 1985, 1986).
——, *Twentieth Century Welsh Poems* (Llandysul, 1982).
Conran, Anthony, *The Penguin Book of Welsh Verse* (Harmondsworth, 1967) .
Johnston, Dafydd R., *Iolo Goch: Poems* (Llandysul, 1993).
Jones, Alun R. and Thomas, Gwyn, *Presenting Saunders Lewis* (Cardiff, 1973).
Jones, Gwyn, *The Oxford Book of Welsh Verse in English* (Oxford, 1977).
Jones, R. Gerallt, *Poetry of Wales, 1930–1970* (Llandysul, 1974).
Loomis, R. M., *Dafydd ap Gwilym, The Poems* (New York, 1982).
Williams, Gwyn, *The Burning Tree. Poems from the first thousand years of Welsh Verse* (London, 1956).

c. Literary studies and histories
(Works in English, or in both English and Welsh)

Bromwich, Rachel, *Aspects of the Poetry of Dafydd ap Gwilym: Collected Papers* (Cardiff, 1986).
——, *Dafydd ap Gwilym*, Writers of Wales Series (Cardiff, 1974).
Charles-Edwards, T. M., *The Welsh Laws*, Writers of Wales Series (Cardiff, 1989).
Davies, W. Beynon, *Thomas Gwynn Jones*, Writers of Wales Series (Cardiff, 1970).
Evans, D. Simon, *Medieval Religious Literature*, Writers of Wales Series (Cardiff, 1986) .
Fulton, Helen, *Dafydd ap Gwilym and the European Context* (Cardiff, 1989).
Griffiths, Bruce, *Saunders Lewis*, Writers of Wales Series (Cardiff. 1979).
James, Allan, *John Morris-Jones*, Writers of Wales Series (Cardiff, 1987).
Jarman, A. O. H., *The Cynfeirdd. Early Welsh Poets and Poetry*, Writers of Wales Series (Cardiff, 1981).
—— and Hughes, G. R. (eds.), *A Guide to Welsh Literature*, two volumes (Swansea, 1976, 1979). Revised edition of volume 1 (Cardiff, 1992).
Jarvis, Branwen, *Goronwy Owen*, Writers of Wales Series (Cardiff, 1986).
Johnston, Dafydd, *The Literature of Wales: A Pocket Guide* (Cardiff, 1994).
Jones, Bedwyr Lewis, *R. Williams Parry*, Writers of Wales Series (Cardiff, 1972).
Jones, R. Brinley, *William Salesbury*, Writers of Wales Series (Cardiff, 1994).

Jones, R. Gerallt, *T. H. Parry-Williams*, Writers of Wales Series (Cardiff, 1978).

Lewis, Saunders, *A School of Welsh Augustans* (Wrexham, 1924; reissued, Bath, 1969).

Morgan, Dyfnallt, *D. Gwenallt Jones*, Writers of Wales Series (Cardiff, 1972).

Morgan, T. J., *W. J. Gruffydd*, Writers of Wales Series (Cardiff, 1970).

Parry, Thomas, *Hanes Llenyddiaeth Gymraeg hyd 1900* (Caerdydd, 1945). English version, translated by H. I. Bell, *A History of Welsh Literature* (Oxford, 1955).

Roberts, Brynley F., *Gerald of Wales*, Writers of Wales Series (Cardiff, 1982).

Stephens, Meic (ed.), *The Oxford Companion to the Literature of Wales* (Oxford, 1986). Welsh version: *Cydymaith i Lenyddiaeth Cymru* (Caerdydd, 1986).

Williams, Gwyn, *An Introduction to Welsh Literature*, Writers of Wales Series (Cardiff, 1978).

Williams, J. E. Caerwyn, *The Poets of the Welsh Princes*, Writers of Wales Series (Cardiff, 1978).

4   Works Relating to the Classical Tradition in Wales

No book-length study of Wales and the Greek and Latin Classics has before been written. Listed here are some books, articles and lectures which treat aspects of the subject. The most important contributions are those of Saunders Lewis, who – although he did not set out to study the classical tradition as such – constantly cast shafts of penetrating light upon that tradition in all periods of Welsh literature.

Davies, Alun Eirug, 'Cyfieithiadau i'r Gymraeg o Ieithoedd Estron ac eithrio Saesneg', *JWBS* X (1966–71), 153–77, esp. 154–5, 165–7, 168–71.

Davies, Ceri, 'Dyneiddwyr Cymru ac Ewrop', *Cof Cenedl* VII, ed. G. H. Jenkins (Llandysul, 1992), 31–61.

——, 'Dysg Ddyneiddiol Cyfieithwyr y Beibl', *LlC* XVI (1989), 7–22.

——, 'Erasmus and Welsh Renaissance Learning', *THSC* , 1983, 48–55.

——, 'Euros Bowen a'r Clasuron Groeg a Lladin', *Taliesin* 78/79 (1992), 87–105.

——, 'Heracleitos: Tri Fersiwn', *Y Traethodydd* CXXVII (1972), 14–18.

——, *Latin Writers of the Renaissance*, Writers of Wales Series (Cardiff, 1981).

——, 'Lewis Edwards, Oes Victoria a'r Byd Clasurol', *Y Traethodydd* CXLII (1987), 115–30.

——, 'Llenyddiaeth Gymraeg yr Ugeinfed Ganrif a'r Clasuron Groeg a Lladin', *EA* LI (1988), 47–70.

——, 'Marwnad Syr John Edward Lloyd a Fyrsil, *Aeneid* VI', *LlC* XII (1972), 57–60. Reissued in M. Hughes (ed.), *Saunders Lewis y Bardd* (Dinbych, 1993), 46–50.

——, 'The 1588 Translation of the Bible and the World of Renaissance Learning', *Ceredigion, Journal of the Ceredigion Antiquarian Society* XI (1988–9), 1–18.

Evans, D. Emrys, 'Edward Richard', *Y Beirniad* (gol. J. Morris-Jones) VII (1917), 252–62.

——, *Y Clasuron yng Nghymru*. Darlith Radio'r BBC, 1952. (Llundain, 1952).

——, 'Yr Epigram a'r Englyn', *Y Llenor* I (1922), 158–86.

Griffiths, J. Gwyn, 'Clasuriaeth Saunders Lewis', *Barn*, Rhif 273 (Hydref 1985), 381–4.

——, *I Ganol y Frwydr: Efrydiau Llenyddol* (Llandybïe, 1970).

——, prefaces to *Cerddi o'r Lladin* (Caerdydd, 1962), *Aristoteles: Barddoneg* (Caerdydd, 1978), *Cerddi Groeg Clasurol* (Caerdydd, 1989).

Jones, E. J., 'Lladin a'r Famiaith yng Nghyfnod y Dadeni', *LlC* IX (1966), 33–45.

Jones, J. J., 'A Bibliography of Translations into Welsh from Foreign Languages (other than English), up to 1928', *JWBS* IV (1932–6), 271–303: Classical Greek, 283–7; Classical Latin, 290–94. Supplement, by I. Lewis, *JWBS* V (1937–42), 231–6, esp.234–5.

Lewis, Saunders, *Braslun o Hanes Llenyddiaeth Gymraeg: I* (Caerdydd, 1932).

——, *Meistri a'u Crefft*, gol. Gwynn ap Gwilym (Caerdydd, 1981).

——, *Meistri'r Canrifoedd*, gol. R. Geraint Gruffydd (Caerdydd, 1973).

——, *Ysgrifau Dydd Mercher* (Llandysul, 1945).

Powell, J. G. F., 'Dylanwadau Clasurol mewn Barddoniaeth Gymraeg Ddiweddar', *LlC* XV (1984–6), 159–71.

——, 'Yr Epigram Groeg a'r Englyn', *Y Traethodydd* CXXXVIII (1983), 59–71.

Pritchard, R. Telfryn, 'Deugain mlynedd a mwy o glasura', *Y Traethodydd* CXLVI (1991), 119–26.

5 Further Bibliographical Guides

Further guidance may be found in:

Carlsen, H., *A Bibliography to the Classical Tradition in English Literature* (Copenhagen, 1985).

Ijsewijn, J., *Companion to Neo-Latin Studies* (Amsterdam, New York and Oxford, 1977).

——, 2nd ed., *Companion to Neo-Latin Studies, Part I: History and Diffusion of Neo-Latin Literature* (Leuven, 1990).

Jones, Philip H., *A Bibliography of the History of Wales*, third edition (handbook and microfiches) (Cardiff, 1989).

Lapidge, M. and Sharpe, R., *A Bibliography of Celtic-Latin Literature 400–1200* (Dublin, 1985).

Marouzeau, J. (fond.), *L'Année philologique: bibliographie critique et analytique de l'antiquité Gréco-Latine* (Paris, published annually).

Contains sections on the history of classical scholarship and tradition.

Parry, Thomas and Morgan, Merfyn, *Llyfryddiaeth Llenyddiaeth Gymraeg* (Caerdydd, 1976).

Pollard, A. W. and Redgrave, G. R., *A Short-title Catalogue of Books Printed in England, Scotland and Ireland, and of English Books Printed Abroad, 1475–1640*, second edition, three volumes (London, 1976, 1986, 1991).

Rees, Eiluned, *Libri Walliae: A Catalogue of Welsh Books and Books Printed in Wales, 1546–1820*, two volumes (Aberystwyth, 1987).

Watts, G. O., *Llyfryddiaeth Llenyddiaeth Gymraeg, Cyfrol 2 (1976–1986)* (Caerdydd & Aberystwyth, 1993).

Year's Work in Modern Language Studies: contains sections on Medieval Latin and Neo-Latin, and also on Welsh Studies.

6 Unpublished Theses

It is both a duty and a pleasure to acknowledge the enlightenment which I have derived from reading the following works:

Davies, W., 'Phylipiaid Ardudwy: with the poems of Siôn Phylip in the Cardiff Free Library collection' (MA Wales, Aberystwyth, 1912).

Emanuel, H. D., 'The Latin Life of St Cadoc: A Textual and Lexicographical Study' (MA Wales, Aberystwyth, 1950).

Geen, A. G., 'The Teaching of Classics in the Schools of England and Wales in the Twentieth Century' (M.Ed. Wales, Cardiff, 1974).

Griffith, W. P., 'Welsh Students at Oxford, Cambridge and the Inns of Court during the Sixteenth and Early Seventeenth Centuries' (Ph.D. Wales, Bangor, 1981).

Gruffydd, R. G., 'Religious Prose in Welsh from the beginning of the reign of Elizabeth to the Restoration' (D.Phil. Oxford, 1953).

James, E. M., '*Secretum Secretorum*: Astudiaeth feirniadol o ddetholiadau Cymraeg a Lladin o'r llythyr ffug-Aristotelaidd at Alecsander Fawr' (Ph.D. Wales, Aberystwyth, 1986).

Lewis, A., 'Evan Evans (Ieuan Fardd) 1731–1788: Hanes ei Fywyd a'i Gysylltiadau Llenyddol' (MA Wales, Cardiff, 1950).

Lloyd, N., 'A History of Welsh Scholarship in the first half of the Seventeenth Century, with special reference to the writings of John Jones, Gellilyfdy' (D.Phil. Oxford, 1970) .

Mathias, W. A., 'Astudiaeth o weithgarwch llenyddol William Salesbury' (MA Wales, Cardiff, 1949).

Owens, B. G., 'Y Fersiynau Cymraeg o *Dares Phrygius* (*Ystorya Dared*) – Eu Tarddiad, Eu Nodweddion a'u Cydberthynas' (MA Wales, Aberystwyth, 1951).

Roberts, G. D., 'The History of the Study of the Classics in Wales in the Sixteenth Century' (B.Litt. Oxford, 1923).

Rowlands, J., 'A Critical Edition and Study of the Welsh Poems written in praise of the Salusburies of Llyweni' (D.Phil. Oxford, 1967).

Rowlands, W., 'Barddoniaeth Tomos Prys o Blas Iolyn' (MA Wales, Bangor, 1912).

Webster, J. R., 'The Place of Secondary Education in Welsh Society, 1800–1918' (Ph.D. Wales, Swansea, 1959).

Index

Aberystwyth 16, 114, 117, 123
Achilles 40, 42, 101, 103
Actaeon 82
Aeneas 31, 32, 40, 82, 101, 133, 136–7, 144, 145
Aeschylus 127, 128, 128–9
Agamemnon 101, 147
Agricola 4, 132, 138
Ajax 42
Alexander (the Great) 21–2, 41, 50–1, 79
Alexander (= Paris) 41
Alfred, King 87
Anacreon, *Anacreontea* 96, 98, 111, 128, 170 n.15
Anchises 32
Andromache 147
Aneirin 19, 145
Antaios 142
Anthology, Greek 128
Antenor 32, 136
Argonauts 82
Ariadne 150
Aristophanes 128
Aristotle 50, 52, 55, 78, 120–2, 129, 130, 131
Arnold, E. V. 117, 174 n.14
Arnold, Thomas 112, 113
Arthur, King 31, 32, 38
Arundel, Earl of 66
Ascanius 31, 32, 54
Assaracus 32, 34
Asser 13
Athanasius, St 176 n.58
Auden, W. H. 115, 135, 146
Augustine, St (of Hippo) 17, 27, 176 n.57
Augustus Caesar 82

Baldwin, Archbishop of Canterbury 36
Barrington, Daines 107
Baxter, William 90, 170 n.15
Bede 27
Bembo 71
Benedict, St 15
Benevento 15–16
Berry, R. G. 132
Bible, The 12, 58, 67, 77, 81, 83, 152–3
'Blue Books' (1847) 110, 112
Boethius 16, 19, 25, 86–7
Borromeo, Cardinal 71
Bowen, Euros 130–1, 144–52, 154
Breuddwyd Macsen 2
Brittany 11
Browning, Elizabeth B. 126
Brut y Brenhinedd 43, 48, 81
Brut y Tywysogion 16, 25, 42, 43
Brutus (of Troy) 31–4, 53–4, 60
Buckhurst, Lord 66, 68
Burgess, Thomas 111
Burton, Robert 88
Byron, Lord 115, 125

Cadfan 3
Cadoc, St 13–16
Cadwaladr 43, 54, 60
Cadwaladr, Rhys 88–90
'Cadwgan, Cylch' (Cadwgan Circle) 133, 142
Caerleon (on Usk) 2, 28–30, 37–8
Callisthenes, Pseudo- 21
Cambridge 39, 53, 56, 58, 70, 115, 116
Capella, Martianus 12
Caradoc (of Llancarfan) 15

Carmarthen 28, 102
Cassandra 131, 135
Cassiodorus 15
'Catamanus stone' 3
Catullus 115, 124, 127, 154
Chaucer, Geoffrey 45, 87
Cicero 16, 33, 39, 63, 66–7, 70, 71,
    72, 73–5, 81, 82, 88, 92, 99
Circe 125
Claudian 109
Claudius 32
Clynnog, Morys 71, 72, 75
Conway, R. S. 174 n.14
Corineus 32
Cornford, F. M. 129
Cowley, Abraham 88–9
Cox, Leonard 56, 166 n.8
Cunedda 3, 139, 142
Curtius: *see* Rufus
Cynddelw Brydydd Mawr 151
Cynwal, Wiliam 80–1

Daedalus 82
Dafydd ap Gwilym 44–50, 51, 89,
    98, 109, 151
Dafydd Ddu (of Hiraddug) 40
Dafydd Nanmor 50, 169 n.84
Dalier Sylw, Cwmni 154
'Damon a Phyddias' 83
Dante 141–2
Dardanus 32
Dares Phrygius 43
Davies, Bryan Martin 154–5
Davies, John (of Brecon), 'Siôn
    Dafydd Rhys' 70, 76–9, 80,
    83, 107
Davies, John (of Mallwyd) 58–9,
    65, 71, 80, 85
Davies, Pennar 133, 135
Davies, Richard, Bishop of St
    David's 58, 66, 70, 76, 77, 85
Davis, David (Castellhywel)
    111–12
Deidameia 42, 49
Dennis, John 104
Dido 34, 42, 82, 101, 151
Diogenes 50
Dissenting Academies 86
Donatus 14, 40, 124
Dryden, John 88, 89, 96

Edwards, Charles 91
Edwards, Hilma Lloyd 177 n.71
Edwards, Huw Lloyd 131
Edwards, Lewis 112–14, 116, 117
Edwards, Owen M. 117
Edwards, Thomas Charles 116,
    117
Einion Offeiriad 6, 40, 71
Eisteddfod, National 119, 120,
    131, 154
Electra 132
Elizabeth I, Queen 82, 87
Endymion 125
Erasmus 52, 55, 64–5, 81, 82
Euripides 119, 128, 154
Evans, D. Ellis 129
Evans, D. Emrys 129
Evans, Donald 154, 179 n.108
Evans, D. Silvan 111
Evans, Ellis ('Hedd Wyn') 127,
    154
Evans, Evan ('Ieuan Fardd') 94,
    103, 104, 105, 106–10
Evans, Evan ('Ieuan Glan
    Geirionydd') 110–11
Evans, Theophilus 92–3

Fates, Three 51, 82
Fielding, Henry 96
FitzGerald, John 130
Fortunatus, Venantius 20
Friars School, Bangor 77, 94
Frogs Classical Society (Cardiff)
    117

Gaisford, Thomas 118
Galen 37
Gellius, Aulus 37
Geoffrey of Monmouth 28–34,
    37, 42, 48, 53, 57, 60, 92
Gerald of Wales (Gerald de Barri,
    Giraldus Cambrensis) 34–8,
    65, 107
Gildas 6–11, 20, 117
Gloucester 35
Gododdin, Y 19–20, 103, 160 n.40
Gogynfeirdd 39–41
Golding, Arthur 67
Gorgon 82
Gray, Thomas 107

Griffiths, J. Gwyn 129–30, 133, 142
Gruffudd ap Maredudd 151
Gruffudd ab yr Ynad Coch 107–8, 141
Gruffudd Hiraethog 81–2, 83
Gruffydd, Elis 79
Gruffydd, W. J. 120, 122, 123, 124–7, 127–8
Guto'r Glyn 50
Gwalchmai ap Meilyr 98
Gwenallt: *see* Jones, D. Gwenallt
Gwinne, Matthew 55

Haverfordwest 39
Hector 40, 41, 42, 48, 81, 101
Hecuba 81, 147
Heine, H. 120
Helen (of Troy) 41–2, 49, 131, 135, 145
Helenus (son of Priam) 31, 34
Hendregadredd Manuscript 44
Henry VII, King (Henry Tudor) 53–4, 60
Henry VIII, King 53
Herbert, George 86
Herbert, Henry 65
Herbert, William 63
Hercules 21, 40, 41, 42, 43, 49, 51, 79, 82
Herodotus 129
Heywood, John 82
Hisperica Famina 17
Historia Brittonum 12, 33
Homer 19, 33, 43, 98, 99–102, 103, 104, 109, 111, 112, 113, 120, 125, 128, 154
Horace (Q. Horatius Flaccus) 33, 37, 64, 65, 67, 81, 82, 86, 88–90, 92, 96–8, 104, 109, 111, 124, 128, 132, 133, 170 n.15
Hrabanus Maurus 19
Hudson-Williams, T. 117–18, 129
Humphreys, Emyr 132
Hywel ap Owain Gwynedd 151

Iaco ap Dewi (James Davies) 90
Icarus 81, 134
Ieuan ap Hywel Swrdwal 52
Ieuan ap Rhydderch 52

Ieuan ap Sulien 16–19, 26–7
Illtud, St 9–12
Intermediate Education Act, Welsh 116
Iolo Goch 51
Ireland 13, 14, 18, 35, 36

Jason 41, 43, 50, 81
Jenkins, E. D. T. 153
Jerome, St 37
Jesus College, Oxford 55, 94, 102, 128, 169 n.63
John of Salisbury 28, 36
John of Wales (Johannes Wallensis) 39
Jones, Albert Evans ('Cynan') 131
Jones, Bobi (R. M.) 1, 154
Jones, David 132
Jones, D. Gwenallt 134–5, 142–4, 153
Jones, D. James 118
Jones, J. Ellis 129
Jones, John Gwilym 131
Jones, John Henry 128–9
Jones, Owen 173 n.85
Jones, Richard Robert ('Dic Aberdaron') 110
Jones, Thomas ('the Almanacker') 88
Jones, Thomas Gwynn 120, 122–3, 127–8
Jones, Tom Parri 131, 142
Jones, William (Llangadfan) 110
Jones, William (Tremadog) 132, 135, 142
Jonson, Ben 88
Jowett, Benjamin 129
Julius Caesar 32, 51, 70, 82
Justinian 37
Juvenal 33, 37, 86, 92
Juvencus 12–13, 19

Keats, John 125
Kyffin, Maurice 66, 67–70, 75, 83, 120

Lampeter, St David's College 111
Laocoon 143–4, 146, 147, 178 n.95
Larkin, Philip 135

Lee, Desmond 129
Leland, John 60
Lessing, G. E. 144
Lewis, R. Morris 120
Lewis, Saunders 20, 74, 92, 93,
      130, 131, 132–3, 133–4,
      135–42, 144
Lewys Glyn Cothi 53–4
Lewys, Huw 66
Lhuyd, Edward 90, 94
'Lichfield Gospel Book' 12
Lifris 13–16
Lily, William 88
Lilly, Gweneth 132
Llanbadarn Fawr 16–19, 27, 28,
      35, 44, 45, 46
Llancarfan 12, 13–16, 35
Llandaff 28
'Llandav, Book of' 13, 28
Llandovery College 111
Llanilltud Fawr (Llantwit Major)
      9–12, 16
Llanthony 39
Lloyd, D. Tecwyn 118
Lloyd, Hugh 55
Lloyd, John Edward 117, 132,
      135–42
Lloyd, Ludovic 56
Llwyd, Alan 127, 154
Llwyd, Humphrey 63, 66, 70, 81
Llwyd, Morgan 91, 113
Llywarch ap Llywelyn ('Prydydd
      y Moch') 41
Llywelyn ap Gruffudd ('the Last
      Prince') 141
Llywelyn Bren 45
Longinus 99, 104
Lucan 19, 33, 37
Lucian 95, 109

Mabinogion, Y 39
MacNeice, Louis 135
MacPherson, James 107
Macrobius 16, 27
Macsen Wledig: see Magnus
      Maximus
Maelgwn Gwynedd 7, 11, 20
Magnus Maximus 2–3, 44
Manorbier 35
Margam 39

Marius 37
Martial 67, 88
Medusa 147
Merfyn Frych 13
Miles, Gareth 154
Milton, John 99, 103, 113
Minotaur 134
Monte Cassino 15
More, Henry 88
Morgan, D. Llwyd 177 n.71
Morgan, John (of Matchin) 93
Morgan, William, Bishop of
      Llandaff and of St Asaph 58,
      81
Morris brothers (of Anglesey)
      93–4, 107
Morris, A. O. 129, 130
Morris, Edward 87
Morris, Lewis 94, 95–6, 97, 102,
      103–4, 105, 107
Morris, Richard 94, 96, 98, 100,
      109
Morris, William 94, 95, 98, 99
Morris-Jones, John 120–2, 131
Morys, Huw 93, 105
Münster, Sebastian 81

'Nennius': see Historia Brittonum
Nepos, Cornelius 43
Nestor 42
Nicolas, Dafydd 93
Niobe 133–4
North, Thomas 67
Norwood, Gilbert 117

Odysseus (see also Ulysses) 82,
      145
Omar Khayyám 120
Ordovices 2
Orestes 132
Orosius, Paulus 21
Orpheus 86–7, 134, 142, 152, 154
Ortelius, Abraham 70
Ovid (P. Ovidius Naso) 13, 17,
      19, 37, 45–8, 51, 67, 82, 86, 92,
      98, 130, 151, 152
Owain Glyndŵr 140
Owain Tudur 53
Owen, Daniel 110, 116
Owen, George (of Henllys) 53, 54

Owen, Goronwy 94–102, 105, 110
Owen, Jeremy 92
Owen, John (epigrammatist) 55, 56–7
Owen, R. Llugwy 116
Oxford 30, 39, 51, 52, 53, 55–6, 58, 70, 76, 92, 94, 102, 107, 115, 116, 123

Pan 126
Paris (France) 28, 35, 39, 123
Paris (of Troy): *see also* Alexander 41, 42
Parry, Richard, Bishop of St Asaph 58
Parry, R. Williams 132
Parry, Thomas 131
Parry-Jones, Henry 128
Parry-Williams, T. H. 123–4
Pedair Cainc y Mabinogi 39, 44
Percy, Thomas 108
Peter, John ('Ioan Pedr') 112, 173 n.85
Petrarch 59, 66, 81
Petronius 37, 88
Persius 37
Phaer, Thomas 56
Phaëton 151
Philomena 82
Phillips, Thomas 111
Phylip family (of Ardudwy) 83, 87
Phylip, Gruffydd 87
Phylip, Phylip John 87
Phylip, Siôn 83
Plato 71–2, 81, 109, 116, 129, 146, 151
Plutarch 67
Polydore Vergil 60–1, 62, 82
Polyxena 42, 49
Powel, David 63, 65, 66
Powell, Griffith 55
Priam 31, 32, 50
Price, John, *or* Prys 60–4, 81, 85
Price, John (Pricaeus) 170 n.3
Prichard, Caradog 142
Priscian 14, 40
Proclus 58
Procne 82
Prometheus 127, 143, 146, 147, 154, 178 n.92

Prudentius 19
Prys, Edmwnd 58, 80–1
Prys, Elis 81, 83
Prys, Tomos 83
Ptolemy 52
Pugh, John (Motigido) 102
Pythia 134

Quintilian 64

Ramus, Peter 91
Red Book of Hergest 44
Rees, Daniel 175 n.21
Rhetorica ad Herennium 67
Rhigyfarch ap Sulien 16, 19, 25–6
Rhodri Mawr 13
Rhys ap Tewdwr 25, 35
Rhŷs, John 128
Rhys, Morgan 93
Richard, Abraham 102
Richard, Edward 94–5, 102–6, 108, 110
Robert, Gruffydd 70–5, 76, 80, 83
Roberts, R. Silyn 120, 123
Roberts, Thomas Francis 117
Roberts, W. Rhys 117
Robinson, Hugh 55
Roman de la Rose 45
Rome 35
Rose, H. J. 128
Rufus, Quintus Curtius 21

Sackville family (*see also* Buckhurst) 68, 69
St David's 13, 25, 36
Salesbury, Henry 59, 65, 71
Salesbury, William 58, 59, 64–5, 77, 80, 81, 82, 85, 120
Sallust 34, 43
Salusbury family (Lleweni) 66
Salusbury, John 82
Samson, St 11
Samuel, Edward 93
Sappho, Sapphic stanza 95, 98, 112
Saunders, William 111
Schiller, Friedrich 126
Schools (in Wales) 54, 94, 102–3, 106, 110–111, 114, 118, 122, 153

Secretum Secretorum 50–1
Sedulius, Caelius 19
Sedulius Scottus 13
Seneca 37, 39, 67, 88, 91
Seven Liberal Arts, The 26–7, 52
Shakespeare, William 55, 88
Shrewsbury 54, 91, 92, 115, 141
Shelley, P. B. 125, 127
Sibyl 134, 136
Sidney, Henry 65, 66
Sidonius Apollinaris 37
Silures 2
Simwnt Fychan 67, 88
Siôn ap Hywel ab Owain 67
Siôn Cent 51
Siôn Dafydd Rhys: *see* Davies, John (of Brecon)
Siôn Tudur 82–3
Sophocles 127–8, 130, 140, 146, 154, 173 n.85
Statius 19, 37
Stradling, Edward 66, 70, 78
Stradling, John 56, 66
Strata Florida (Ystrad Fflur) 44
Suetonius Paulinus 2
Sulien, Bishop of St David's 16–19, 25–7
Swift, Jonathan 93, 96
Swinburne, A. C. 116, 125, 126
Symbolists, French 147, 151

Tacitus 2, 4, 129
Taliesin 5–6, 8, 19, 20–1, 40, 44, 50, 79, 145
'Taliesin, Book of' 21–3
Tantalus 134, 142
Terence (P. Terentius Afer) 37, 67, 70–0, 130
Tereus 82
Tertullian 93
Thelwall, Simon 67
Theocritus 105–7, 108, 109
Theodulf (of Orléans) 19
Theophrastus 130
Theseus 150
Thomas, A. Maximilian 130
Thomas, Ebenezer ('Eben Fardd') 119
Thomas, Gwyn 154

Thomas, William (Italian scholar) 75–6
Thomas, William ('Islwyn') 119
Thucydides 116
Traethodydd, Y 112–13, 120, 130
Trioedd Ynys Prydain 41–2, 48, 81
Tudur Aled 50, 52, 151
Tydeus 42

Ulysses (*see also* Odysseus) 42, 101
University of Wales 116–18, 129, 153
Urien 5, 20

Valéry, Paul 130
Valla, Lorenzo 63
Vaughan, Henry 86–7
Vaughan, Robert 90
Vaughan, Rowland 65
Vaughan, Thomas 86
Vaughan, William 56
Vespasian 32
Virgil (P. Vergilius Maro) 9, 17, 19, 20, 32, 33–4, 37, 49–50, 51, 56, 65, 67, 92, 98, 99, 100, 101–2, 103, 104, 105, 111, 130, 132–3, 133, 136–42, 144, 152, 173 n.85, 177 n.76

Walahfrid Strabo 19
Walter of Châtillon 51, 79
Walter Map 39
Watkins, Richard 55
Welsh language 3–4, 6
Westminster School 54
Whitford, Richard 52
William I, King 25
William of Malmesbury 28
William of Newburgh 60
William of Ockham 51
William, Dafydd 93
Williams, Hugh 116–17
Williams, Moses 90, 94
Williams, Rhydwen 142
Williams, Waldo 142
Williams, William (Pantycelyn) 93
Wilson, John ('Christopher North') 112

Winchester College 54, 55, 56
Wynn family (of Gwydir) 66, 110
Wynn, John 77
Wynne, Ellis 91–2, 93

Ystorya Dared 43, 44, 48, 81
Ystrad Fflur: *see* Strata Florida
Ystradmeurig 94, 102–6, 108–9, 111